A Blistered
Kind of Love

Published by
The Mountaineers Books
1001 SW Klickitat Way, Suite 201
Seattle, WA 98134

The Mountaineers Books is the nonprofit publishing arm of The Mountaineers Club, an organization founded in 1906 and dedicated to the exploration, preservation, and enjoyment of outdoor and wilderness areas.

First edition, 2003

Published simultaneously in Great Britain by Cordee, 3a DeMontfort Street, Leicester, England, LE1 7HD

Manufactured in the United States of America

Project Editor: Mary Metz
Copy Editor: Christine Clifton-Thornton
Cover and Book Design: Ani Rucki
Layout: Ani Rucki

DISCLAIMER
This book is a compilation of notes and memories; as such it is full of subjective perception and opinion. Still, we have done our best to truthfully recreate our summer's adventure. For the sake of not boring the reader comatose, however, we must admit to taking a degree of creative license. Additionally, some names have been changed (to protect the "innocent," and ourselves from lawyers).

Library of Congress Cataloging-in-Publication Data
Ballard, Angela, 1973–
  A blistered kind of love : one couple's trial by trail / Angela
Ballard, Duffy Ballard.
     p.   cm.
  ISBN 0-89886-940-4 (hardcover)—ISBN 0-89886-902-1 (trade paper)
  1. Ballard, Angela—Journeys—Pacific Crest Trail. 2. Ballard,
Duffy—Journeys—Pacific Crest Trail. 3. Hiking–Pacific Crest Trail. 4. Pacific Crest Trail—Description and travel.
I. Ballard, Duffy, 1972– II. Title.
  GV199.42.P3B35 2003
  917.9—dc21

2003010156

A Blistered Kind of Love

One Couple's
Trial by Trail

Angela &
Duffy Ballard

THE MOUNTAINEERS BOOKS

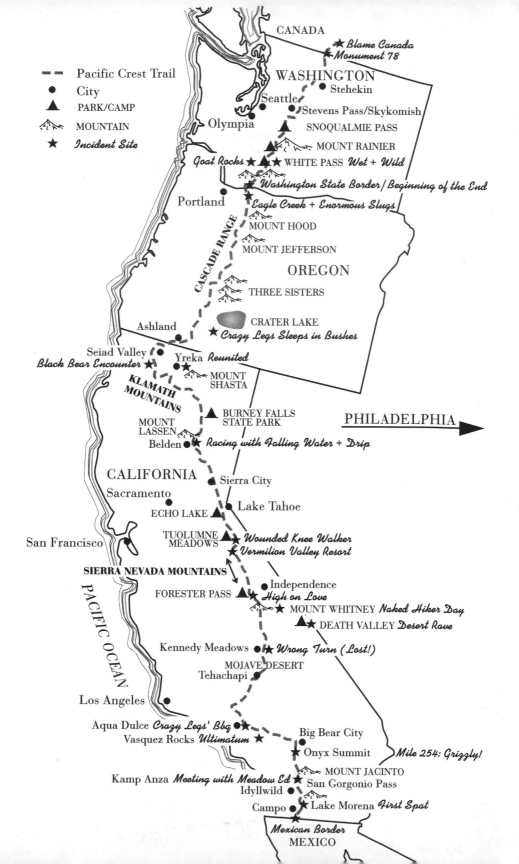

CANADA

★ *Blame Canada*
Monument 78

WASHINGTON

● Stehekin

Seattle ●

● Stevens Pass/Skykomish

Olympia ●

SNOQUALMIE PASS

▲▲ MOUNT RAINIER

Goat Rocks ★ ▲ ★ WHITE PASS *Wet + Wild*

★ *Washington State Border / Beginning of the End*

Portland ●

★ *Eagle Creek + Enormous Slugs*

MOUNT HOOD

CASCADE RANGE

MOUNT JEFFERSON

OREGON

THREE SISTERS

Ashland ●

CRATER LAKE

★ *Crazy Legs Sleeps in Bushes*

Seiad Valley ●

Black Bear Encounter ★

● Yreka ★ *Reunited*

KLAMATH
MOUNTAINS

MOUNT
SHASTA

▲ BURNEY FALLS
STATE PARK

PHILADELPHIA ▶

MOUNT
LASSEN

Belden ● ★ *Racing with Falling Water + Drip*

CALIFORNIA

Sacramento ●

● Sierra City

ECHO LAKE ▲ ● Lake Tahoe

San Francisco ●

TUOLUMNE
MEADOWS ▲▲ ★ *Wounded Knee Walker*
★ *Vermilion Valley Resort*

SIERRA NEVADA MOUNTAINS

● Independence

FORESTER PASS ▲ ★ *High on Love*

★ MOUNT WHITNEY *Naked Hiker Day*

▲ ★ DEATH VALLEY *Desert Rave*

Kennedy Meadows ● ★ *Wrong Turn (Lost!)*

MOJAVE DESERT

Tehachapi ●

PACIFIC OCEAN

Los Angeles ●

Aqua Dulce *Crazy Legs' Bbq* ● ★

Vasquez Rocks *Ultimatum* ★

● Big Bear City

★ Onyx Summit *Mile 254: Grizzly!*

MOUNT JACINTO

Kamp Anza *Meeting with Meadow Ed* ★ San Gorgonio Pass

Idyllwild ●

Campo ● ★ Lake Morena *First Spat*

★

Mexican Border

MEXICO

Pacific Crest Trail
● City
▲ PARK/CAMP
🏔 MOUNTAIN
★ *Incident Site*

Contents

Acknowledgments

First, we'd like to acknowledge the peanut. What a fantastic legume. Without it, our trail diet would have been dangerously unappetizing and protein-poor. We'd also like to thank those who've helped make the Pacific Crest National Scenic Trail (PCT) a reality. Visionaries like John Muir, who saw the importance of protecting our nation's wilderness areas, and the builders and protectors— members and staff of the Pacific Crest Trail Association and beyond—who lobby for and maintain the 2,655-mile trail.

Of course, we must thank everyone who supported our crazy notion of hiking from Mexico to Canada. Phil and Roberta Ballard were instrumental at every step, allowing us to turn their home into re-supply headquarters, believing when it was illogical to do so, mailing packages, and providing moral support. Duffy's brother, Chris, deserves particular mention because his 1998 literary project, *Hoops Nation*, was a seminal inspiration, and his wisdom as a writer has since proven invaluable.

We are also extremely grateful for the love and support of Angela's family. Special thanks to her parents and to her brothers and sisters-in-law (for constant encouragement, advice, and affection). Mile by mile, we were followed and supported by many friends and loved ones. We owe a large debt to all of those who aided our March of Dimes charity effort and who sent thoughts and words to spur us northward.

Next, we'd like to acknowledge Duct tape and Spenco 2nd Skin. Without these wondrous inventions, our feet and certainly our thru-hike wouldn't have survived—and no trail love, not even a blistered kind, would have been possible.

During our months in the wild, we met many generous souls who offered help while asking nothing in return. So here's a toast to Bob, Donna, Meadow Ed, and all the other trail angels who brightened our path. You are the spirit of the PCT. And while we're at it . . . here's to trekking poles. Without you, we would've spent much of the summer on our asses.

During the sometimes agonizing birth of this book, many took time out from their own busy literary careers to help us focus and improve our manuscript. Chris Ballard, Karen Berger and the folks at *GORP.com*, Alexandra Cann, and Erik Larson; and Mary Metz, Christine Clifton-Thornton, and Alison Koop at The Mountaineers Books—we owe you much. We must also extend our gratitude to the Savage family and the Barbara Savage Memorial Award for helping us turn our literary dream into a reality. Thanks, as well, to whoever invented the baby wipe. We're certain you've helped keep us together.

We'd also like to send our appreciation to those who allowed their names, experiences, and writings to be included in this book—in particular, Toby McEvoy for his witty insights into long-distance hiking as recorded in his journal and Luke Snyder for his jokes.

Finally, we must thank and acknowledge our summer's constant guide, the direction north. Keep up the good work.

Prologue

DR. JOHN WILLIAM LOWDER'S unwitting premonition shook me. "When I die," he said to a friend, "my wish is to be in the mountains, alone, and to have a few hours with God." Lowder, a sixty-nine-year-old outdoorsman, was walking from Mexico to Canada along the Pacific Crest National Scenic Trail (PCT) when he and fellow hikers faced a snowstorm in California's Sierra Nevada Mountains. Ignoring his old rule to never hike alone, Lowder separated from his younger companions; no one's sure why. Perhaps he hoped to out-hike the brewing storm. Possibly his judgment was compromised by exhaustion. Most likely a combination of factors caused the veteran backpacker to take a chance—to set out on his own toward the small town of Lone Pine.

Along the way, he lost the trail in the snow and fell two hundred feet down a steep, icy slope, breaking both legs and one arm and taking severe blows to the head. Amazingly, he survived the fall, climbed into his sleeping bag, and began treating his wounds. Still, he didn't survive the night. He spent his final hours in the mountains alone.

I looked away from the computer screen and around my cluttered studio: *Backpacker* magazine's latest *Gear Guide* lay amongst peanut butter Power Bar wrappers and a dog-eared copy of *How to Shit in the Woods*. I knew that hiking the Pacific Crest Trail was going to be the experience of a lifetime, but I didn't want it to be my last.

Initially, my primary worries had been about leaving my job and upsetting my mother and father. Then I heard about Lowder, bear attacks, and snakebites, and suddenly, unemployment and familial discord didn't seem so bad.

X ▪ ▪ ▪ X

A Blistered Kind of Love

Although our dream of going on a really long walk had taken shape slowly, by the time I read about Lowder we'd reached a point of no return. Duffy and I were inextricably tied to the trail, as was our future. Looking back, I'm not sure which came first, Duffy and I falling in love with each other or falling in love with the idea of hiking the PCT. I guess the two life-changing attachments developed in tandem, and from the very beginning, bipedal travel was a fundamental part of our lives together. We'd started off as winter running partners who met despite rain, sleet, and face-cracking cold to jog the streets of Philadelphia, and during each jaunt we shared enough secrets that by spring we were inseparable.

One of our first romantic getaways was to Duffy's parents' cabin on California's rough and craggy coast. Perched on a hill overlooking the ocean, the cabin was a little lonely and bedraggled, the rotting and weather-warped door reluctant to open. Once inside, Duffy sifted through his childhood memories while I poked around, checking the dates on old magazines and flipping through books until a particular tome caught my eye—*The Pacific Crest Trail*, by William R. Gray.

The book's cover was bent and water-stained, but the photographs inside remained vivid. Soon we were sitting on the porch, alternating between gazing at the beach below and the spectacular images of the Pacific Crest Trail in the aged book. Reading captions like "Snowmelt thundering down Woods Creek" and "Mist swirls around a treeless ridge of the Goat Rocks," I was enchanted and enthralled. I longed to witness elks sparing in the Cascades, to gather wild berries as I walked, to see butterflies resting on snow, and to "adopt the pace of nature." Duffy's eyes sparkled.

"What are you thinking?"

"Nothing," Duffy replied mischievously. "It's just that I've heard of this trail and have been thinking of doing it."

"Doing it? Doing what?"

"Well, it's two-thousand-something miles long, and it would take months, but I was thinking it would be cool to hike the whole thing—from Mexico to Canada."

"You're crazy." I turned my attention to the book's prologue. In it Gray describes hiking the Pacific Crest Trail as a "calling," to be embraced for reasons ranging from love of wilderness and kinship with nature to lust for a physical test. The rewards of answering the call, he writes, are intensely personal: "the pride of surmounting a difficult pass, the simple luxury of falling asleep in a silent area of rocks, trees and stars." The experience, he concludes, can change a person in ways that can't be foretold or imagined.

When we returned to Philadelphia, I showed the book to Duffy's parents. They'd never seen it before. Someone must have borrowed the cabin for a night and left it there. I can't help but think it was left for us.

X ▪ ▪ ▪ ▪ X

Duffy and I had been planning our hike for almost a year before I finally told my parents. I knew that quitting my job and disappearing into the deserts and mountains of the West with my boyfriend wouldn't make them happy and was deeply afraid of even broaching the subject.

When I did finally bring it up, I explained that Duffy and I were going to embark on a pilgrimage of sorts and hopefully, someday, write a book about it. Their reaction was what you might expect from many parents: They were horrified and said so. I tried to explain that this was going to be good for me, that I needed to take a risk, and that it was a smart career move to quit my advertising job and attempt something extraordinary. They'd traveled a lot as youths; maybe they could empathize with my wanderlust? But my parents are protective, and for them there was no getting around the fact that I was taking off with a man they'd never met to backpack along a trail they had never heard of. Nothing I said eased their minds, and I felt like I was speaking through a wall. Everything was muffled and confused.

As I drove back to Philadelphia from visiting my family and breaking the news, I replayed the confrontation in my head and cried. I wasn't a perfect daughter. There were things about the woman I'd turned out to be that I knew my parents were unhappy with, but I tried not to purposefully disappoint them. By hiking the PCT, I was going against their wishes, and that was a hard thing to do. That didn't mean, however, that I wasn't going to do it, and when my tears dried I was more committed to our hike than ever.

After that, my parents and I didn't speak for a few months. It wasn't an entirely intentional separation; it just kind of happened. I guess I needed time to cool off and adjust. When you're little, you think your parents are infallible, and even into early adulthood you tend to trust that they're right—and mine often were. But in this case, I was fairly confident that they weren't. I say fairly because I still had fears—of bears, bugs, bandits, and the like. Potential danger, however, lurks everywhere you go, and I truly believed that trekking the Pacific Crest Trail was the appropriate next step for Duffy and me. The months of relying on one another for food, warmth, and shelter, as well as for safety and companionship, would bring us even closer and help us to determine whether we were cut out to spend the rest of our lives together. But by prioritizing the man I loved, I was damaging my relationship with my parents. It was a heart-wrenching trade-off. Only time could prove whether it was a worthwhile one—or not.

X ■ ▪ ▪ ▪ X

 ONE EVENING IN THE FALL OF 1998, while flipping through a popular men's "lifestyle" magazine, I came across a headline that captivated and taunted me—*Be a Man of the World: The 10 Adventures of a Lifetime.* The list included a voracious bite of everything macho—mountains and motorcycles, Cadillacs and kayaks, animals and air travel. The writer dared me to carry out one of these adventures and overcome years of pathetic suburban impotence. The challenge struck a cord. It was bad enough to be a prematurely balding and single twenty-something, but to be further mocked by a magazine that I depended on to unlock the secrets of female pheromones was too much.

"Dude," I thought to myself, "you can do this . . . just throw down a strong *cojones* elixir and scamper right up to the peak of K2. Or kayak your lazy ass down the 2,750-mile Mekong River in China. Or get your manliness in gear with a little help from man's best friend by dog-sledding 150 miles to the North Pole."

I pondered these options one by one. I'd recently read *Into Thin Air,* by Jon Krakauer, and a quick review of the story convinced me that I wanted no part of a 29,000-foot peak—especially not one described as "a mountaineer's mountain . . . high, technical, mean." And while I'd done some kayaking in the past, I recalled that it hadn't taken much more than a portly dragonfly to tip over my kayak. This sort of boating résumé didn't exactly qualify me to be the first ever to conquer the Mekong "from source to sea." How about dog-sledding? I sure did like dogs—but I didn't like the idea of minus twenty degree temperatures and a landscape so glaringly white that I couldn't remove my glacier goggles.

There was one choice, however, that maybe wasn't so impossible: hiking the Pacific Crest Trail. That might be feasible for a mere mortal. It sounded easy enough—strap on a backpack and put one foot in front of the other. After all, it was just walking.

A whole lot of walking; 2,655 miles of it, in fact. Some quick math indicated that this path to validating my Y chromosome would require hiking twenty miles a day for five months over some of the most isolated wilderness in the U.S. That sounded like a trip better suited to a descendant of Daniel Boone than someone actively invested in the amenities of modern life. Five months on the trail would require many sacrifices—twenty weeks without Direct TV, web surfing, or automated coffee makers. One hundred and fifty nights and none of them spent on the couch with chips, beer, and a ballgame. Over four hundred dried, dehydrated, and downright dour meals. Quite daunting, really.

At least I had one thing going for me—I'd been raised in the 1970s by parents who still believed that they were living in the 1960s. This gave me three distinct advantages over my peers: a wardrobe rich with tie-dye; a "family" van with a bed built in the back (I'm told I was conceived on this bed); and frequent opportunities to commune with nature. When my brother Chris and I were still at an early age, my parents would pack us into our earth-toned 1971 Dodge for weekend excursions. These trips often took us down Highway 1 to Big Sur, where my parents had bought ten acres of undeveloped land from an LSD-entranced local for $100 an acre and built a small cabin overlooking the Pacific Ocean. There, Chris and I spent our days scrambling in and out of steep wooded valleys and along a creek that teased its way through the roots of oaks and redwoods. Eating dinner on the pint-size cabin's deck, we'd watch the ocean slowly suck the sun out of the sky. When the sun had set and the moon started to rise, my parents would hike down the hill to their swinging bed, which creaked below twisted oaks. Back up on the deck and snug in our sleeping bags, Chris and I would slowly drift off to sleep under star-speckled skies.

X ▪ ▀ ▪ X

Several months after first reading about the Pacific Crest Trail, I could barely recall my initial "I'll prove I'm a man, you puny magazine writer" response. But thoughts of the trail still lurked in my subconscious, occasionally bursting forth. Then I read Bill Bryson's story, chronicled in his popular book, *A Walk in the Woods*. Similarly drawn to a long-distance hike, Bryson attempted to tackle the Appalachian Trail (AT), which stretches 2,100 miles, from Georgia to Maine. To do this, he had to overcome numerous obstacles, including a complete ignorance of backpacking and a large, flabby behind.

As unprepared as Bryson was to thru-hike (a term used to describe an end-to-end hike of a long-distance trail such as the AT), the hiking partner he recruited was more so. Steven Katz, referred to simply as Katz, was a middle-aged burnout whose years of partying like a nineteen-year-old had left him soft and directionless. Within hours of starting the AT at its southern terminus, in Springer, Georgia, Katz was wildly jettisoning provisions from his pack in a desperate attempt to keep up with Bill, who we can confidently presume was not setting any speed records. Bryson and Katz were unable to complete the Appalachian Trail–in fact, they covered less than half of it–but nevertheless their story was inspirational. If these goofballs could hike over 870 miles, then I was pretty sure I could, too. Additionally, Bryson's account of the continuing invasion of the East Coast wilderness by strip malls and theme restaurants was a painful reminder that I shouldn't assume that our nation's backwoods would always be there for my enjoyment. Better to see them before they disappeared.

The inspiration was there, but unfortunately there were still quite a few barricades between the Pacific Crest Trail and me. My active enrollment in medical school and relative lack of financial resources were among these, but were trivial compared to the question of who would hike with me. I certainly had friends who would have loved to share my beef jerky and fig bars, but the problem was that they were all too busy with career-building nonsense. And there was no way in hell I was going to conquer 2,655 miles of desolate, mountainous, rattlesnake-infested wilderness on my own. There I'd be on the first night, securely wrapped in a minus ten degree rated sleeping bag with a knife protectively tucked under my parka, then along might come a gust of wind to rustle my tent and conjure up images of the mysterious finger-chopping witch in *The Blair Witch Project*. Moments later I'd be racing madly through the desert, stabbing at darkness. No, hiking alone wasn't a very good idea.

X ▪ ▪ ▪ X

I am pretty sure that my dream of hiking the Pacific Crest Trail would have remained just that if I hadn't started dating Angela. For the first time in my life I'd met someone with whom I wasn't afraid to make a commitment. Sure, hiking the PCT was only a five-month commitment, but it felt like much more. Five months together in the wild would greatly, and perhaps unnecessarily, challenge our relationship. I was prepared to accept the risk. Was Angela?

Angela wasn't very outdoorsy. She grew up in the New York City suburbs, and her parents hadn't owned a van with a built-in bed or sponsored activities like tie-dye or communion with nature. In fact, given her upbringing, I got the sense that she considered a run in our local city park a hardcore backcountry experience. But what she lacked in practical experience she made up for in spunk. From the moment we found William Gray's book in my boyhood cabin, the idea of a trek mobilized her infectious energy and adventurous spirit. I was amazed at her voracious appetite for long-distance hiking books, and was shocked when I discovered that she'd begun to save money for the trip.

At first I thought her interest was based primarily on the romantic notion of escaping the rigidity of her life. But as the months went by and we moved beyond the "honeymoon" phase of our relationship, talk of a trail adventure persisted, as did Angela's hunger for a new set of technical texts on backpacking. Contrary to my fears, the more Angela learned about my quirks and the inconveniences of living in the outdoors, the more committed she became.

Later, I was inspired by the strength she displayed in handling her parents' disapproval. Rationally, I didn't blame her parents for withholding support; they hadn't met me, and as far as they knew I could be as wacky and irresponsible as a high school dropout following the Grateful Dead. Emotionally, I harbored some resentment, primarily on Angela's behalf, but also because the conflict made everything else more complicated. There was a bright side, though: As I watched Angela struggle with conflicting loyalties and emotions, my own concerns about school, money, and finger-chopping witches became less overwhelming. Things would work themselves out. For better or worse, we were going to do this.

[1]

180 Snickers Bars

 I'D TRIED ALL THE LOCAL supermarkets and health food stores, but none were selling corn elbows or corn spaghetti. According to Ray Jardine, long-distance hiking guru and author of *The Pacific Crest Trail Hiker's Handbook*, corn pasta is the ultimate power food. Jardine and his wife, Jenny, have hiked the Pacific Crest Trail three times and once held the record for the fastest complete hike: 2,655 miles in three months and four days. With this sort of résumé, I wasn't about to doubt their dinner choices, a fact that resulted in me spending many futile hours searching for corn pasta.

Of all the things we had to worry about while planning a five month hike, organizing approximately 1,260 trail breakfasts, snacks, lunches, and dinners was—while intimidating—at least something I could control.

During the eight months prior to our departure, it seemed that most of our weekends were spent planning and shopping. "What do you want for breakfast during week two? Energy bars or Pop Tarts?" I asked Duffy on one of the many Saturdays when I found myself wheeling our huge shopping cart down the aisles of our local bulk food club, which sold three-gallon jars of mayonnaise, four-case packs of V8 juice, and big-screen TV-size boxes of Pop Tarts.

Monday to Friday, I worked as a writer for an advertising agency in Philadelphia. I'd worked there for nearly four years and really liked it. I also enjoyed my little single-girl's apartment and stopping at the corner café every morning for a cup of coffee. Life was orderly and predictable. But while iced lattes and an occasional icy beer were nice, my new shiny green ice axe was so much more exciting.

An ice axe is a lightweight mountaineering tool shaped like a conventional axe but with several key differences, including a point at the end of its shaft called a "spike," and, at its head, a long serrated blade called the "pick" and a blunt, spoon-shaped "adze." Due to the snowy and icy conditions often encountered by hikers in several mountain ranges along the Pacific Crest Trail, ice axes are considered to be mandatory equipment. This is especially true in the Sierra Nevada Mountains of California, where the PCT climbs a series of difficult mountain passes ranging from 10,000 to 13,200 feet above sea level. Even into late summer, Muir, Mather, Forester, and other passes can be covered in knee-deep snow and glassy ice—meaning we'd have to keep our axes in hand and, if we slipped, be ready to perform ice axe self-arrest.

To perform self-arrest, you use your body weight to plunge the serrated blade of the axe into the icy mountainside (that you're in the process of whizzing down). Afterward, you ideally find yourself halted midslope, clinging to your axe and eyeing the bone-crunching rocks below—relieved that you're no longer hurtling toward them. During a brief mountaineering lesson at a nearby outdoor retailer, our instructor, Dave, remarked that while performing self-arrest, one should be careful to throw body weight *behind* the axe, not *onto* it. The greatest danger when learning self-arrest, he explained, is accidentally landing on the axe and gouging a hole in your face.

"When done correctly, nearly fifty percent of self-arrests are successful!" Dave exclaimed with a Grizzly Adams grin. One out of two didn't sound so fantastic to me, especially if success depended upon correct technique. Preferring to avoid any similarly unfriendly statistics, I changed the subject.

We needed a camp stove, the smaller and lighter the better. Dave recommended an MSR Whisperlite Internationale and fired it up for me. The resulting roar reminded me of a jet engine and caused many of my fellow fleece-clad shoppers to turn and stare. "I'll take it!" I yelled, expecting uproarious applause but getting only more stares.

Later that afternoon I tested our new toy. Sitting cross-legged on the driveway at Duffy's parents' house, I alternated between peering at the contraption in front of me and the instructions in my lap. When I was sure I'd read every-thing five times, I turned the dial on the stove and watched white gas trickle into its circular trough. My hand shook as I lit a match and tentatively inched it towards the hissing spout. The smell of gas grew stronger. My mind flashed to my sophomore year in college, when my roommate singed off her eyebrows lighting our oven. I leaned my head as far away from the stove as I could while still extending the match toward it. After several seconds of fearful stretching I finally applied the flame to the stove's pilot. Nothing.

Shaking my head, I turned to watch Duffy trying to pitch our tent on the lawn. If we couldn't light a silly stove in the backyard, how were we going to light it in a driving rainstorm? I loved Duffy like no one before, but at that moment, doubt stole in. I knew that he'd been on a couple backpacking trips and even learned a repertoire of knots during an outdoor leadership course, but it wasn't like he could write *The Definitive Guide to Surviving in the Wilderness*.

"Duffy, help, please," I whined. After fifteen minutes of tinkering, we finally got the stove lit and placed our titanium pot over the tumultuous blue fire. We whipped up some chewy wagon-wheel pasta, and as I choked it down it occurred to me that we were out of our minds.

X ▪ ▪ ▪ ▪ X

Ahead lay 2,655 miles of wilderness ranging from parched desert to muddy rain forest. And behind? I could count on my two hands the number of miles I'd hiked in my life. Nine. Including two miles up and two miles down Turkey Mountain in my New York hometown. Not a very impressive feat, consider-ing that a turkey can do it. I'm fairly confident, though, that your average Thanksgiving turkey cannot hike the Pacific Crest Trail.

Zigzagging its way from Mexico to Canada, the PCT crosses three states (California, Oregon, and Washington), three national monuments, seven na-tional parks, twenty-four national forests, and thirty-three federally mandated wildernesses. Along the way it ascends more than fifty-seven major moun-tain passes—lowish points in otherwise impermeable mountain ranges—and skirts the shores of innumerable bodies of water—lakes, tarns, ponds, creeks, streams, and rivers. Temperatures on the route range from over 100 degrees F in the deserts to below freezing in the High Sierra and North Cascades. The trail's lowest point is 140 feet above sea level, at the Columbia River Gorge between Oregon and Washington. Its highest is 13,200 feet, at Forester Pass in California's Sierra Nevada Mountains. All told, the PCT boasts the greatest elevation changes of any of America's eight National Scenic Trails as it passes through six out of seven of North America's ecozones as well as sixteen different plant communities in California alone. These include creosote bush scrub, valley grassland, chaparral, Joshua tree woodland, ponderosa pine forest, and mountain meadow. Wild animals known to inhabit the regions surrounding the trail include coyote, marmot, pika, black bear, elk, mountain goat, bobcat, and cougar.

Our northbound hike would begin about forty miles east of San Diego, amidst chaparral-covered hills and just yards from the U.S.–Mexico international border. Once home to Digueno Indians (who survived by eating cacti and yucca root), the border region of California is now populated mostly by border patrol, ranchers, illegal aliens (passing through), and, in late spring, approximately three hundred Canada-bound hiking hopefuls, many of whom—I assumed—were subsisting on that infamous and elusive corn pasta.

X ▪ ▪ ▪ ▪ X

After feeding the rest of our chewy, driveway-cooked, non-corn pasta to the dog, I moved inside to our re-supply headquarters–Duffy's old bedroom. "Re-supply" is the term used by distance hikers to describe detours into towns to pick up supplies–often in the form of food-laden re-supply packages. For months, working in our re-supply HQ, I alternated between staring at Duffy's tattered stuffed animals, dusty high school basketball trophies, and the backpacker's mess hall that was oozing out of boxes, creeping over chairs, and covering every inch of carpet before me. Military Meals-Ready-to-Eat (MREs), energy bars, Snickers bars, cereal bars, instant potatoes, mac 'n' cheese, cheesy crackers, dried fruits, dried peppers and other vegetables, dried spaghetti sauce, turkey jerky, freeze-dried meals–stuff that had been dried and then dried again, because it just wasn't dried enough. Even our drinks were dry. There were bags of instant coffee, hot chocolate mix, powdered milk, and Tang, lots of delicious Tang. Sealing everything up into what I hoped were airtight Ziplocs, I spent four days carefully distributing delightfully dry camping meals into sixteen re-supply boxes.

But even after each box got its food rations it wasn't nearly complete. There were more piles to be picked through—a thousand ibuprofen tablets, a thousand multivitamins, seventy-six AA and AAA batteries, thirty-six rolls of film, a twenty-four-pack of toilet paper, fourteen rolls of athletic tape, two bottles of povidone-iodine solution for our med kit, and six of the same for purifying water.

While I filled boxes, Duffy weighed every piece of gear, down to the quarter ounce. Then he began generating lists: lists of re-supply points, lists of food and equipment, lists of lists. All of these were subsequently downloaded onto our Palm Pilots—primarily for the purpose of reminding ourselves how good we were at making lists.

Other logistics also needed to be taken care of before we could disappear from normal life. Visa bills had to be paid in full if we wanted our credit ratings to survive our adventure. We needed to acquire air-ambulance and medical insurance (it can cost more than $50,000 to be airlifted out of the wilderness). Apartment subletters had to be found and debriefed. Health and dental check-ups had to be scheduled and attended (we'd heard of one couple whose hiking trip had been interrupted by an urgent need for a root canal). Duffy had to register for fall classes and I had reams of paperwork to complete regarding my leave of absence from work. And on and on.

It was all vastly annoying. The whole point was to get away from this sort of drudgery. I dreamed of savoring majestic vistas with looking-glass lakes, but instead I was explaining to Jennifer at Comcast Cable why I wouldn't be watching much HBO that summer.

Worst of all, planning for a long-distance hike seemed as potentially fruitless as it was frustrating. Historically, only five percent of PCT hikers actually make it the whole way, and out of those who quit, most do so in the first couple weeks. In the past few years, with the increasing popularity of lightweight backpacking techniques and refined itineraries, success rates have approached twenty-five percent, but one out of four is still pretty discouraging.

The combination of the magnitude of the planning effort and the odds of success was disquieting. Taking care of the logistics would be immensely gratifying if the trip worked out, but if it didn't—well, then the reward wouldn't be a completed trip but a planned one. The result of the uncertainty was a sensation not unlike that which you might feel if you planned a wedding but were forced to accept a caveat from the groom indicating there was only a one in four chance he'd show up.

In an effort to improve our odds, we enrolled in *Hiking 101* at a local community college. I figured that it would be a good practical introduction for me and, at a minimum, a decent review for Duffy. We arrived for the first class notebooks in hand and pencils sharpened, ready to learn the holy commandments of hiking. Our companions in this mission were a group of middle-aged urbanites and an instructor who was still reliving his days in the military. There were eighteen people in all: fifteen women, Duffy, our instructor, and one other guy, who wasn't representing his gender in the most enthusiastic manner. He was a wispy gentleman with pasty skin and a half-hearted pyramid of facial hair hanging from his chin. He looked as though he might buckle to the floor under the weight of a sunscreen-filled fanny pack.

Our instructor was a gruff and weathered former colonel in the Air Force. During his thirty-nine years in the Force, he informed us, he'd taught many raw recruits the skills of outdoor survival and interrogation. To punctuate this point, he pulled a green hat with white lettering from his canvas sack.

"We seized this hat from a Russian soldier. Do you know what it says? 'Excrement Happens'—and in the woods it does." The colonel scanned the troops and did not look pleased.

"Let's get something straight from the start." Dramatic pause. "The outdoors is not Walt Disney World." Another pause. "When you go out there, it is not like going to the amusement park for the afternoon." Longer pause. "The animals you see will be real. They *will not* be people in fuzzy costumes."

Satisfied that he now commanded our attention, the colonel gave us the details regarding a series of day hikes, which complemented the classroom instruction. On Sunday we were to meet at a Dunkin' Donuts near the trailhead. The colonel wanted to make sure that this reconnaissance would go smoothly.

"We will meet at the Dunkin' Donuts at oh-nine-hundred sharp," he commanded. "Note I said *at* the Dunkin' Donuts." Nice long pause. "Not *in* the Dunkin' Donuts. Now, if you want to go and sit *in* the Dunkin' Donuts and have your four-hundred-calorie glazed cruller, you can do that. But I will not, I repeat, will *not* come to look for you there." The colonel stopped and slowly spread a glare around the room.

Our gruff leader spent the rest of the evening reviewing hiking clothing and equipment. While explaining the usefulness of 1972 L.L. Bean flannel shirts and blue jeans, he pulled these items out of a weathered bag. Pretty soon there was a large pile of tired clothing on the table, including a musty thermal undershirt, several pairs of thinning wool socks, and two industrial-strength leather boots. He continued unloading a first-aid kit and a pair of wool pants that made my legs itch just looking at them. The whole time I half-expected him to pull out a hand grenade or a bazooka. He didn't, but it wasn't long before the subject of artillery was broached. The colonel had gone off on a tangent to explain safety requirements on our weekend hikes and the perils of straying from the group.

"I don't like people falling behind. I carry a .45 and if you fall behind too much . . . well, as a squad commander, you are allowed a ten-percent loss." The room went deathly quiet. I think that's when we decided not to join our classmates on the weekend excursions; somehow filling re-supply boxes seemed quite a bit safer.

For the next four Monday evenings *Hiking 101* continued to be an excellent source of amusement. Not excellent enough, however, for Duffy to miss *Monday Night Football*, so I endured the rest of the colonel's tirades on my own. Unfortunately, the course didn't really offer a whole lot of practical information for the aspiring long-distance hiker. The colonel seemed to have a fantastic recall of the outdoor survival techniques he'd taught fifteen years earlier, but he hadn't completely updated his résumé for the new era of Polartec jackets and ultralight travel. To prepare ourselves for our quest, we were going to have to take matters into our own hands.

X ▪ ▪ ▪ X

"I'm not gonna lie; it concerns me that you've never backpacked," Duffy remarked quietly. We were alone, peeling apples to dry in our food dehydrator, but his tone seemed to indicate that he was afraid someone else might hear. "You might not like it," he added.

I was floored. Duffy never talked about his fears, especially if they had to do with me—or us. I'd figured he must be nervous about embarking on a three-state hike with someone who was even more of a novice than himself, but if he was nervous enough to mention it, we could be in big trouble. Duffy was having doubts; obviously he wasn't sufficiently impressed by my conquest of Turkey Mountain.

Somehow, I'd have to prove to him that I could hack it.

It was autumn, just seven months before we were due to depart for the West Coast and the start of our long summer's walk. Duffy had created a spreadsheet detailing the miles we'd need to cover between water sources in the desert.

"Some days," he said, "we'll have to walk more than twenty miles in the sun to get from one soggy creek bed to another." There was an expectant pause as he tried to gauge my reaction. I shrugged my shoulders and feigned indifference.

I'd read just about every Pacific Crest Trail and backpacking-related book I could get my hands on, including *The Complete Book of Outdoor Lore* by Clyde Ormond, *The Pacific Crest Trail: A Hiker's Companion* by Karen Berger, and *Soul, Sweat and Survival on the Pacific Crest Trail* by Bob Holtel. But Duffy wasn't sold. "Sure you read the manual," I could almost hear him thinking, "but can you drive the car?" It was time for a trial run.

Living in Pennsylvania, the natural choice was a weekend on the Appalachian Trail, the Pacific Crest's older, eastern sister. On one of our many trips to the outdoor gear store, I found a book that listed all the best Appalachian Trail hikes in our area and picked a route along Blue Mountain Ridge, past Bear Rocks and Bake Oven Knob to Lehigh Gap.

A few days later, after hours of loading, unloading, and reloading our rented backpacks, my first overnight outdoor experience started with a spurt and sputter. It took us about two hours to drive to the trailhead, where we parked and then made it as far as the edge of the woods before being greeted by signs saying "Beware of Hunters" and "Hikers advised to wear fluorescent orange." None of our new moisture-wicking hiking clothing was remotely orange. Soon we were back in the car headed to Wal-Mart.

It was a Friday afternoon around three o'clock, and Wal-Mart's parking lot was packed. It was as if the only people working in town were the half a dozen Wal-Mart cashiers. Morbidly captivated, we took in all the mega store had to offer—including a high-tech video surveillance system with four cameras in the women's bathroom alone.

With a gasp of simultaneous relief and surprise, we found an entire aisle dedicated to florescent orange clothing. We tried on hats, shirts, jackets, even socks, but settled on three-dollar plastic vests. By the time we got back to the trail and started hiking it was 4:30 in the afternoon. The light would soon be fading.

Near Blue Mountain Ridge, the Appalachian Trail climbs a rocky knife-edge and weaves in and out of boulders piled high by glaciers. Actually, I don't think the word *trail* applies to the route we stumbled along. Imagine a wall about five feet high, pieced together with rocks about the size of pumpkins but not nearly so smooth. Now picture someone tipping over that rock wall and making you walk over the resulting mess.

"During the last ice age," Duffy read from photocopied pages of a guidebook, "Pennsylvania experienced a climate that frequently froze and thawed layers of rock. This periglacial cycle caused immense slabs of stone to fracture, leaving a 'sea of rocks', or felsenmeer."

Occasionally Duffy would shift his glance from the rocks underfoot to the meaty packet in his hands in order to give such tutorials, but mostly we just hiked—and hiked quickly. We were determined to reach Bear Rocks before dark. The one-gallon water jugs strung to my pack bounced off my butt with every step. Duffy had insisted that carrying extra water would be good practice for the desert, but I think he was really trying to figure out how much weight I could handle.

We followed the trail's white blazes for about an hour, but as we neared an immense rock outcropping (the knife-edge) the white marks abruptly disappeared. When we finally located them again, I had to chuckle at the absurdity of the next test.

The white blazes, and the trail, continued directly up the slippery, cold gray rocks—rocks piled precariously on top of one another for as far as I could see. We scanned for an alternate route, but the surrounding terrain was equally treacherous. There was nothing to do but crawl. The sun was dipping low and the wind picking up. We had to make it to the other side of this ridge before it got dark. Hiking over these rocks in daylight was dangerous; add the challenge of darkness, and I was afraid we might leave rural Pennsylvania in body casts. With my heavy backpack leaning one way and the rest of my body struggling to go another, I dragged myself along ledges, hopped from boulder to boulder, and clung to scraggly, naked trees. When we finally got over the knife-edge (with only a couple punctured water bottles as evidence of our peril), our feet were throbbing and our stomachs were growling.

We stumbled upon Bear Rocks just before nightfall and began making camp. Minutes later, a group of high school boys arrived and eyed us maliciously. I got the sense that they'd had their sights set on our campsite. Feeling uncomfortable, we turned our backs to make dinner.

We still hadn't mastered cooking on our MSR Internationale, and the pasta turned into porridge. But it was hot and filling, and that was good enough. After eating, Duffy built a half-hearted campfire from a collection of damp twigs and fall foliage. We watched it fizzle out after half an hour and then ducked into our tent to snuggle under our sleeping bag and cuddly soft fleece blanket. This was my first night camping with Duffy, and I enjoyed the romance of the moment immensely—until the hollering and crashing began. Through the thin nylon of our tent, I could see lights bobbing amongst the trees around us. Feet rushed through leaves and brush. Voices called to one another in the coal-black night.

"It's those kids," Duffy whispered. When they finally quieted down, Duffy fell asleep. Not me; I heard every leaf rustle for the next eight hours.

It started to rain. The leaves rustled louder, twigs snapped, and I thought I heard footsteps. Convinced those high school kids were coming back to play tricks on us, I lay on the hard ground as stiff as a corpse. The corner of our tent started to leak, and my toes became cold and wet. I couldn't figure out where the noises were coming from. Suddenly, something brushed up against the tent just above my shoulder. Terrified, I stared at the patch of nylon, waiting for a hand to press against it or a knife to come slicing through.

Finally, as early morning light illuminated the tent, I caught some snippets of sleep. When we awoke, the source of my terror was revealed. Scattered around the perimeter of the tent was a dusting of granola. We'd left our trail mix outside and a squirrel or chipmunk had a fine feast—hence all the night-time rustling. And that soft touch, the ghostly hand running its fingers along the tent wall—that was our rain fly flapping in the wind.

"Did you sleep at all?" Duffy was still groggy.

"Oh, yeah," I said cheerfully. "It's so peaceful out here." I was determined not only to pass this exam but to get bonus points for optimism.

A cold rain appeared to be settling in for the weekend, and Duffy suggested we cut short the rest of our trip.

"Whatever you want," I said with a smile. My fingers and toes were going white and numb from standing in the bone-chilling drizzle. Soon, I knew, they'd turn blue and start to throb. For the past few years, I'd suffered from Raynaud's phenomenon, sometimes called Raynaud's Disease or simply Raynaud's. Raynaud's, named for the French physician Maurice Raynaud who first recognized it in 1862, refers to a cold- or stress-induced interruption of blood flow to the fingers, toes, nose, and ear lobes. For reasons not completely understood, some people's blood vessels hyper-react to cold. This means that anything from snow flurries to an iced drink can lead to painful and sometimes debilitating symptoms. In severe instances, ulcerations and infections can occur, leading to gangrene. Nine times more common in women than in men, Raynaud's affects approximately twenty-eight million Americans.

Usually, Raynaud's was just an uncomfortable inconvenience for me, relieved by holding a steaming cup of tea or taking a hot shower. But in the wilderness, I worried about how I would bring feeling and blood back to my hands and feet, especially at 12,000 feet. What if I couldn't? Would I develop frostbite? Or gangrene? I'd sought medical advice (from both Duffy and a fully licensed M.D.), but because people don't really know what causes Raynaud's, there aren't many known treatments. Taking medicines usually used for high blood pressure can help (I'd been taking them for more than a year and found only mild relief), but mostly physicians recommend preventing exposure to cold conditions and objects. Well, it was too late for that now, so I shoved my hands under my armpits and hoped for the best.

"These are hypothermic conditions, all right," Duffy remarked. He was jumping up and down around our campsite. "Rain, wind, and temperatures just below fifty degrees. It's not worth the risk." Whatever the reason, I was happy to get out of the miserable, wet weather as soon as possible. My nose was getting raw from wiping away the runniness.

We hiked purposefully the rest of the day, determined to move fast enough to stay warm and to make it back to the car before we were thoroughly soaked. With lighter packs (we dumped our "training" water) and thoughts of central heating to inspire us, we made good time. When we got home we took long, hot showers, huddled over bowls of soup, and slept soundly. We hadn't completed our proposed route, but we'd survived our first thirty-six hours in the wilderness.

X ▪ ▪ ▪ X

Months later, the sweet, sharp aroma of tomato sauce oozed beneath my apartment door into the cramped stairwell. I'd been dehydrating spaghetti sauce all week, trying to add at least one stretchy tomato "leather" to each of our resupply boxes. In a few weeks, we'd be so sick of those slimy, salty roll-ups that we'd throw them out or give them away. But for now, the whir of my dehydrator was a constant companion.

Alone in my tomato-scented apartment, I packed my personal belongings and made room for my subletter. Soon I'd have no job and no rent to pay; everything I needed to survive would be on my back. Surrounded by wilderness, there'd be no traffic to fight, no ringing telephones, no emails, and nobody to answer to but my hiking partner. It sounded like freedom—so why did I feel so trapped? After quitting my job, alienating my family, and spending my savings on equipment, I felt frequent flutters of fear. If this didn't work— if Duffy and I didn't work—I had no Plan B.

Under the strain, I started grinding my teeth in my sleep but otherwise kept quiet. I didn't want to discuss the worst-case scenario with anyone for fear of it becoming a self fulfilling prophecy. Could I hike alone if I had to? And if so, how would we divide equipment, funds, and food? Should I be insisting on the long-distance hiking equivalent of a prenuptial agreement?

X ▪ ▪ ▪ ▪ X

We finally touched down at the San Diego International Airport on May 7. We had made arrangements, using a Pacific Crest Trail email forum, for an ex-Navy commander named Bob to pick us up. He was to be our first "trail angel." Trail angels are sometimes said to be the "unsung heroes" of the PCT, helping hikers with food, water, rides, laundry, showers, and much more. During the dark times, when hikers waver between continuing on and giving up, the support, encouragement, and "magic" provided by a trail angel can make all the difference.

Often anonymous, trail angels help thru-hikers for no other reason than, in the words of one angel, "the satisfaction of helping another human being . . . making their journey better and in the process becoming woven into that journey." Frequently, trail angels find spots where hikers are liable to run into trouble and then, like magic, solve the problem—for instance, by providing water in the desert. In this way they seem like guardian angels, appearing just when they are needed most.

In Bob's case, this meant picking up hikers at the airport, giving them a place to stay, and then driving them to the trail's southern terminus, near Campo.

We rescued our packs from the strap-eating conveyor belts at baggage claim and, exhausted from the previous day's preparations as well as the cross-country flight, staggered outside into the bright southern California sunshine. Bob was already parked at the curb, his minivan sporting a *Pacific Crest Trail* placard.

"Welcome to paradise!" Bob exclaimed when he spotted our bulging packs, trekking poles, and Duffy's *Lawrence of Arabia*-like sun hat. Beckoning us, he grinned and shouted, opening his thick arms out wide to reveal sweaty armpits and a sumo wrestler tummy.

At Bob's bungalow we made ourselves comfortable on the patio, spread our gear around us, and began to meticulously weigh the pros and cons of each item one last time. Pieces of gear deemed worth their weight were carefully positioned in our packs. Discarded stuff went into Bob's "hiker box." Hiker boxes, we learned, could be found at popular re-supply locations up and down the trail. Although they were always called "boxes," they often weren't boxes at all but rather barrels, bags, or buckets. Though their shape and size varied, their contents quickly became predictable—discarded hiker junk. Heavy, tasteless, and mysterious grains, socks, old shoes, used paperbacks, multi-vitamins, and leaky sandwich bags filled with more anonymous grains. Bob's hiker box contained all of the above as well as shampoo, candles, and *corn pasta*.

"I couldn't find this stuff anywhere!" I exclaimed. "And they're throwing it away?"

"Must taste terrible, 'cause everybody leaves it. Do me a favor and get it outta here," said Bob.

Duffy gave me a look that said, "Don't you dare." He'd never been very enthusiastic about corn pasta, and he'd seen me cry over the weight of my pack more than once. Sitting in the hot tub with his pony-size golden retriever, Nugget, Bob watched our preparations.

"Don't be scared of illegals," he said suddenly. "If ya run into any, just grab your camera, pretend it's a cell phone. They believe three things about America," Bob gestured to the southern horizon. "The cops are always around the corner, everyone has a cell phone, and that those phones always work. If they think you're calling the border patrol on 'em, they'll skedaddle.

"Also, you should know that there's been some talk of killer bees coming up from South America." Bob was stroking Nugget's big wet head and seemed to be talking more to him than us. "But no hikers have been stung yet, so you should be okay. Watch out for the rattlers, though; there's a lot of them out this year. I've always wanted to kill one and eat it myself; heard it tastes like chicken. By the way, what would you like for dinner tonight? Last real meal for a while. . . . "

We decided to head to our favorite fast-food establishment, Jack in the Box, and piled into the car. Over burgers, fries, and strawberry shakes, Bob told us about a hiker he'd dropped off just a few days earlier, Ricky Rose. Ricky carried a sixty-pound pack containing a cell phone and global positioning system (GPS), as well as a bulletproof, rubberized laptop. I'd worked hard to get my pack down to thirty-five pounds and still winced under its weight.

"You'll catch up to Ricky in no time," said Bob. "Can't miss him. Skinny, bushy beard, big pack." I wasn't sure that such a description was going to be much help. It seemed like that's what all male thru-hikers might end up looking like.

During dessert, Bob advised us to also keep a lookout for Bruce, a middle-aged gentleman who suffered from Parkinson's disease. Bruce's goal was to hike the length of the California Pacific Crest Trail, a distance of more than seventeen hundred miles. This despite the fact that he'd been suffering from Parkinson's for fifteen years and was receiving progressively less relief from his medicine. To prolong the pills' benefits over the long-term, Bruce took them only twice a day. On the trail, this meant he'd have an hour and a half in the morning to break camp, put on his pack, and get going before the onset of incapacitating tremors, slowness, and clumsiness. After his evening dose, he'd have another symptom-limited hour and a half to set up camp, cook, and get into bed. In between, he would lack the dexterity to perform simple maneuvers such as adjusting his pack straps, unwrapping a Power Bar, or tying his shoes. By comparison, my worries seemed minuscule.

Following dinner we returned to Bob's house for an early night. Lying on a twin bed in Bob's teenage son's room, I listened to Duffy's rhythmic breathing. Our last few days at home had been hectic and I knew I had to sleep, but my mind was racing. Had I packed enough dried milk for the three or four days it would take us to reach Mount Laguna, the first town along the trail? What if the seasonal creeks dried up? When would we see our first rattler? How did illegal immigrants survive out there without maps and gear? What were my parents doing? Tears welled in my eyes, as they often did when I thought about my mom and dad. Guilt weighed on me heavier than a freshly loaded pack. "Soon," I thought, as I drifted into a tumultuous, shallow sleep, "just a few more hours and then I'll disappear into the wilderness."

[2]

Meadow Ed

I'VE BEEN TOLD that when breaking in a pair of leather hiking boots, it's best to proceed with caution. Wear them around the house a couple of times, then maybe wear them for a day in the office, and finally take them out for a series of three- to five-mile hikes. In theory, the leather should slowly soften and mold to your feet for the perfect fit. Sure sounds comfortable, but I've never met or heard of anyone who has successfully bent the will of a pair of new leather boots. On the contrary, boots typically bend the will of feet by inflicting torturous hot spots and blisters. Perhaps it's this fortitude of spirit that warrants their status as expensive retail items.

Similarly, the southern PCT doesn't break thru-hikers in easily; instead, it begins with fifteen dry, waterless miles through high desert. But heat and lack of water aren't hikers' only concerns—there are also rattlesnakes, mountain lions, killer bees, and illegal immigrants to worry about. Thirst, fear, and pain will greet you on the PCT, and like a good ol' pair of leather boots stuffed with callused, hoof-like feet, they'll stay with you until you've been thoroughly broken in.

X ▪ ▪ ▪ X

On the morning of May 8, we traveled east toward the small California border town of Campo. For weeks I'd been preoccupied with trail worries, but on this morning fear took a backseat to grogginess. It was 4:45 in the morning and we were whipping along the dark curves of Highway 94 in Bob's Dodge van, feeling slightly ill from breakfast sandwiches and frequent stomach-revolving shifts in direction. We'd had a short, fitful night of sleep; excitement, nerves, and strange surroundings made us fidgety, so much so in Angela's case that she sat bolt upright in bed at about 12:30 in the morning and chirped at me to get moving. She chirped and chirped, despite my pleas for her to consult her watch. At last, after a dozen or so chirpies, she checked the time and reluctantly lay back down.

Angela and I weren't the only ones on the groggy side. Bob was making the pre-dawn trip to Campo for the twenty-second time that spring (we were his thirtieth and thirty-first hikers), and the cumulative effects had made him a little sleepy—sleepy enough to disregard a sharp curve in the road and take the Dodge screeching into the oncoming lane. Luckily, Campo to San Diego isn't a big commuter route, and there wasn't any westbound traffic to collide with. Our only fatality was Bob's mug of coffee.

Fifteen minutes later, Bob pulled the van up next to the wooden PCT monument, which stands twenty feet from a corrugated steel fence marking the Mexican border. Running alongside the fence is a well-maintained dirt road used nightly by Border Patrol officers to scout for footprints. The monument itself was a cluster of five rectangular pillars of varying height with a series of inscriptions that read, "Southern Terminus Pacific Crest National Scenic Trail," "Established by Act of Congress on Oct. 2, 1968," "Mexico to Canada 2627 Miles 1988 A.D.," and "Elevation 2915 ft."

It was cold and windy and we were anxious to get started, so we snapped a couple of photos, said our good-byes to Bob, and then were off toward Canada—a mere 2,655 miles away (the trail has grown by twenty-eight miles since 1988). As we set out from the border, I wore a pack containing our tent and ThermaRests, five days' worth of food, a gallon of water, and an assortment of personal items. It had weighed in at fifty-three pounds that morning on Bob's scale. Fifty-three pounds of pressure on my shoulders and hips wasn't so comfortable—about as comfortable as sitting next to an eight-hundred-pound dairy cow for a twelve-hour Greyhound ride. But for the time being, the discomfort of a heavy pack was superseded by the excitement of starting our great adventure.

We moved at a steady pace over undulating trail in the face of blustery winds, which stirred up clouds of caramel-colored dust. My nose caught an occasional whiff of sweet sagebrush. Every so often, I glimpsed suspicious pieces of litter—juice cans and candy bar wrappers with Spanish lettering, ragged blue jeans, an Oakland Raiders baseball hat. There were no signs of those who had discarded these treasures, but I assumed they weren't fellow hikers. I'd done enough research to know that very few long-distance hikers wear blue jeans or Raiders paraphernalia.

A week before our departure from Philadelphia, I'd read an account of a hiker who, while walking at night, was chased by a gang of men. He avoided capture by locking himself in a small shed. The assailants didn't give up, however, and spent an hour attempting to break in while the frightened hiker (who happened to be an ex-marine) braced himself against the door. As morning broke, he burst from the shed, brandishing a knife whittled from wood and raced away from his tormentors. Despite the fact that this assault occurred in Chariot Canyon, some sixty miles north and a three-day hike away, I was fearful of a similar confrontation. Bob had asserted that the Chariot Canyon attack had been perpetrated by local "yahoos" rather than illegal immigrants, whom he thought were "much more interested in avoiding hikers than in stealing their stuff." That didn't help much. Illegals and yahoos? I didn't want to try my luck with either of them.

The United States and Mexico share a two-thousand-mile border, and while estimates vary widely as to the number of illegal immigrants that attempt to cross this border each year, they run as high as *seven and a half million*. By comparison, the number of *legal* Mexican immigrants is currently capped at seventy-five thousand per year. A significant percentage of the illegal U.S–Mexico border-crossers, probably in the range of sixty to eighty percent, attempt to cross into either San Diego or neighboring Imperial Counties. Approximately 400,000 of these are picked up by U.S. Border Patrol (USBP) each year and shuttled back over the border, where many will make plans to try again. Within San Diego County, there are more than two thousand Border Patrol agents for sixty-six miles of border, enough for one per every two hundred feet or so. In addition, the USBP has at its disposal high-tech infrared equipment that can pinpoint the location of a jack rabbit down to a centimeter. Despite the large work force and cutting-edge technology, evidence seems to support the claim that, even in San Diego County, the USBP carries a batting average around the Mendoza line (.200 or so), meaning that only one out of every five border-crossers is caught. The Immigration and Naturalization Service (INS), while long acknowledging the difficulty of estimating the flow of illegal immigrants, has generally publicized a higher apprehension rate than this. But information from the U.S. census of 2000 showing higher than expected numbers for total population and particularly for the Hispanic population, seems to refute these claims.

Compounding the illegal immigrant problem is the illegal cargo some carry. Approximately seventy-five percent of illicit drugs in the U.S. enter via transport across the U.S.–Mexico border. Drug cartels often "mule" their cocaine and other recreational pharmaceuticals across within the stomachs and intestines of those dreaming of a better life. "Mules" are people who smuggle drugs by ingesting securely wrapped containers of extremely pure substances. These poor folks, already risking capture by Border Patrol, assault by anti-alien vigilantes, exposure, dehydration, and starvation, take on the further peril (not to mention discomfort) of passing latex-coated cocaine through the behind. Consider that in the year 2000 alone, there were five hundred documented border-crossing deaths, most of them from environmental exposure. Who knows how many died and weren't found? Drug "mules" are willing to risk all of this for $1,000 and the chance for a new life in America—quite a gamble to take to enter a country that goes out of its way to punish both illegal drug distribution and illegal immigrants.

X ▪ ▪ ▪ ▪ X

As midday approached, the wind abated and sunshine bore down. We completed a gradual traverse of Hauser Mountain and then a steamy, knee-rocking canyon descent. By one in the afternoon we'd reached the canyon floor and Hauser Creek. It was the first water supply of the day, and a remarkably unimpressive one at that—a stagnating pool swarming with gnats and surrounded by mud pocketed with cattle hoof marks. Our lunch consisted of raisins, energy bars, and dried meat sticks. I'd soon discover that a meat stick is the perfect protein bolus for a ravenous hiker. At first, the contents of the dried meat stick were a mystery to me, but after a summer of these tasty and wholesome treats I think I finally figured out the secret recipe—eight parts beef, four parts pork, two parts rat brain, and one part human foot. After a treat like that you can't help but feel sleepy, and on that afternoon, under live oak and sycamore trees, we took a peaceful nap.

A couple of hours later, we began the last leg of the day's hike to Lake Morena. Several steps into a 1,000-foot vertical ascent of Morena Butte, I abruptly halted. Placed neatly at the edge of the trail were two D batteries, a tube of aloe, and a brand-new pair of wool socks. These were not south-of-the-border possessions; no, they were evidence of another Canada-bound hiker, most likely one trying to remedy decisions that had led to a very heavy backpack. Perhaps these were signs of Ricky and his sixty-pound load? I chuckled, picked up the aloe, and set off up Morena Butte.

It was our first real climb and I attacked it with gusto, plowing forward with the aid of forceful trekking-pole lunges. Every thirty seconds or so I'd glance at my watch altimeter to gauge our progress and yell the update to Angela behind me. By the time we reached the apex of the butte I was huffing and Angela was wheezing.

A brisk interchange ensued. Angela was upset at the pace of our climb and my disregard for her shorter and slower stride. I tried to explain that I was merely climbing the hill at my own comfortable rate and that she needn't feel obligated to keep up with me. This explanation didn't help. Angela felt strongly that she shouldn't ever fall outside of trekking-pole range of me while on the trail. But this just wasn't going to be possible. One of the first rules of long-distance hiking is that you must hike at your own pace. Unfortunately, my (long-legged) pace was rarely going to be Angela's (short-legged) pace. Angela wasn't satisfied and pleaded with me to slow down. "I'll always wait for you to catch up," I said. It was the best she was going to get.

This was our first on-trail spat, and I knew there would be many to follow. I hoped, however, that we could quickly reconcile our divergent hiking styles. If not, we might soon be taking diverging paths back to Philadelphia. These thoughts spun around in my head as my legs carried me down to Lake Morena, an expanse of refreshment within the thirsty hills. The Lake Morena campground offered luxuries that we would find at few other camping spots along the trail—soda machines, picnic tables, bathrooms, and hot showers.

Soon after arriving, we received a visit from Ricky. Fortyish, with dark black hair and a toothpick-inspired frame, Ricky limped up to us on a knee tightly bound with an ACE bandage. Ricky then rapidly filled us in on the compelling story of . . . Ricky. He started with his charity effort, B2B (Border 2 Border) 2000, which was designed to raise money for the Krusty Burgers for Kids Fund and had already garnered many, many sponsors—forty-four in all. These included NASA, AlpineAire Foods, Outfitters Jerky, AloeUp Skincare Products, Crescent Moon Snowshoes . . . Ricky seemed intent on naming all forty-four of them and probably would have if I hadn't interrupted to ask about his computer.

"Yup" he responded, "I've got a six-pound, solar-powered, bulletproof laptop. You can drop the beast from eight feet onto granite and it will still purr like a kitten." And the D batteries and aloe left on the trail?

"Well, had to ditch that stuff once my knee started acting up. I thought another hiker might want 'em."

"Who wants to carry D batteries?" Angela whispered to herself as much as to me. I wondered how AloeUp Skincare would feel if they knew that their aloe had been jettisoned just fifteen miles into the PCT. Apparently, Ricky's unpacking had been too little, too late, because he was planning to rest a day or so at Lake Morena to let his knee settle down. Satisfied that he'd thoroughly filled us in on his operation, Ricky turned a critical eye to our gear.

"So, MSR stove, huh?"

"Yup, Internationale," I said.

"Good choice. That's what I have, too. It's the best choice, it really is. You can use any sort of fuel. Titanium pot? That's a necessity. But the fuel bottle . . . no titanium? What, couldn't afford the few extra bucks for titanium? Come on, really should have titanium." Rick apparently wanted us to apologize for the oversight, but I wasn't in the mood to beg forgiveness for a few extra ounces of fuel bottle, certainly not from a guy who was carrying a six-pound laptop.

"Yeah," was all I could muster.

Angela looked stressed. "Maybe we do need a titanium bottle."

"What are you guys carrying for grub? I have more freeze-dried meals than I know what to do with. You should have seen the day that AlpineAire dropped them off—we had to clear out a large area on the driveway. I am eating nothing but freeze-dried. Well, nothing but freeze-dried for dinner, beef jerky for lunch."

"We have a mix of stuff—some from Mountain House, some instant potatoes, some MREs," I reported.

"MREs? Meals-Ready-to-Eat? Those military rations are heavy, man, real heavy. Freeze-dried is the way to go. You should dump the MREs and pick up some freeze-dried." Angela was looking pale but Ricky didn't notice and continued.

"You know, by my GPS calculations, the distance from Campo to Lake Morena was really only eighteen point one miles, not twenty point three."

I noted a slump in Angela's shoulders.

"We didn't *really* need to hear that, Ricky." I was wishing he would hand me a titanium fuel bottle so I could hit him over the head with it.

"Well, you know that guidebook is always getting it wrong. I bet you could find a mistake on every single page." He was referring to the definitive guide to the PCT, Schaffer's *The Pacific Crest Trail*. Only the most brazen hiked without it. We'd painstakingly divided its two thick volumes into nine sections, which we taped into colorful poster board covers. I thought of these sections as our lifeline and, no matter what Ricky said, wasn't prepared to admit that they might be inaccurate.

Later, standing around a campfire with a couple of other hikers, Ricky regaled us with more about Ricky. The fire was comforting on a cool night, but eventually we had enough of his pontification about routefinding and snowshoeing in the Sierra snowfields and excused ourselves.

Fog moved off the reservoir and settled over the campground. I could see moisture developing on the roof of our tent, but I was too tired to put on the rain fly. I awoke in the middle of the night to see prominent beads of water suspended on the nylon ceiling. "Maybe I can flick the water off," I thought, and tapped the tent with my middle finger. Drip, drip, drip. Mutters and rustling next to me. Several hours later, there was movement in the nearby trees. I sat bolt upright and accidentally smacked the ceiling with my head. A shower of moisture descended. The rustling outside stopped, so I dropped back onto my now-soggy fleece pillow. Angela chirped twice in displeasure and then the night was quiet.

When morning finally emerged, we moved deliberately. Packing up our fog-moistened gear was both slow and unpleasant. It took us an hour and a half to break camp. Once we finally got hiking, things got dryer, but not much better. Heat descended on us early and rapidly escalated. But while our morning hike was miserable, there was one stroke of good fortune: In leaving Lake Morena, we left behind NASA's finest PCT hiker, Mr. Ricky Rose.

With sore and reluctant legs, we suffered through ten miles and ninety-plus-degree heat on a shadeless and overgrown trail. We took a midday break at Kitchen Creek, a short walk down Kitchen Creek Canyon Road, laying out our space blanket footprint under an aged black oak. Kitchen Creek, unlike Hauser, was running well, forming cool, inviting pools. Our initial plan had been to hike another four miles to Cibbets Flat Campground that evening, but several hikers had advised us that the Border Patrol considered this to be a popular layover spot for drug-trafficking mules. Sleeping with mules seemed risky, so after several hours of relaxation under the oak it wasn't difficult for us to rationalize staying put for the night.

Dinner was freeze-dried chili mac from Mountain House; within minutes a bag of brown, dusty macaroni morphed into a hearty meal. We remarked on its excellence while exploring Kitchen Creek in the twilight.

I listened for the mating call of the Arroyo toad, an endangered species native to the seasonal creeks of Southern California. We'd been told that this was the height of the spring mating season. The Forest Service certainly took this seriously, having closed Boulder Oaks Campground, five miles to the south and posted "Do Not Disturb" warning signs near Kitchen Creek. But if there was mating going on at Kitchen Creek it was not of a vociferous nature; we heard nothing but satisfied after-silence. The twilight pinks and oranges reflected off the rocky hills and the creek bubbled peacefully. We retired to the tent and, taking a cue from the toads, slipped quickly and quietly into sleep.

X = ▪ ▪ ▪ X

"I saw a skunk last night. He looked at me through the tent. I was *sooo* scared I couldn't even breathe. He was right there!" Angela was animated in telling her story of a late-night visitor.

"What? I don't think there *are* skunks around here. It must have been a raccoon. Did it have eye patches?"

"I don't think so, but it had a stripe on its nose. It sure looked like a skunk."

"Chigger, you should have woken me up. I would have protected you from that vicious . . . raccoon." Chigger was an affectionate nickname I had for Angela. I often display affection in odd ways.

"It wasn't a raccoon!" she insisted. "And if I had tried to wake you up, the skunk would have sprayed us."

"Couldn't be much worse than we already smell."

"Speak for yourself."

As we walked back up Kitchen Creek Canyon Road to the trail, we continued to debate the identity of our curious friend. Schaffer's guidebook didn't mention skunks in the area, and I was about to press the point when we spotted a van coming toward us. It was an ancient, white VW clunker, barreling down the hill. As it passed, the driver and passenger gave us wide grins and enthusiastic waves.

"I bet they just dropped off some illegal cargo," I remarked.

Or perhaps they had just successfully passed a Border Patrol checkpoint. Under Operation Gatekeeper, instituted in 1994, the U.S. government has adopted a policy of considering certain roads near the border as *being* the border. Kitchen Creek Canyon Road was one of them.

We kept a keen lookout for border-crossers that morning, but all we saw was chaparral. Before hiking the PCT, I'd never heard of chaparral, and at first I thought the name referred to one particular plant. Chaparral, however, is the name for a plant community that is prevalent in the high desert and foothills (3,000 to 5,500 feet) of Southern California. Chaparral consists of a collection of extremely hearty and drought resistant shrubs and small trees—manzanita, sage, ribbonwood, mountain mahogany, chamise, sumac, mountain lilac, and poison oak, to name a few. These plants share a number of characteristics—long roots to search the rocky subsoil for water, stiff evergreen leaves to limit water loss, and sharp, calf- to waist-high branches to scrape the bejeezus out of hikers' legs.

As we hiked through a sea of skin-scarring shrubbery, our views were occasionally enlivened by spiny yucca plants and red-stained gneiss, sprinkled with white forget-me-nots. In the early afternoon, the topography began to change as we ascended into the Laguna Mountains, and scattered Jeffrey pine trees offered us a hint of the sublimely alpine. Traipsing toward Mount Laguna, the first re-supply stop on the northbound PCT, we amused ourselves by counting the critters around us. Lizards of all shapes, sizes, and colors dominated the data collection. Most of them scurried frenetically about the trail—all but the horned lizards, often called horny toads. Yellow-brown in color, round in shape, and with a regal crowns of horns, many of these horny toads sat stoically in the middle of the trail, color and texture allowing them to blend in almost seamlessly.

By midafternoon we'd counted fifty lizards, thirty-three butterflies, a smattering of bunnies, a couple of black beetles, and one large ebony snake. We didn't count the bees, though; there were just too many of them. We were switchbacking up chaparral-infested foothills when they started swarming and buzzing around us. I thought immediately of Bob's report of the recent arrival of killer bees.

"It's just a matter of time," he'd said, "before they nest someplace on the trail, and just a matter of time before a hiker disturbs 'em and gets the royal sting treatment."

Killer bees, also known as "Africanized Honey Bees" or "Africanized bees," are descendants of African bees imported in the mid-1950s by Brazilian scientists attempting to breed honeybees better adapted to the South American tropics. As if dutifully following a bad Hollywood horror script, some of the bees escaped and began breeding with local Brazilian bees. Killer bees were born from this fateful match and rapidly multiplied, extending their range throughout South and Central America at a rate of two hundred miles a year.

Their amazing proliferation is attributed to two behavioral adaptations. First, killer bees are much less discriminating in their choice of nests than native bees, willing to utilize just about anything they might come across—hollow trees, walls, porches, sheds, attics, utility boxes, garbage containers, abandoned vehicles, and perhaps even PCT trail registers. Second, they aren't shy about engaging in group-sex rituals (also known as "swarming") on a more regular basis than their comparatively chaste cousins.

In the early 1990s, the Africanized bees began invading North America. The first swarm was found in October of 1990 in Hidalgo, Texas. Subsequently, colonies were found in Arizona and New Mexico in 1993 and finally in California in 1994. Now, more than eight thousand square miles of Imperial, Riverside, and San Diego Counties are colonized with killer bees. In July of 1993, eighty-two-year-old Lino Lopez attempted to remove a killer bee hive from an abandoned building on his ranch in Harlingen, Texas. He was stung more than forty times and became the first U.S. death attributed to the ill-tempered bees from Africa. More deaths have followed, and I hoped that Angela and I wouldn't become the first thru-hikers to join the list.

Amidst the swarming and occasional collisions, I noticed that these bees didn't look much like honeybees; they were darker in color and larger. Later I learned that this discrepancy was a *good* thing, since killer bees closely resemble the friendly and harmless European honeybee. They may be just a smidgen smaller than your average backyard flower friend, but only an expert can tell the difference.

I pushed the brim of my hat down and walked faster up the switchbacks. Bees bounced off me freely as I motored forward. Every so often I looked back at Angela to be sure she wasn't being engulfed by a swarm and carried off; that sort of disappearance would be hard to explain to her family. I didn't know much about Angela's parents, but it seemed clear that they thought our hike was foolhardy. Losing their daughter to a bee swarm certainly wouldn't help sway this opinion.

We hiked through bees for several miles without suffering a single sting or kidnapping. One good thing about all those bees—their fury of movement helped distract me from the pain of the long climb up to Mount Laguna.

Like Campo and many other towns near the PCT, Mount Laguna is a small settlement. For the most part, when it comes to towns along a Pacific Crest hike, small is better. In a petite town, hikers tend to experience less culture shock, and re-supply is more convenient because the facilities, and really the whole town, are centralized in a small area. Plus, in small towns there are fewer people to offend with hiker-stench.

The Mount Laguna residents didn't complain about our hygiene. With all the hikers passing through at this time of year, they were probably accustomed to our unique form of air pollution. And the locals certainly didn't threaten to toss us out of town on account of our unkempt appearance, something that Chigger had fretted about all afternoon. Our first town stop was brief. We weren't picking up a box in Mount Laguna, and no matter how we tried to rationalize it, we didn't feel we'd earned the luxury of a hotel stay. We purchased sodas and chips from the general store and sat outside recovering from the morning climb.

During our first day of hiking we'd decided that we absolutely had to lighten our packs, and in a more drastic way than had Ricky Rose. The grueling climb up into the Lagunas had accentuated this urge to purge, as did the lineup of lightweight packs we saw propped against the steps of Mount Laguna's general store—packs that were dwarfed by our bulging behemoths. If a backpack skirmish were to break out, my Mountainsmith and Angela's Gregory would have a tremendous advantage in size and weight. As it turns out, though, backpacks are generally docile creatures and would rather pick their fights with those who carry them than with each other.

Several of the lightweight packs scattered about were not much bigger than what the average junior high student carries to school. I recognized their brand as GoLite, an ultralight gear company inspired by Ray Jardine. Ray Jardine is *the* celebrity in the long-distance hiking world; his name and ultralight (and corn pasta) advice is well known throughout the thru-hiking community. Like most of our Pacific Crest brethren, we'd dutifully read Jardine's books—*The PCT Hiker's Handbook* and *Beyond Backpacking: Ray Jardine's Guide to Lightweight Hiking*. But while we were well versed in the "Ray Way" of hiking, we hadn't exactly been following all of his recommendations. We'd figured that we were too green to risk packing ultralight. Now, however, we were ready to give semilight a shot.

I bought two boxes at the Mount Laguna post office and we filled them with unneeded luxuries. Into one box went an extra titanium pot, a collapsible water jug, two pairs of hiking socks, and a large handful of Angela's underwear. We sent this box home to Philadelphia, hoping that my mother would not be curious enough to open it. Into another box we put stuff to send ahead to Idyllwild, 140 miles north—my wilderness medicine field guide, Angela's Palm Pilot, our Counter Assault "grizzly tough" pepper spray (carried primarily for drug-trafficker deterrence), a pair of dirty khaki shorts, and a number of items from my very complete (and very heavy) first-aid kit. As I heaved my pack, which I'd started sarcastically calling "Big Red," back on, its burden didn't seem at all diminished. Perhaps Angela's felt better?

"This pack is still *too* heavy," she sighed.

A day and twenty miles of hiking later, our packs remained obese and our supposedly semilight operation was ready for a night in town. Bullied and nearly beaten by winds whipping across a parched meadow, we hiked off-trail for a mile before reaching the rusty barbed-wire gate that led to Sunrise Highway. Our plan was to hitch a ride into the resort town of Julian, seven miles up the highway. Once famous for its gold mines, Julian is now known for its pie shops and apple cider. A piece of boysenberry pie, piled high with vanilla ice cream, would be a delicious change of pace. We hiked for several miles along the highway before a Chevy pickup with a built-on camper came to our rescue. Angela jumped in the back while I sat in the front with the driver and admired a collection of mementos neatly arranged his dashboard—quartz crystals, eagle and hawk feathers, and a sequoia cone. Our driver's name was Tim, a young guy with an innocent and earnest face. He lived in Julian, where he was house-sitting with his girlfriend and commuting to San Diego for school. At the moment, however, he was returning from a week of meditation and fasting in the Anza-Borrego desert. I was intrigued. Why had he chosen the desert for his fast?

"The fast is my way of dealing with fear. The desert is a tough place. I have great fear of the desert. That's why I went there."

My initial reaction was, "Wow, this guy's a little loopy." But after a moment of consideration, it made sense. I remembered my own desert "vision quest" ten years previous and how intimidated I'd been, and then asked myself: Why was I hiking through the desert again? Why was I walking to Canada? Facing my fears certainly played a role—facing fears of the unknown, of commitment, of finding my limits and pushing past them.

As Tim rolled the camper into Julian, Angela was busy in the back, nosing through a hippyish milieu—tapestry curtains, incense, and literature, lots of Buddhist literature. Angela filled me in on a few of the selections once we got to town. There was the classic *Living Buddha, Living Christ,* the renowned *Tibetan Book of the Dead,* and the provocative *What is Zen?* None of these, however, sounded as practically useful as *Adventures in the Chemistry of Consciousness: The Joyous Cosmology* by Alan Watts, a work reviewed by *Contemporary Psychology* as "The classic book on the hallucinogenic drugs LSD, mescaline and psilocyine. Alan Watts describes with startling clarity and poetic beauty his drug-induced experiences." Tim seemed to have been supplementing his desert fast with Buddha and conscious-altering substances. Given our experience in the desert so far, I guess I couldn't really blame him.

X ▪ ▪ ▪ ▪ X

We had an excellent evening in Julian, starting with a shower at the Julian Lodge and continuing with a six-pack of Sierra Nevada. Actually, we didn't make it through the six-pack; it only took two beers, combined with three and a half days of constant sun exposure and sixty-two miles of hiking, to put us into TV-entranced comas. Eventually, we got around to some grocery shopping and dinner at the Boar's Head Salon, a cowboy-friendly joint in an otherwise touristy town. A dinner that didn't include freeze-dried food was a big relief to my stomach.

In these first few days of hiking, we discovered that freeze-dried meals, while surprisingly tasty, do funny things to the GI tract. A couple of hours after a meal, we'd erupt into such a gaseous concerto. My booming bass and Angela's tender soprano must have delighted our wilderness audience of lizards and the like. Before our trip, I thought Angela was incapable of a fart. On the trail, I was relieved to discover that she was capable of quite melodious, if not pleasantly aromatic, flatulence. It was starting to look like our trip might turn into the *Long Summer's Fart*. Thankfully, though, we were fart-free that evening, which allowed us to explore Julian without offending the locals.

The next evening, we began our most challenging stretch of trail thus far, a 23.8-mile waterless trek through the San Felipe Hills to Barrel Springs Campground. For the first time we were in true desert, the Anza-Borrego. We began in high spirits, refreshed by our day off, and made good progress in the twilight up Granite Mountain. The only impediment to our buoyant mood was our water supply. We'd been unexpectedly unable to supplement it at a "water cache" at Scissors Crossing, the intersection of Highways S2 and 78, at the base of the San Felipe Hills. Trail angels and PCT-friendly locals maintain a number of water caches along dry sections of the trail. Cache locations are advertised on the Internet and propagated by word of mouth. We had no difficulty finding the Scissors Crossing cache, the first on the northbound PCT, but were dismayed when we saw that it was completely dry. More than forty plastic one-gallon jugs lay in the sand, bone dry, pointlessly secured by a rubber-coated serpentine chain and lock.

It is in part because of experiences like ours that water caches are controversial in the long-distance hiking community. Critics note that hikers are more likely to engage in irresponsible water-carrying practices if they know of caches along the trail. If these hikers carry less water than recommended (two gallons per day) over a waterless stretch and then find an empty cache, the result could be quite thirsty indeed. Long-distance hiking "purists" (a term Angela explains at length later) also charge that water caches detract from the natural challenge of the trail and make it more accessible to hikers who perhaps aren't properly equipped, mentally or physically, for the task. Of course, most hikers are overjoyed at the sight of a water cache, and the presence of one at a location like Scissors Crossing can save them either a trip into town to re-supply or from carrying two days' worth of water. We arrived *from* town, but had done so without a full store of water, counting (irresponsibly) on the presence of a cache.

But for the time being we had enough water to maintain hydration, so I focused my attention on the changing habitat. Here in the "true" desert, chaparral gave way to cacti, yucca plants, and agave—asparagus-shaped plants rising four to eight feet in height. We switchbacked past a forest of ocotillo shrubs, plants that the guidebook described as a "bundle of giant, green pipe cleaners." Octillo shrubs spend most of their lives covered with spiny and lifeless branches, but perhaps half a dozen times a year, always two to three days after a rainstorm, they "sprout vibrant green clusters of delicate leaves along their entire length." The ocotillo is a perfect example of the unique adaptation seen in the desert environment. With less than two weeks of rain a year, and summer temperatures of up to 120 degrees, it is incredible that much of anything can live out there, but on that evening the San Felipe Hills were bursting with highly specialized life.

After three miles of energetic hiking we found a cozy and scenic campsite on a dry creek bed, surrounded on three sides by granite boulders. With our tent snuggled in between the boulders, it was like being in a sauna—the rocks, after absorbing the sun's heat all day, now radiated it. We hung our sweaty clothes on them and sat down to admire the view west across San Felipe Valley to the lush Volcan Mountains. From our boulder-protected perch, the Volcans looked tantalizingly wet and green. An extension of the Laguna Mountains, the Volcans act as a barrier to cool and moist air moving east from the Pacific Ocean. Coastal air settles and precipitates on the mountains, spawning a verdant tapestry. On the eastern side of the mountains only hot, dry air remains, and in this air the San Felipes bake day after day. Unfortunately for hikers, the trail does not pass through the Volcans. Back in the PCT's planning stages, the Forest Service wasn't able to convince private landowners to allow the trail to be routed through the Volcans and instead had to plan this waterless stretch through the Anza-Borrego.

The next day, I was cursing those landowners and the U.S. Forest Service as a pleasant early morning walk along gradual switchbacks turned into a steamy, shadeless midday trudge. It seemed ironic to me that the Forest Service went to great lengths to protect the mating grounds of the Arroyo toad but didn't seem overly concerned about hikers dying of heat stroke in the Anza-Borrego Desert. Even with an early afternoon nap under a few tall shrubs and the discovery of an unexpected water stash near the W-W Ranch, we were thirsty, dirty, and exhausted when we finally reached Barrel Springs Campground after a twenty-one-mile day.

The "springs" were not the vision of refreshment that I'd dreamed of all afternoon. In fact, they were nothing more than a pipe-fed concrete tub that was home to an extended family of tadpoles. I was disappointed but in no mood to complain; and complaining wouldn't have helped produce a tadpole-free oasis. So I sat on the edge of the tub and cleaned up as best I could.

Several hours after our arrival at Barrel Springs, with twilight deepening and dinner on the stove, two hikers arrived. They stumbled into camp, heads down and postures screaming defeat. They were so exhausted that they barely acknowledged arriving at their destination and only glanced at the spring-tub before throwing their packs down on a flat spot and collapsing.

X ▪ ▀ ▪ ▪ X

We were up early the next morning, attempting to get a jump on the heat of the day. The late-night stragglers were also packing their gear. I recognized them as a couple we'd seen from a distance, camped near the Scissors Crossing water stash. They both looked to be in their mid-twenties and sported matching hiking shirts—long-sleeve, white, button-down, polyester ones, seeped with dirt.

"Hikers?" asked the lanky fellow. He had the scruffy beginnings of a trail beard and wore a tight shell necklace.

"Yeah. I'm Angela and this is Duffy."

"Hey, I'm Chris. When'd y'all start?"

"May eighth, and you?" I asked with trepidation.

"May tenth." Yikes, these two were really moving; no wonder they'd looked so worn out the previous evening.

"Where are y'all from?"

"Philly, you?"

"I'm from Texas. This is my girlfriend, Stacey; she's from Pittsburgh," he said, pointing toward his hiking partner, a blond with a long, single braid and a friendly, slightly cherubic face.

"Why are y'all hiking the PCT? Why not the AT, seeing that you're from out that way?"

We'd heard this question before. Angela launched into our well-practiced response: The Appalachian Trail is too crowded; we didn't really care for the summer humidity in the east; the Sierra Nevada is incredibly beautiful; the PCT offers so many open vistas, et cetera, et cetera.

"Y'all hiking light?" Chris asked.

"Well, not really. We haven't really perfected the system yet."

"Yeah, it's difficult, isn't it?" exclaimed Stacey. "We've tried really hard—not carrying a tent and making one of those tuna-can alcohol stoves—but my pack still seems heavy."

"Stacey even left behind the deodorant. Not that I can tell much of a difference; she smells either way."

"Chris!"

"Stacey, you told me you was an earthy girl. And if that's true I am obligated to treat you like dirt. What'd ya expect?"

"Ignore him."

"Did you guys find any water at Scissors Crossing?" I asked.

"Yeah, there wasn't much left. We took the last four gallons and camped under that cottonwood."

"*Four* gallons?" I was shocked; we'd never carried more than two gallons at one time. Greedy water hoarders—they'd grabbed the last of the Scissors Crossing stash. I was a little irritated, but no harm was done and they seemed nice enough, so I decided not to hold a grudge.

That morning we hiked in tandem with Chris and Stacey, and our conversation, like several previous and many to follow, turned to the hiking business: itinerary lengths, water purification techniques, footwear choices, and other topics that a normal pedestrian would find numbingly esoteric. I eventually found solace in this routine. Such conversations validated the trip and the months of planning. It was encouraging to know that we weren't alone in considering the delicate pros and cons of water filtration versus iodine treatment and that some hikers were willing to spend entire afternoons building alcohol stoves out of soda cans. With long-distance hiking, comfort is found in others' reassurance that you're not completely crazy.

Over the next few days we ran into Chris and Stacey frequently, and although they'd gained ground on us before Barrel Springs, we were starting to find our trail legs and were now moving at a comparable pace. Shared snack breaks and campsites gave us the opportunity to learn more about them and to practice our trail jargon.

Stacey had met Chris in his native Texas while working for the Student Conservation Association. Through her work, Stacey had met many forest ranger and backpacker types, and she'd developed an interest in long-distance hiking. It wasn't too hard to convince Chris, unemployed at the time, to join her, so they'd hiked nine hundred miles of the Appalachian Trail the previous summer and now were gunning for a Pacific Crest thru-hike. At least, Stacey, with her detailed re-supply spreadsheet and itinerary, was gunning; as far as I could tell, Chris was along for the walk. He did a lot of the talking, but it was pretty clear who ran the show.

Listening to Chris' frequent talk, I noticed that we all shared not only a common trail language, but also an immediate (and exciting) goal—reach the next re-supply and trail angel operation, "Hiker's Oasis," at Kamp Anza. We zipped through Warner Springs and meandered along Agua Caliente creek before falling behind Chris and Stacey near Tule Canyon, where Angela and I spent a cold and windy night. The next day we battled our way through the outskirts of Anza to Hiker's Oasis.

Kamp Anza is an RV park approximately five miles off-trail in the middle-of-nowhereville, also known as Anza, California. One hundred and forty-four miles into the Pacific Crest Trail, Kamp Anza was our first mail re-supply point. We'd chosen Kamp Anza, rather than Warner Springs, thirty-four miles to the south, because we'd heard good things about Hiker's Oasis, an RV trail angel site run by Paul and his wife, Pat. By the time we arrived, we'd been fully whipped by the cool Anza winds and were relieved to take shelter on the front porch of the Oasis. The porch looked out over a luscious green lawn, the only one around for miles and miles, home to a potpourri of tents and tarps and presided over by a large American flag. Paul and Pat were the only somewhat permanent residents of Kamp Anza and therefore had a unique incentive to cultivate and maintain a lawn and garden in otherwise arid surroundings. So, in a very real sense, their lawn was an oasis—perhaps not one that normal people would choose to take holiday at, but a hiker's oasis nonetheless. As evidenced by the collection of mobile nylon on the lawn, we were not alone. Joining us at the Oasis were seven other hikers, including Chris and Stacey, and one itinerant trail angel, known simply as Meadow Ed.

Meadow Ed did not resemble an angel in most respects; he was more Santa Claus-like than angelic in appearance—a round fellow, round in the face and very round in the belly. Ed's face was insulated by a whitish-gray and rather unruly beard, which distracted from his lightly haired scalp. His narrow eyes were nearly hidden behind bulging cheeks and round spectacles. Meadow Ed's belly hung proudly and unobstructed over squat legs contained in loose sweat pants. All in all, he was a picture nearly antithetical to that of a long-distance hiker—which was appropriate, because although Ed enjoyed hanging out with hikers, he didn't appear to be much of a hiker anymore. Ed normally based his trail angel work out of Kennedy Meadows, in the Sierra, but when he heard that Pat had left the Oasis for a couple weeks during prime hiker season (for family reasons), Ed had traveled south to give Paul a hand.

While Paul puttered inside, Ed oriented us to the laundry and washroom facilities and laid out the rules of the house. We were *not* allowed inside the RV without an invitation from Paul; we were *not* to sleep on the deck; we were *not* to drink, cuss, or smoke; and most importantly, we were *not* to threaten the vitality of the Oasis by pissing on the lawn. It was immediately clear that Ed himself was perhaps not setting such a good example; his breath held the scent of whiskey. But, minutes later, I forgave him the inconsistency when he produced two steamy cups of hot chocolate, a big bowl of ramen topped with turkey gravy, and a basket of garlic bread. We dug in aggressively, occasionally taking a breath to chat with our fellow hikers. After our shoveling slowed, Ed extracted our hiking résumés. Upon hearing that we were babes in the long-distance hiking world, he set about educating us. I never did figure out exactly how much of the trail Ed had hiked, but from the beginning it was easy to see that he was heavily invested in spreading its lore.

Ed started by giving us the play-by-play of upcoming trail. After Anza we would head into the San Jacintos, which offered steep climbs up Spitler and Apache mountains and then an equally steep descent down Devils Slide Trail for a town stop in Idyllwild. This was the section of the trail where Marge, also known as the "Old Gal," had recently suffered a nasty fall. Next was another mountain range, the San Bernardinos. Before we reached them, however, we would face a descent out of the San Jacintos and the greatest loss and subsequent regain in elevation on any portion of the trail. We'd plummet from over 9,000 feet in the San Jacintos down to San Gorgonio Pass at about 1,000 feet, and then head back up to 8,500 in the San Bernardinos. In the process, Ed told us sternly, while scratching at the few tufts of hair on his head, we should be sure to find the Pink Motel in West Palm Springs.

"The Pink Motel," he said, "is a junkyard house in the middle of sand and chaparral. It's a grade-A trail angel spot, but not easy to find." He marked it on our map before continuing his verbal tour through Section C of our guidebook and the San Bernardinos. He looked at me gravely as he did so. I stared back and was concerned by the sight of his poor dentition.

"You know, you'll see grizzly bears in Section C."

"Holy shit," I thought, "is he kidding? Grizzly bears, down here?"

"*Grizzly* bears?"

"Yes, grizzlies, most hikers see them," Ed continued in the solemn tone.

"Don't y'all listen to him," broke in Chris. "He's talking about some sort of animal farm. There ain't no wild grizzlies down here."

Ed grinned. "Yeah, there's an animal park near Onyx Summit, right next to the trail. Owner's got a grizzly caged. He's a Hollywood animal trainer and he keeps his animals out there. He has cougars, too, and tigers."

"The tiger was in the movie *Gladiator*," Stacey pitched in. I thought that was an exciting piece of news and had Ed mark the location in our guidebook.

Meadow Ed talked us all the way up to Agua Dulce, at mile 450, before taking a break. He didn't rest for long, though. Our next lecture was about Scott, the aspiring "yo-yo" hiker. A yo-yo hike is a double hike, a Mexico–Canada–Mexico odyssey in one hiking season. So far, no one's been able to pull it off, though several have tried. But according to Ed, because of the very low snow levels in the Sierra, this might just be the year. Scott (nicknamed "Let It Be") was attempting the yo-yo for the fourth and probably final time. If he didn't succeed this time, he probably never would; rumor had it that Scott would exchange his yo-yo hiking shoes for wedding rings in the fall.

"Just another example of how some women try to keep men from achieving greatness," Ed jokingly lamented. I thought it demonstrated great greatness that Scott could avoid finding steady employment for three years in a row and still locate a woman willing to marry him. Ed told us that his "sources" indicated Scott had already signed the trail register at Tehachapi (mile 555) and that he'd be in Kennedy Meadows (mile 700) soon. That put him a good 450 to 500 miles ahead of us and made me wonder whether we'd make it out of California before seeing Scott yo-yoing his way back to Mexico.

I asked how old Scott was. Ed told me he was only twenty-eight, and then went inside the RV to get his PCT scrapbook so that he could show me a picture. He was back a minute later with Paul and each held a photo album in their hands. They bragged back and forth about their photo collections and in particular about competing autographed pictures of Let It Be. As I looked through the albums, complete with lists of trail register signings for several years, it occurred to me that Paul and Ed followed Pacific Crest Trail hiking as if it were a competitive sport. For them the "standings" were the trail registers with the lists of names and dates, and the "disabled list" was gathered through word of mouth and conjecture. "All-stars" were hikers like Scott, the fastest and most determined people on the trail. With such rabid fan support, no wonder some hikers seemed to get caught up in turning their hike into a competitive event. I wondered if Ed and Paul privately amused themselves by placing bets on how far different hikers would make it. Considering that Ed had asked us to call Paul when we finally got off the trail, it wouldn't have surprised me a bit. How far did they think we'd get?

The next morning Ed sat with Angela and me on the porch.

"You'll cry," he warned Angela. Then he looked at me. "You'll cry, too. This trail can break you." He fixed his glance on our tent. "And sometimes that tent is going to seem awfully small for the two of ya."

"Thanks, Ed, that's very encouraging," I replied.

"Well, I've seen many couples torn apart on this trail. You guys are connected by an umbilical cord there," he said, pointing at the tent. "You may want to pull away . . . but what then? Two people, one tent, one stove."

"One sleeping bag," Angela added. I glared at her.

"Duffy, I hope I will see you guys in Kennedy Meadows. I throw a party on June 15, Ray Day. Drink up, and then head into the mountains. And that's when we see who the *real* hikers are. Thirteen thousand feet, glacier traverses, and stream-crossings—and I am not talking about the type of stream-crossing that you and your little brother used to get a kick out of while standing over the toilet."

I gave his joke a token smile. "We'll see you there, Ed, umbilical cord and all."

[3]

The Race is On

BEFORE SETTING MY TREKKING SHOES on the Pacific Crest Trail, I did plenty of reading—twenty-seven books' worth, to be exact. These included John Muir's *My First Summer in the Sierra*, Cindy Ross' *Journey on the Crest*, and a collection of short stories about misadventures in the wild called *No Shit, There I Was*. I didn't limit my research to paperbacks, though; I also scoured the Internet and newspapers for tidbits—anything that would help me prepare for the journey ahead. By the time we got out of Bob's van at the Mexican border, I thought I had a decent idea of what to expect. But I quickly discovered that the printed page couldn't adequately prepare me for life on the trail. In particular, the printed page absolutely failed to prepare me for meeting Meadow Ed. But while Meadow Ed came as a surprise, he instantly became an integral part of my hike. His visage would hang over me for the rest of the summer, pushing me forward. Unwittingly, he became one of my greatest motivators, albeit in a twisted, "I'll show you" sort of way. Meadow Ed was skeptical about our chances, and I suppose, considering our condition when we first met, I couldn't really blame him.

X ▪ ▪ ▪ ▪ X

The night before we reached Kamp Anza had been difficult. Dirt seeped into every nook and cranny of our bodies, clothing, and gear. I could feel it between my toes and on my scalp, like sand after a windy day at the beach. It was only our ninth night en route to Canada, and our 139th mile, but already I felt farther away from home than I'd ever felt before.

Wind whipped through the canyon where we camped and pummeled our tent all night. Adding to the wind's roar was the constant flapping of our rain fly and periodic showers of sand against the tent walls. Snuggled beneath our shared sleeping bag, we slept fitfully until a gust tore out our tent stakes, causing the whole darn thing to cave in.

"Save the women and children!" Duffy yelled. I awoke with a start, and all restful slumber was ended for the night.

When dawn finally broke, the cold wind hadn't let up and we had to keep moving to stay warm. We didn't pause for breakfast because we had none. We didn't have lunch, a snack, or dinner, either. What we did have was pancake mix—just the mix: no butter, no frying pan. By midmorning, I was starved and thought I'd try making pancakes in our pot. Duffy (being a more experienced cook) tried to talk me out of it, but I stubbornly continued combining flour and water and heating the concoction. The result was lumpy and burnt. I ate it anyway, until I started to feel sick. Duffy gave me a smug look.

"I told you, Chiggy."

I didn't know it yet, but similar provision miscalculations would plague us for weeks to come. But this was our first experience with hiking hungry, and it would be short (or so I told myself)—just a three-mile hike to a jeep road and then a five-mile road-walk to our next re-supply, at the Hiker's Oasis at Kamp Anza.

When we got to the jeep road, it was as deserted as it was dusty. The desolation was made all the more complete by an absolute lack of street signs, and soon we were lost in a maze of dirt roads, barbed wire fences, and anonymous ranches. The horizon was hazy. I stared at a cow skull strapped to a fence and just couldn't believe how cold it was. The temperature and the terrain didn't match. Duffy plodded stoically a hundred yards ahead. Lagging behind, I stumbled over my numb, Raynaud's-ridden feet and wiped tears of frustration from my eyes.

Farther down the road, as we rested against weathered fence posts, a white car with government plates slowed to a stop beside us. From inside a large woman with long braided hair peered at us suspiciously. She worked for the IRS and was searching for a local rancher who needed an audit.

"You guys okay?" she asked. We nodded. She seemed about to offer us a ride but then hesitated. "I probably shouldn't pick up hitchhikers in a government car. You guys aren't wackos, are you?" I tried to reassure her of our sanity, but explaining that we were in the process of hiking to Canada didn't seem to help and she drove away.

X ▪ ▪ ▪ ▪ X

Many wrong turns later, we arrived at Kamp Anza's Hiker's Oasis. Sitting on the Oasis' front porch, we shared hot chocolate and turkey with ramen noodles with Meadow Ed. While he lectured about what lay ahead, I signed his scrapbook, jotting down my reflections on trail life so far. All told, Meadow Ed and I spent about ten hours making each other's acquaintance, but even by the time we left, I don't think he knew my name. Nope, I was merely "Duffy-me-boy's" girl. Women solo-hikers and women hiking teams got his attention and respect, but the female half of a couple—well, it seemed like she might as well be deadweight, because she clearly wasn't pulling it.

Don't get me wrong; Meadow Ed's hospitality was incredible. He made yummy hot cocoa, and watching him cruise around Kamp Anza in an old golf cart was a welcome diversion. But the fact that he never called me by name and always asked Duffy all the questions rubbed me the wrong way. For the rest of the hike, would I be looked at as Duffy's albatross? Hadn't I walked the 144 miles to get here? Wasn't that hulking purple pack in the corner my burden to carry—and hadn't I carried it?

I thoroughly enjoyed the hot showers, laundry facilities, and trailer-cooked meals (courtesy of chef Ed) at Hiker's Oasis, but when it came time to leave, I was more than ready. Now I had even more to prove—to Meadow Ed and to myself.

Farewells were brief, and we told Meadow Ed that we'd see him soon—in Kennedy Meadows, approximately 550 miles away. After a night of sleeping on the grass at the Oasis, the dusty trail seemed especially harsh, but there were mountains to look forward to: The jagged saurian ridges of the San Jacintos lay on the near horizon.

X ◦ ▪ ▪ ▪ X

Like many backpackers, I spent a lot of my hiking time looking down—at the ground and at my feet. And with good reason: There were rocks, roots, and snakes to watch for. Some might say I could have stayed home to stare at rocks and my dirty shoes, but I saw the scenery and a whole lot more—I just had to stop walking to look at it.

After just a few days of downward-facing, I could identify coyote droppings, the heart-shaped tracks of whitetail deer, slither marks and shed skins of snakes, horny toads, lizards doing pushups (I never did figure out why they do this), and the squiggly bottomed footprints left by a rare, 180-pound, big-eared, bipedal creature named Duffy. Even when I couldn't see Duffy, all I had to do was look down and there were his size eleven and a half prints. I found the tracks from his hiking shoes comforting whenever we were separated, which so far seemed to be most of the time.

Scanning the ground during our trek toward the San Jacintos, I noticed something curious. It looked as if someone was pulling a little red wagon. Or maybe it was a wheelchair? If Bill Irwin, a blind man, could hike the Appalachian Trail (with his Seeing Eye dog, Orient, in 1990), I figured it was possible that someone might attempt the PCT in a wheelchair. The tracks, thin lines dug in the sand, continued for mile after mile and caused me increasing consternation. I was curious to know what was creating them and whiled away eight miles coming up with possible explanations. A new type of pack with wheels? A ranger measuring distances on the trail with a wheeled meter? Two very long, very straight rattlesnakes? The guessing game kept me somewhat distracted until the afternoon started getting hot—real hot. Sweat poured down my forehead and temples and out from under my khaki hat. I could feel it making paths through the dirt on my face.

While trying to wipe gritty perspiration off my forehead before it dripped down my nose, I turned a corner and saw Duffy talking to two round, middle-aged women. One stood with an enormous white pack that looked like a giant marshmallow strapped to her back. I recognized it as the ultralight Kelty Cloud, packed to such capacity that only its color could be considered light. The other woman was collapsed on a rock nearby, staring into space. I recognized her exhausted stance as much like my own.

Ms. Marshmallow was from Anaheim and hiking the PCT in sections. She'd hiked over a thousand miles the previous summer and this season was tackling Sections A and B, from the Mexican border to San Gorgonio Pass, a total of 212 miles. Her friend was visiting for a couple of days. Marshmallow's pack was filled to the brim because she was carrying enough food for her entire month-long journey. At first I didn't believe it was possible for one to carry a month's rations, but then I looked back at her gleaming pack. It was big, all right, and appeared to be exceedingly weighty.

Just then, she reached inside the puffy whiteness. She was up to her bicep in it and seemed to be searching for something until, with a dramatic *swoosh* of her arm, she pulled out two red, shiny apples and handed them to us.

Fresh fruit on the trail. How decadent. How heavy. How delicious. We gaped at her and immediately sat down to eat the ruby treasures. Marshmallow grinned and waved good-bye, and then she and her friend trundled off. As they left I noticed the exhausted sidekick dragging her trekking poles along behind her, one in each hand, creating perfectly parallel trenches in the sand.

The next day, after a night at a trash-ridden campsite, we were bound for the town of Idyllwild, more than twenty-five miles away. By lunch we'd covered the ten miles to Apache Spring, our next water source. Duffy hiked half a mile downhill to the spring while I conked out by the trail.

Pretty soon, a tall, sinewy, older gentleman with a single trekking pole, a minuscule pack, and a hint of a limp came cruising by, looking slightly off balance but moving quickly. He introduced himself as Dave, a carpenter from Washington. "Folks are calling me 'Fast Dave,'" he said with a chuckle. We exchanged pleasantries and then he followed Duffy down the side trail toward the spring.

A few minutes later, three young men came charging up. In the lead was a muscular guy with a shaved head, wearing gear from a running shoe company, complete with a skimpy pair of shorts, the kind those Kenyan marathoners wear. Behind him, the other two looked more like what you might expect from college kids out for a hike. But, man, were they moving fast and in a regimented fashion, sort of like an army troop. They called themselves the "JourneyFilm Crew," and all three were carrying packs manufactured by GoLite, the ultralight gear company that utilizes Ray Jardine's designs.

By deconstructing traditional backpacking items down to their essence and finding excellence in structural rationality, simplicity, and ultimate utility, Ray Jardine has revolutionized the way people look at long-distance hiking and its accompanying gear. With a degree in aeronautical and astronautical engineering, Jardine designed space–flight mechanics before retiring early to pursue outdoor endeavors. Along the way he put his expertise to use designing methods and tools to make his mountaineering, rock climbing, hang gliding, sea hiking, and long-distance hiking hobbies more enjoyable. In the case of rock climbing, while conquering some of the most challenging climbs on the planet, he invented a nifty little tool, the "friend," that has since helped many climbers scale rock faces once thought impossible. That was in 1978. Nearly ten years later, desiring to continuously "expand his horizons" and "live in a realm far beyond the norm," he turned his attention to long-distance hiking, a new challenge to which he could apply his unstinting logic.

When Jardine says "ultralight," he means it. He calculates his pack weight down to the last ounce and has no patience for the extraneous. Don't bother with bringing a tent, asserts Jardine; a tarp provides more than enough shelter. What brand of backpack is the best? None—Jardine suggests that you make your own (or buy the GoLite model). If, however, you're foolish enough to risk purchasing a pack from a mainstream retailer, be sure to cut off all those fancy straps and clips or they'll conspire to weigh you down. Boots are much too heavy and cumbersome; sneakers will do the trick. And even these, it seems, can be made lighter. Jardine recommends shaving the brand logos off sneakers to reduce their weight and to cut down on backwoods marketing. (Jardine is staunchly against backwoods marketing.) Surely I will need to bring along items of basic hygiene—a toothbrush, perhaps? Jardine will grudgingly grant you the luxury of a toothbrush—but not toothpaste (too heavy, too loaded with chemicals). All in all, when it comes to gear and personal items like the toothbrush, Jardine's philosophy is "cut and whack."

"Cut off anything you will not use," writes Jardine in *Beyond Backpacking*. "Be assertive, and remember that if you whack too much you can always sew it back together. Do the same with all your gear, cut and whack to your heart's content: the toothbrush handle, the maps (cut away whatever portions you will not need, not just the borders), cut the bandana in half, chop a small wedge from a bar of soap."

Jardine is extreme, but he also gets results. On the last of Jardine's three Pacific Crest hikes, his base pack weight (without food and water) was a paltry nine pounds, and he and his wife Jenny flew up the country averaging better than thirty miles a day.

The three JourneyFilm Crew youngsters looked like sincere members of the cult Jardine and paused for only a second to bark a question at me— "Seen Fast Dave?" I yipped back in the affirmative and said that he'd gone down to get water from the spring. The boys grinned at each other and began to haul ass down the trail once again. But before they were out of sight, one of them turned back and yelled to me, "Tell Dave that the JourneyFilm Crew was here."

"Men," I thought, "always in competition." When Dave returned with his water, I didn't mention the JourneyFilm Crew. I didn't want to feed the voracious gossip monster that lurked in the shadows of the PCT community.

This monster rears its head whenever two or three hiking groups come together, whether at a water source or in a town. After a little over a week on the trail, I knew how the first several minutes of every conversation with a fellow thru-hiker would go. It would start with a seemingly innocent question. "When'd ya start?" Based on the response, the inquisitor would do some quick calculations to figure out how many days we (the competition) had been on the trail, how many miles we'd hiked so far, and our average miles per day, all leading to an answer to the all-important question: "Are they going faster or slower than me?"

I'm making a gross generalization here, but this is how our conversations began about ninety percent of the time. And I must say, we weren't innocent; we played the game, too. I just loved it when a guy, puffed up with machismo, flaunting his Jardine-approved pack and smirking at my bulging one, would ask the inevitable questions, only to find out that—yikes! a girl—a girl with a big fat pack—was going faster than him. This didn't happen all that regularly, but when it did, it was I who puffed up with pride.

Unfortunately, I wouldn't have such satisfaction with the JourneyFilm Crew. Among those into thru-hiker "standings," they had a right to gloat. They started their trip on May 10 at 10:06 in the morning, approximately fifty-three hours behind us—and there they just went, kicking up dust in their wake. The Crew included Kimmo, a photography student from Finland whose previous adventures included biking across the U.S.; J. B., a film student; and Joe, a biology student. Their initial goals had been to successfully thru-hike the PCT and create a documentary of their trip. This changed slightly when they met Fast Dave, "the toughest guy we've seen yet," they wrote on their website. "He motivated us to hike faster and faster until we reached a point when JB and Kimmo hallucinated of beating the record for the fastest thru-hike [three months and four days], set by the legendary Ray Jardine and his wife Jenny." In the interest of their newfound quest, the JourneyFilm Crew ate most of their meals while walking and used a stopwatch to time their breaks. "Kimmo can't stand it when other hikers pass us," J. B. once said.

The need for speed and the ensuing hunger and exhaustion would lead the JourneyFilm Crew into many adventures—and mishaps. More than once the team ran out of food, resulting in a member of their party collapsing on the trail. Fortunately, in each case another hiker happened to show up in time to supply a Power Bar or two. In Yosemite, at Tuolomne Meadows, Kimmo left his wet sneakers drying by a campfire while he went to search for a room for the night. J. B., who was also drying by the fire, fell asleep, and when Kimmo returned he found his shoes smoldering (and J. B. still sleeping). Without a footwear retailer for more than sixty miles and no time to wait for a new pair to be mailed, Kimmo tried Duct-taping his shoes' insoles to his feet. Not surprisingly, this didn't work. Eventually a sympathetic shopkeeper gave Kimmo an old pair of work boots. They were two sizes too small, but Kimmo wore them anyway. The hike must go on, especially when there's a record to break.

Back in the seventies, Peter Jenkins wrote the best-seller *A Walk Across America*, in which he detailed his walk from New York to New Orleans. Traveling mostly on roads, Jenkins' route was a unique and often solitary one. Ours, on the other hand, was along a dedicated trail traveled by three hundred others trying to get to the same destination within approximately the same time frame. But despite these differences, Jenkins' trip was in many ways similar to ours—a quest of sorts, although we weren't quite sure what for. On his way to New Orleans, Jenkins, like us, confronted obsessions with speed and mileage. In response he wrote, "I was opposed to becoming 'mileage crazy.' Mileage craziness is a serious condition that exists in many forms. It can hit unsuspecting travelers while driving cars, motorcycles, riding in planes, crossing the country on bicycles or on foot. The symptoms may lead to obsessively placing more importance on how many miles are traveled than on the real reason for traveling. . . . On foot, in a van, on a fleet motorcycle or on a bicycle, a person must be very careful not to become overly concerned with arriving."

X ▪ ▪ ▪ ▪ X

Soon after the JourneyFilm Crew sped off, Duffy returned with water and we hiked on and up into the San Jacinto Mountains. Much of the tread through the San Jacintos had been blasted into the face of the mountains, dangerous work during which one trail worker died. As our climb took us higher and along cliffs, I avoided looking over the steep drop-offs and focused instead on keeping my balance on the loose scree. Every once in a while, our footfalls would send a rock careening over the edge and down the cliff side. Often, a felled tree or rockslide would block the path and we'd have to climb over it. That's when the troubling story of Marge (the "Old Gal") would scuttle across my consciousness.

"Marge broke her leg somewhere around here," Duffy noted as he picked his way over a three-foot expanse of freshly tumbled rock.

"Thanks for reminding me." I surveyed the scene and my nervousness increased.

Marge had slipped on a loose rock in a pile just like this, jamming her foot and breaking her leg as she fell at an awkward angle. When a rock slips from a slide like the one we were traversing, it's sometimes called a "Judas Rock." If the wrong rock plays Judas, an unsuspecting hiker may become the guest of honor at her own Last Supper.

It was May 18, two weeks since the Riverside Mountain Rescue Unit had rescued Marge from this area. The seventy-two-year-old was attempting to trek all of Section B—alone. Her loved ones had advised against this, but Marge reasoned that there would be many other hikers on the trail if she needed assistance. And she was right, there were; they just happened to be three days behind her.

During that time, Marge dragged herself, her pack, and her broken leg thirty feet to a flat spot, where she made a makeshift camp. "The whole process took about four hours. It's amazing what you can do on your butt," Marge later wrote in an email to a friend. "My fear the first night," she added, "was cougars. I'd never thought of cougars before but for some reason that was my big fear so I was sure not to moan or cry out when I moved my injured leg. I didn't want a cougar to realize I was injured."

The second night, Marge awoke at four in the morning to planes flying overhead and spent an hour trying to flash SOS signals at them. "I tried to pray but could not remember the simplest of prayers," Marge recalled. "All I could say was 'Dear God' over and over."

Around nine in the morning on her third day, Marge had only half a cup of water left, eight sticks of gum, nine Tums, and two inches of toothpaste. "I thought about the great life I'd had," she later wrote, "my marvelous kids etc. And if I died? That was ok. I had a very deep feeling of acceptance and peace."

That same day, at about 12:30 in the afternoon, help finally arrived. Kathy and Ed, two thru-hikers from Spokane, Washington, had met Marge earlier in the year via the online Pacific Crest Trail community and had been impressed that the seventy-two-year-old was still hiking. They'd seen her entries in trail registers and thus were aware that she was a few days ahead of them. So when they came around a corner and saw an older woman sitting on the trail with her gear spread out around her, they knew it was Marge.

What they didn't know was that she'd broken her leg and had been sitting there for nearly seventy-two hours.

Once they realized what had happened, they gave Marge water, nuts, and energy bars. Then they sped off to get help. At about 4:30 that afternoon, Ed met a day hiker with a cell phone and called 911. By 7:30 that evening, two rescuers arrived at Marge's side with a special stretcher equipped with a big trail wheel called a "Stokes" litter. More rescuers arrived at intervals and took turns pushing and pulling the litter down a steep, little-used side trail. The trail was so narrow that Marge's rescuers sometimes slid off it and into bushes. By the time they got to a waiting ambulance at 2:30 in the morning, the rescuers' arms and faces were so bloodied it seemed as if they'd need medical attention, too. Later, in a thank-you note Marge wrote to the Riverside Mountain Rescuers, she joked that if there ever were a "next time," she'd like to recommend Cadillac suspension.

Ruminating over Marge's story during the next seven miles, I felt alone and scared. Duffy's long legs were proving capable of covering ground quite quickly, with my short stubs leaving me lagging behind. What if I fell off one of these cliffs? How many miles would it take for Duffy to even notice I was missing? What if I took a water or rest break, fell farther behind, and got lost? These worries urged me to hike faster and forego breaks, but they also made me feel as if our romantic adventure was turning into a forced march. Was Duffy succumbing to the speed-hiking mentality? This jogged my insecurities. Maybe he resented me for holding him back. I could hear Meadow Ed now, "Duffy-me-boy . . . is that umbilical cord strangling you yet?"

With Meadow Ed's voice running through my head, I came upon a snow-patched saddle where Duffy had stopped to wait for me. He was leaning against a boulder and casually kicking a mound of snow with his toe. I tried to figure out how long he'd been there. Not long enough to take off his pack. I was relieved; I wasn't so far behind after all.

To our right was the notoriously steep and treacherous Devils Slide trail that would take us three miles down to an Idyllwild trailhead. From there we'd head four miles, by road, into town and to the hiker-friendly Tahquitz

Inn. By the time we descended to the trailhead and began trudging down the desolate roads toward town, night was falling.

Passing empty vacation homes, our trekking poles made *clack-clack* sounds on the pavement. My feet were burning and Duffy's knees were killing him, the joints grinding like engine parts needing oil. For Duffy, steep descents were proving to be one of the most painful aspects of thru-hiking. Sometimes he'd stop, lean on his trekking poles, and just gasp. It was pitch dark when we finally we made it into the outskirts of town.

A young woman came out of a Mexican restaurant, got into her car, and drove forward ten yards before screeching back to us in reverse.

"Wanna ride somewhere?" she asked.

"Yes, please!" I was so relieved; we'd find the hotel much faster by car. The girl started chucking Twizzlers, McDonald's bags, sweaters, and books off of her front seat and into the even messier backseat.

"No, really, we can walk," Duffy said, giving me a strange look. I was puzzled. Didn't Duffy want a ride? I sure did—enough to sit in a backseat trash bin. Reluctantly, he finally climbed into the Honda hatchback and the girl careened out of the parking lot. She drove so fast that we sped past the Tahquitz Inn twice before noticing it.

When she pulled over, *onto* the curb, Duffy jumped out like a jackrabbit and glared at me. "Are you crazy? I was sure we were gonna die. Did you smell the booze?"

I certainly did not. All I smelled was myself. Besides, Duffy had been looking pale with the pain from his knees. I just wanted us to find a place to dump our packs and put our feet up. It wouldn't have mattered to me if she was drunk, stoned, or just plain insane, I still would've gotten in the car. After doing a twenty-eight-mile day, I was in desperate need of a bed.

At least we'd made it. We checked into a room and collapsed on its couch. We probably lay there for at least an hour before mustering the energy to shower. I watched the grime spiral down the drain in an almost hallucinogenic state, amazed at the amount of dirt coming off my body.

The next morning my feet were still throbbing. Hot spots on my heels and little toes stung and the top of my left foot sent out intermittent sharp pangs. But lying in that soft bed, on clean white sheets, the trail seemed like that sweet romantic dream again. When I got up, however, the dream shattered. My leg muscles were tight, like knotted rubber bands pulled taut, and I buckled over.

It took a couple hours of running errands, stretching while waiting in various checkout lines, and reclining in the sun while writing emails (on our handheld email device) for my calves and hamstrings to loosen up. Walking back to our room, I noticed the JourneyFilm Crew sleeping outside the Tahquitz on the grass. "They're not going so fast now," I smirked, and then stopped myself.

I'd been sucked into the competition. The race was on.

[4]

Pink Motel

BY THE EARLY 1930s, Clinton C. Clarke was too bent with age to enjoy backpacking. A Harvard graduate with a degree in literature, a successful oilman, and an avid Boy Scout, Clarke could still quote from *Huckleberry Finn* and light a fire in a blustery wind, but his hiking career was pretty much over—or so he thought. He was only fifty-eight—an age at which today's men clutch bottles of Viagra ordered off the Internet, learn to swing dance, or head west in Winnebagoes—but Clarke's perception of frailty left him with nothing better to do than dream of hiking and dispense advice. "Start hiking early, by eight o'clock," Clarke instructed backpackers. "Go slowly at first. Always rest by standing in the sun (if you sit down you will lose pep.) Drink a little water, a raisin under the tongue will help." These recommendations may seem humorously outdated now, but Clarke's Depression-era dream of the Pacific Crest Trail does not.

Clarke dedicated his final years to the vision of a border-to-border trail along the mountain ranges of California, Oregon, and Washington, "traversing the best scenic areas and maintaining an absolute wilderness character." Why did Clarke devote the sunset of his life to the promotion of a pastime he could no longer enjoy? Maybe it was because he had made his fortune squeezing black gold from the ground and wanted to repay his debt to Mother Earth, or maybe all that Mark Twain had gone to his head. Whatever the reason, Clarke worked until his last days to preserve a slice of the American West from man's meddling. The Pacific Crest Trail, first proposed to government officials in 1932, took six decades and millions of dollars to complete.

Clarke didn't live to realize his dream, but given his altruistic dedication, this seems somehow appropriate. His tombstone might as well quote from Twain, "Always do right, it will gratify some and astonish the rest."

The initial foundation proposed by Clarke and his supporters to federal officials for the PCT was a link between two existing northwestern trails, Oregon's Skyline Trail and Washington's Cascade Crest Trail, and two California trails, the John Muir Trail and the Tahoe–Yosemite Trail. But with the country in the midst of the Great Depression and lacking a popular mandate for long distance trails, the response from Washington, D.C. was tepid. At the time, the potential costs of trail construction, mapping, and rights-of-way across private land were beyond the will and thin wallet of the federal government.

Very gradually, though, like a glacier receding from Yosemite Valley, the idea picked up steam. Clarke founded the Pacific Crest Trail System Conference in 1932 to lobby for and map the trail; its founding members included the Sierra Club, the Boy Scouts, the YMCA, and a young photographer named Ansel Adams.

In the summer of 1935, Clarke commissioned a survey to begin tracing the trail, heading south from Monument 78 at the Canadian border. "Their instructions," wrote Robert Cantwell in a 1963 *Sports Illustrated* article, "called for them to locate a wide, easy grade, to lay out the trail so it passed through scenic country, to keep to the summit ridge, to note all wildlife, to check good hunting grounds and to test the fishing in streams and lakes." Five forest rangers tackled the initial eight miles of survey, diligently noting their discoveries: "a porcupine, a fool hen with chicks, a whistling marmot, eleven mountain goats and a herd of seven deer." With this attention to detail, it's no wonder that the work of mapping and trailblazing took decades.

In part because the Boy Scouts were occupied maintaining their own trails and the Forest Service was busy counting fool hens, much of the subsequent work fell to volunteers from the YMCA. One such volunteer, Warren Rogers, caught Clarke's "footpath–fever" at the age of twenty-three and never lost it. After the initial sections of the trail had been mapped out, it was Rogers who explored them, overcoming the limitations of a body crippled by childhood polio.

During the slow spawning of the PCT, Clarke remained the project's fig-urehead, holding court in his Pasadena home (he was nicknamed the "Arm-chair Hiker") with Rogers as his eyes, ears, and feet in the field. When Clarke passed away in 1957 at the age of eighty-four, Rogers continued campaigning for the completion of the PCT. Keeping the Pacific Crest Trail alive, according to Rogers' son, was his father's purpose in life.

Finally, in 1965, amid the sixties' fervor for everything earthy, President Lyndon Johnson announced his intention to develop a national system of trails. As is often the case in Washington, this announcement led to an earth-shattering development: the commission of a commission. The commission published a report, "Trails for America," that recommended building four na-tional scenic trails—the Appalachian Trail, the Continental Divide Trail, the Potomac Heritage Trail, and the Pacific Crest Trail. Some years later, President Johnson signed the National Trail Systems Act, which named the AT and the PCT our first National Scenic Trails. Still, there was much work to be done.

In 1970, eighteen-year-old Eric Ryback became the first person to attempt a PCT thru-hike—despite the fact that only half of the trail had been com-pleted. Hiking south from Canada in blue jeans, without a guidebook and with an eighty-pound pack, Ryback struggled against hunger, exhaustion, and loneliness. Ultimately, he claimed success and documented the hike in his book, *The High Adventure of Eric Ryback*. Whether Ryback did indeed complete a border-to-border thru-hike is still a matter of debate within the PCT commu-nity. Some dispute the veracity of his claim, noting that Ryback accepted rides for portions of his trip. Schaffer et. al., the authors of the PCT guidebook, rec-ognize Richard Watson's 1972 effort as the first successful thru-hike. Given the patchwork nature of the trail in the early 1970s, however, the notion of thru-hiking was at that time certainly nebulous at best.

Due in part to the publicity generated by Ryback's adventure, trail con-struction boomed throughout the 1970s. The federal agencies (the Bureau of Land Management, the Forest Service, and the National Park Service) respon-sible for managing most of the land on the PCT's course finally agreed on some important management guidelines, and between 1972 and 1980 nearly a thousand miles of trail were built. The trail was officially completed in 1993, twenty-five years after its designation as a National Scenic Trail and thirty-six years after Clinton Clarke's death. Work continues, just as Clarke would have hoped, and a new legion of dreamers envisions a trail unencumbered by private land restrictions and protected from suburban sprawl.

X ▪ ▪ ▪ X

On the morning of May 21, I was roused from my own dreams by an angel's chirps.

"Happy *berrrtday*, Duffy! Happy, happy twenty-eighth! Happy *berrrtday*!" Angela repeated, delivering a compact pat to my bum. "Rise and hike, *berrrtday* boy."

It was a comfortable morning at 7,500 feet in the western San Jacinto Mountains. We'd camped on a flat bed of pine needles under the cover of Jeffrey and Coulter pines. It was a beautiful spot, filled with an invigorating pine scent, and we broke camp in a jovial mood. We had our sights set on a birthday celebration at the Pink Motel, the junkyard trail angel refuge that Meadow Ed had described to us at Kamp Anza. It would be a twenty-one-mile hike, but entirely downhill. We were somewhat low on water—three liters for the two of us—but I wasn't particularly troubled, even though we faced a sixteen-mile waterless stretch. Of course, it would have been nice to fill up before we left, but this campsite offered no such opportunity.

The night before, I'd accidentally marinated our instant potatoes in a Dead Sea–like salt solution, and we'd each needed a liter and a half of water to counteract the brackish spuds. Angela lobbied for a two-mile detour to Black Mountain Camp for more water, but I convinced her that it was unnecessary, reasoning that we'd handled the San Felipe Hills with an equivalent amount of water and that today would be easy downhill walking. What I failed to figure into my blasé calculations was that the farther we descended toward San Gorgonio Pass and its 1,000-foot elevation, the hotter it would get. In fact, for every 1,000 feet of elevation lost we should have planned on a gain of three to five and a half degrees. In just six hours we'd drop from our comfortable mountain perch into a smoldering valley inferno.

X ▪ ▪ ▪ ▪ X

There are many things for a novice hiker to worry about when setting off on a distance hike, most of them involving the prefixes "hyper-" and "hypo-." To start with, there's hypothermia, hyperthermia, and hypo-nutrition. Then there's hypo-hydration, hyper-exhaustion, and hyperextension (of mission-critical joints). And finally, there are hyper-high falls, hyper-intense bear encounters, and, for a boyfriend like me, confrontations with my (occasionally) hypersensitive female. So far, we'd been lucky and avoided any serious, non-estrogen related exposures to anything from the "hyper-"–"hypo-" family. We'd covered nearly two hundred miles unscathed. But while some of my fears had been alleviated, there was one menace that still loomed large. Snakes. Snakes with rattles . . . and sharp fangs designed to deliver poisonous venom.

Rattlesnakes are members of the pit viper (crotalid) family of poisonous snakes and come in sixteen speciated flavors. Although these sixteen species vary greatly in size, skin pattern, and behavior, they all share three basic characteristics: dry, hollow segments of tail skin that make a loud, scary noise when wiggled; heat-sensitive organs located on the sides of their heads that allow them to locate and track prey; and erectile fangs, often over half an inch in length, that can inject a complex soup of destructive proteins.

And while one or more rattler species can be found in each of the forty-eight contiguous states, California is fortunate to be home to six species—the sidewinder, the speckled, the red diamond, the Pacific, the western diamondback, and the Mojave green.

I've never liked rattlesnakes of any specie. In fact, ever since a pre-adolescent encounter, I've been deathly afraid of them. Perhaps this is because our seminal meeting occurred when I was at the unfortunate age of eight. I say "unfortunate" because at eight, I was neither particularly brave nor very rational. Rather, I was enormously impressionable and harbored an exaggerated fear of animals, both wild and domestic. Large family dogs with wagging tails would sometimes cause me to turn tail and flee. And *wild* animals such as bears, crocodiles, and rattlesnakes, well—I considered them to be deadly efficient boy-killing beasts. To make matters worse, I was well aware of the presence of rattlesnakes in my native California and was sure that if I were ever bitten by one I would face a grotesquely painful death.

I saw my first rattler while hauling gear down to my family's Big Sur cabin. He was a five-footer and percussed loudly. I was duly petrified—and that was even before he started advancing up the trail toward me! Desperate, I flung my sleeping bag and screamed shrilly, but my assailant wasn't deterred. He kept slithering right for me. Did he mistake me for a gigantic lizard sandwich? I continued to scream and was just about to wet my Underoos when my father, right behind me on the trail, came to the rescue. He lobbed a number of large rocks at the snake, nearly hitting him dead-on. After about the fourth rock, the rattler got the idea and retreated. He'd never been close enough to *physically* hurt me, but psychologically, well—that was a different story.

Twenty years and a medical-school education later, I'd evolved a more complete understanding of the rattlesnake. Now I knew that a rattlesnake bite is not instantly fatal and that up to forty percent of bites are completely dry of venom. According to the *The Merck Manual of Diagnosis and Therapy*, more than eight thousand people in the United States are bitten each year by poisonous snakes, but fewer than six actually die. Most of the fatal bites occur among children, the elderly, and members of religious sects who handle venomous snakes. Rattlesnakes are likely more afraid of people (especially those in odd religious sects) than we are of them and are usually anxious to avoid confrontations. In fact, the majority of bites in the U.S. result from people's attempts to prove that they are faster than the snake—which, considering that a rattlesnake can strike in 1/256th of a second, means the only thing these folks prove is that they know how to end up in an emergency room. Wilderness experts will tell you that if you give a snake six feet he won't bother you, but, as my childhood experience taught me, this isn't *always* the case.

Before starting our hike, I'd educated myself on the proper treatment of rattlesnake bites. The treatment algorithm goes like this: First, grab a Sawyer Extractor and start sucking. The Sawyer Extractor, if used correctly and within the first five minutes after a bite, may remove up to thirty percent of envenomation. I say "may" because the Extractor has never been shown to be of any definitive benefit to humans. In essence, though, it remains a safer and more attractive option than the technique glorified in pop culture—having your friend suck out the venom by mouth. Next, apply a compression wrap (not a tourniquet) to the affected extremity (most bites are on the hands, feet, arms, or legs) with an Ace bandage. Finally, the victim should be evacuated to an emergency room for evaluation and immediate treatment (if necessary) with equine antivenin or the synthetic Crofab. These antidotes bind to and neutralize the venom, preventing or lessening tissue destruction and clotting abnormalities.

So, yeah—now I knew a lot more about snakes, and knowledge *is* power, but in my case not powerful enough to overcome boyhood terror. Especially not after reading in the guidebook that rattlers can be found virtually anywhere along the California section of the PCT. Landmarks with names such as Rattlesnake Canyon, Rattlesnake Springs, and Rattlesnake Trail didn't help much, either. The guidebook described Rattlesnake Trail as "little-used." Gee, I wonder why?

During our first two weeks on the trail I'd vigilantly scanned the ground for rattlesnakes, and during those two weeks I hadn't seen a single one. It was ironic, then, that I should hear my birthday "gift" before I saw him. The sharp and loud percussion came from my right as I rounded a curve in the trail. I skipped quickly to my left, darted forward, and spun to face the menace. I looked at him closely for a second: His fork-shaped bubblegum-pink tongue was flicking rapidly and contrasted severely with the tire-tread darkness of his coiled body. He was a Pacific rattlesnake and sat tucked back against a collection of boulders, hidden from view to those coming down the trail. Fortunately, his position was slightly off-trail, and I'd been able to move safely outside of his six-foot striking range. Angela, however, was rapidly approaching.

"Angela, *wait! Stop! Snake!*" Hearing my screams and the snake's rattle simultaneously, she came to an abrupt and startled halt.

"I hear him, but where is he?"

"He's behind the boulders . . . you'll be okay. Walk on the outside of the trail."

She hesitated as the rattling resonated. "Are you sure?"

"Yes, *yes, of course!*" I realized that I sounded frantic and tried to calm my voice. "Just walk to . . . the edge . . . of the trail."

Angela paused for a moment and then scampered over to me, looking back at the reptilian rascal. She clung to my elbow as we walked a few yards down trail and far out of the snake's striking range. I dropped my pack and with quivering hands removed our camera from its case. A couple photos later, I relaxed and started to feel mischievous. I picked up a grapefruit-size rock and tossed it against the boulders above our slithery nemesis. As the missile struck, the snake rotated with incredible speed, lifted his head, and cranked up the rattling. It was an impressive display of quickness—but also a sign of vulnerability.

"I don't think it would be too hard to kill that sucker," I said.

"Duffy, *no!*"

"Do you remember reading about the hiker who'd kill snakes with a slingshot, then cook them over a fire? That guy looks big 'n' meaty. I bet barbecued rattler would be pretty good . . . remember, Bob said they taste like chicken." What better way to overcome my childhood nightmares than with a Pacific rattlesnake feast?

"Duffy, *no!* Don't you dare."

"Oh, I won't hurt him," I said, heaving another rock. He spun again.

"Let's go, Duffy! *Come* on."

I thought about launching a final bomb, but felt a pang of pity. I turned back to the trail and, with the rattling still reverberating between my ears, we continued north.

As we walked, Angela and I excitedly discussed the encounter. She'd never heard a rattler before and described her reaction as a "spine-tingling primeval alarm." I agreed, and despite my newfound bravado soon resumed nervously scanning the trail in front of me.

Within an hour, though, the rising temperature began to dull my reptile detection system. By midmorning the thermometer on my watch read 105 degrees and the trail had descended out of conifer protection and into unshaded chaparral. Our late-morning snack of peanut butter crackers and dried fruit required a good deal of water to wash it down, and when we finished we were left with just over a liter for the two of us. A couple hours later, and ten miles into the sixteen-mile waterless section, we polished off the last tepid drops of our supply. Soon, our hike became a pulsating, parched stumble. Following a seemingly never-ending series of gradual switchbacks, we made our way through boulder-studded chaparral. With each step I kicked up clouds of dust that seeped into my nose and mouth. Far below I spied Snow Canyon Road, where there was supposed to be a water fountain. To the west of the road, dark speckles represented the small village of Snow Creek. It looked both tantalizingly reachable and painfully far away.

As we continued our indirect descent, I glanced periodically at my watch, noting the temperature as it creeped up to 119 degrees. The heat of the mid-day sun radiated off everything—rocks, manzanita bark, the reflective pattern of my boots, even the dirt in front of me. Worst of all, a serious thirst had set in; my mouth was drier than a case of saltines.

We stopped several times to rest under oddly shaped boulders that cast smidgens of shade, but without water, even sitting was torture. Finally, we passed a spacious and invitingly dark cave, but it was already occupied. Marshmallow, head resting on her Kelty Cloud, snoozed alongside her equally somnolent pole-dragging friend. I desperately wanted to wake them up and ask for water, but they looked much too comfortable to bother. Angela thought dried peaches would help (she often suggested food to remedy unpleasant circumstances), but instead of taking my mind off my thirst, they sucked up all remaining saliva, increasing cottonmouth production to an all-time high. Half an hour later, Angela began to decompensate. Her steps and breath became labored and her face turned an unhealthy shade of red. She was on the verge of tears. I was starting to get scared—scared for myself and very scared for Angela. I'd never seen her look this exhausted, not even after finishing the Philadelphia half-marathon in humid 95-degree weather. She was tough, but not infinitely tough, and in these conditions I had no idea how long it would take for her to completely break down. And what if we didn't find water at Snow Canyon Road?

Angela's trekking poles balanced nearly motionless in her hands and she barely bothered to look up from the trail. I stopped her under a slice of boulder shade and told her to sit.

"Stay here," I said, "and I'll come back with water."

She didn't like that idea. I could tell she was petrified at the thought of being left alone. I explained that I still had some energy left and it would be best for both of us if I used it to find water as fast as possible. It couldn't be more than a couple miles to Snow Canyon Road. I didn't bother to mention the horrible possibility that I might not find water there. Reluctantly she agreed, softly nodding her head. I told her I loved her and promised that I would be back soon, and then took off at a trot. I was afraid to leave her, afraid that by the time I returned she'd be as dried and wrinkled as a dehydrated peach, but nevertheless I sped forward with singular purpose. Thoughts of rattlesnakes dissipated and were replaced with visions of frosty Oranginas. I wound down more switchbacks and then more switchbacks; they seemed to go on forever. Was I switchbacking into the depths of hell? Just when I had become convinced of the inevitability of my fiery demise, I passed through a forest of huge boulders and saw it. . . .

A metal spigot rose four feet out of the sandy ground. Judging from the pool of liquid sitting in its well, it was in working order. I sprinted the last twenty yards, turned its squeaky handle, and ducked my head. Scalding hot! I violently spat out the mouthful and let the faucet flow for a few seconds before trying again. Heavenly! I drank long and deep, but not to complete satisfaction. I needed to get back to Angela before she withered away.

I filled two liter containers and started running back up the trail. I rounded several switchbacks and then I saw her. She was spent—hyperventilating, with eyes deeply sunken and brimming with tears—but walking. Before even uttering a meek "Hello," she gulped down a liter of water. Later, she told me that after I'd left, she'd cowered under a boulder and cried in desperation. After several minutes of hysteria she'd decided that it was better to push on and hope I would be around the next corner. In her quest to find me, she'd sped up with each passing switchback until she was trailing only half a mile or so behind.

Those six miles were the most difficult and painful of our trip thus far. In retrospect, the distance seems insignificant. What is six miles without water during a twenty-mile day? I later got some perspective while reading *The Long Walk*, the story of Polish cavalry officer Slavomir Rawicz. Rawicz, after escaping from a World War II Soviet work camp in Siberia, walked four thousand miles to find freedom in India. Along the way, Slavomir and seven companions crossed the Mongolian border into China by way of the "burning wastes" of the great Gobi Desert. For *twelve days* they walked without water, losing two of their party to hyperthermia along the way. I didn't believe it was possible for anyone to survive twelve days without water, but somehow Rawicz did. He describes the torture of moving in "throbbing discomfort, mouths open, gasping in the warm desert air over enlarged, dust-covered tongues. I eased the sticky pebble round my sore gums to create a trickle of saliva so that I could swallow." Finally, they found an "oasis." It wasn't a river, lake, or metal water spigot, but "no more than a slimy ooze," an "almost dried-out creek, the moisture compounded with mud at the bottom of the channel not more than a couple of yards wide." Rawicz and his friends pushed down the mud to collect small handfuls of murky water. They drank it, "sand and mud and all, in ecstasy."

Compared to Slavomir Rawicz, our six miles were supremely wimpy and our water faucet an abundant oasis. Knowing this, however, does not make the memory of that day any less painful or any less scary.

After drinking two liters of water each, we started to feel human again and became anxious to find a crack of shade. After several minutes of searching we discovered a slim, sandy cave between two giant boulders. We collapsed inside of it and over the next few hours took turns braving the inferno to procure more water. As we rested and rehydrated, Zach, a Cal-Berkeley student we'd met in Idyllwild, ambled by. Zach looked beaten down by the elements, but I'm sure we looked worse—stretched out and motionless on our ground cloth, faces flush with defeat. He joined us in the cave and sat cross-legged, writing in his journal. We were too tired to provide much conversation. After an hour, Zach left to brave the heat again; he wanted to get to the

Pink Motel before dark. That seemed sensible to me, but returning to the merciless sunshine was just not an option for us. Finally, as the sun sank lower on the horizon, we emerged from our lair and began the five-mile trudge to the Pink Motel.

X ▪ ▪ ▪ ▪ X

The Pink Motel is not a motel—at least not in the "bed, bath, clean towel, and fresh linen" sense. It's really more of a "Motel 6 Lite," an abandoned two-room house about a mile from where the PCT intersects Interstate 10 in the nearly deserted town of West Palm Springs. The Pink Motel features unique landscaping: It's surrounded by a junkyard, a cemetery of blown and bald tires, stripped-down cars born before the days of the Ford Administration, and an assortment of other relics—a VW Bus, a Winnebago, and a two-person speed boat that looks sad to be so far from home. From its appearance, few would guess that the Pink Motel is a hospitality establishment, but its name is not all that misleading—it's a dirt-washed, pink stucco hiker asylum. A retired couple, Don and Helen, own the partially abandoned structure and garden of scrap metal and, since 1988, have opened the "second home" to PCT hikers seeking shelter from this nasty section of trail.

When we finally arrived, we couldn't see much of the Pink Motel. It was 9:30 at night, quite dark, and there were no neon "Vacancy" billboards to guide us. Instead we passed several "Keep Out" warnings. Our ears became saturated with the sound of wind roaring through rusted metal. We contoured around this eerily noisy junkyard to a small, one-story house. I entered through the creaky screen door and came to an abrupt halt. A whitened, bony man, naked but for a pair of grungy, once-white undies, rose off a couch directly in front of me. "Oh no," I thought, "this isn't the Pink Motel, it's an old hick's junkyard paradise. I hope he doesn't own a sawed-off." I took a step back and prepared to turn and run, but then caught a glimpse of familiar faces crashed out on several adjacent couches—Chris, Stacey, and Zach. My tension melted.

Chris gave us a brief verbal tour of the place before sinking back into his couch. The bony old man was asleep again and snoring loudly. The next morning I learned that this old-timer was actually an accomplished thru-hiker, a veteran of both the AT and the PCT.

Due to our late check-in, we missed out on the Pink Motel's couch suites. They were all booked, so we spent my birthday night on a soft if not completely clean carpet. Two weeks and 212 miles from Campo, a night on a floor seemed like a fantastic luxury to me. I slept soundly, confident that we'd survived the worst this desert could dish out.

[5]

Ultimatum at
Vasquez Rocks

 **THE HOSE HELPED.** I stood in the moonlight, balancing on my right leg as I tried to wash the dirt out from between the toes of my left foot. Zach, Chris, and Stacey, were inside. I could hear the murmurings of conversation and an occasional snore. Standing in quickly muddying sand, watching tiny head- and taillights stream along Interstate 10 in the pass below, I held the hose high over my head. Water ran down my back and buttocks. Coyotes *yip, yip, yip, yowrooooo*'d in the distance.

Finally, I dragged myself away from the starscape and the cool running water to take my place on the Pink Motel's living room floor with Duffy. The old toothless man snored and gasped on the couch nearest us while occasional rustles indicated our roommates were restless. Duffy, on the other hand, was out cold.

X ▪ ▪ ▪ ▪ X

We set off at seven the next morning. We hiked two miles and then veered off-trail to refill our water bottles at the Mesa Wind Farm, home to many of the 4,900 wind turbines in the area. Annually, each turbine produces the energy equivalent of a thousand barrels of oil.

The temperature was already rising precipitously, and after hiking for only forty-five minutes we'd put a serious dent in our water supply. I remembered reading that seventy-five percent of the human brain is composed of water and took that to mean that if I felt like my brain was boiling in the desert heat, it probably was.

We'd each gulped down several liters of water the previous evening, but dehydration still lingered. Our blood had thickened and was moving slowly through our circulatory systems, a phenomenon Duffy called "he-mo-concentration." Staring at the blue-green yarn-like veins in my wrists, I could almost see the lethargic "he-mo-concentration" within. I was all dried up. Even my joints seemed crackly and stiff.

Both Duffy and I knew that it could take two or three days to recover from deep dehydration and heat exposure such as we'd just experienced. We also knew that we were at the greatest risk of succumbing to heat-related illness two to four days into a heat wave. But medical knowledge be damned—there we were, back in the desert sun. In our one-track thru hiker minds, it was our only choice. We had a limited amount of time to get to Canada, and we weren't going to let a minor setback like nearly passing out from lack of water delay our progress.

In ambient temperatures greater than 110 degrees, the average human can survive for three weeks without food but only three days without water. (Slavomir Rawicz and his companions in the Gobi were clearly not average.) In such extreme heat, a person risks not only dehydration but also hyperthermia and heat exhaustion. Heat exhaustion can strike in a matter of minutes, causing symptoms such as shallow breathing, vomiting, dizziness, weakness, dry throat, confusion, flushing, and racing heartbeat. Remain in hot conditions long enough, and heat exhaustion may progress to heat stroke, a serious condition that, if not rapidly remedied, causes virtually all of the body's major organ systems to shut down. In the words of Robert Young Pelton in *Come Back Alive: The Ultimate Guide to Surviving Disasters, Kidnappings, Animal Attacks, and other Nasty Perils of Modern Travel*, "Your body is similar to an automobile. Just as an engine has an operating temperature range, a coolant, and a fuel system, so does your body. . . . The problem is that when you overheat, you don't pop a hose, you die."

To avoid reaching such a fatal malfunction, the body puts its approximately four million sweat glands to work. Sweat contains sugars, sodium, and potassium—a concoction known as electrolytes. Electrolytes keep the nerves and muscles functioning properly. Lose too many electrolytes through excessive sweating and you can suffer muscle spasms, cramps, and extreme fatigue. Yup, that all sounded familiar.

Exercise physiologists say that, on average, the body requires two to three liters of fluid each day. On a *normal* day, that's enough to recover losses. But if your days aren't so normal—let's say you're hiking twenty miles over rough terrain—your water requirement doubles, to four to six liters. If you (perhaps inexplicably) attempt to do this in extreme heat, the total jumps to seven to eleven liters of water per person per day. Between us, Duffy and I were carrying six liters of water. Duffy didn't seem overly concerned, stating that we'd pick up more along the way, but I wasn't sure if he really had any idea how much we were supposed to be drinking. Had he really paid attention in medical school?

I'd heard that the combination of heat and lack of water can drive a man (or woman) insane but never really believed it until those couple days in the desert. Tears (precious, water-wasting tears) were my constant companions, and a handful of miles became seemingly insurmountable obstacles. At least, though, I wasn't mentally fried enough to consider drinking my own urine (said only to work if you boil it first) or worse, the poisonous fluids from the machines in the Pink Motel's junkyard. And I definitely wasn't crazy enough to kill. Other desert adventurers have not remained as levelheaded.

On August 4 of 1999, Raffi Kodikian of Doylestown, Pennsylvania, and his buddy, David Coughlin of Millis, Massachusets, drove into Carlsbad Caverns National Park, New Mexico, for a night of camping. The ranger who issued them a backcountry permit advised them to take one gallon of water per person per day. Instead, they hiked into Rattlesnake Canyon with three pints of water and a bottle of Gatorade. The next day, when they tried to hike back to their car, they got lost. Much of what happened over the next four days remains a mystery.

On August 8, park rangers, after just a ten-minute search, found Raffi Kodikian. He was lying on his back in a tattered tent. He wore nothing but a pair of bloody shorts. Heavy rocks were strewn about, evidence of an SOS signal. An unopened can of baked beans sat nearby. A few yards from the tent was a mound of stones. Underneath laid the dead body of David Coughlin. He was twenty-six. "I killed him," Raffi told the rangers.

Later, police discovered Raffi's journal. "I killed + buried my best friend today," wrote Raffi. "David had been in pain all night. At around 5 or 6, he turned to me + begged that I put my knife through his chest. I did. . . ." Raffi went on trial for murder in New Mexico on May 8, 2000—the same day we began our hike from Mexico to Canada.

At the time of the trial, David's family said they were choosing to believe Raffi's story as it was laid out in his journal entries. "We have no reason why Raffi would have wished David harm or pain," a Coughlin family statement said. "Moreover, we cannot presume to know what transpired, or the thoughts and emotions the two experienced during the days before David's death. To be sure, we have questions. However, we find it difficult to believe there was any malicious intent."

The brain, as I mentioned earlier, is seventy-five percent water. Without adequate water, "your mental capacity goes down the toilet in a day or two," reports Gregory Davenport, author of *Wilderness Survival*. Throw in excess heat exposure and the result can be life-threatening stupidity.

In Raffi and David's case, environmentally-induced stupidity prevented them from locating a trail leading to their car—a trail that was a mere 275 yards from their camp—for four days. It also prevented them from taking simple, perhaps obvious, steps toward figuring out their location. For example, had they hiked to the top of a nearby ridge they could have seen the trail, the road, and possibly their car—which was only a mile and a half away.

According to Raffi, after two days of being lost, when buzzards started circling overhead, he and David discussed suicide. On the third day, David puked up mucus and bile for several hours and on the fourth, he begged Raffi to kill him.

"I put my knife through his chest," Raffi wrote in his journal. "I did, + a second time when he wouldn't die. He still breathed + spoke, so I told him I was going to cover his face. He said OK. He struggled but died. I buried him w/love. God + his family + mine, please forgive me."

David didn't write anything in his journal indicating that he wanted to die, and investigators wonder how he could have been in so much pain, so near death when Raffi seemed fine. In fact, shortly after being "rescued," Raffi is reported to have cracked a few jokes. The doctor who performed the autopsy on David concluded that he'd suffered "moderate to severe dehydration." There was also evidence of other trauma—twelve blunt-force injuries, including a large contusion on the back of his head.

During Raffi's trial, medical experts testified that while David's hydration level was low enough to cause significant distress, he almost surely would have survived if it weren't for Raffi's "intervention." Experts were surprised that an unopened can of baked beans was found at the campsite. Anyone suffering from severe dehydration would be expected to consume any available source of liquid. During the trial, Raffi was asked if he knew what he was doing when he killed his best friend. "What I thought I was doing was keeping my friend from going through twelve to twenty-four hours of hell before he died," he replied. Whether that statement really captures his true intent will likely forever be a mystery. Regardless, Kodikian was found guilty of second-degree murder and sentenced to two years in prison and five years probation. And to think, it all started with a seemingly innocent adventure in the desert.

X ▪ ▀ ▪ X

Back at the Mesa Wind Farm, my own twelve to twenty-four hours of hell were underway. Beneath scorching skies I trudged seven shadeless miles toward Whitewater Canyon, our next water source. The switchbacks down the canyon wall were interminable, and a panoramic view of idyllically lush and green Whitewater Trout Farm didn't help. The guidebook had made it clear that hikers weren't welcome at the farm, so we had no choice but to follow the trail up the sandy alluvium of Whitewater Creek. Whitewater Creek itself was nowhere to be seen.

Inching along, my feet sank in the soft sand. I'd nearly finished off my water bottle and what was left was hot, like shower water. Duffy was way ahead of me, appearing strong while I wilted underneath the sun's rays and my pack's weight. I cried as I went, staggering more than walking. My peripheral vision started to fade and I felt like I might faint at any moment. Periodically, I'd lean over on my trekking poles, close my eyes, and tell myself I could do it—*had* to do it. Finally, Duffy stopped and turned around. It took at least fifteen minutes for me to catch up with him. When I did, I told him I could go no farther.

"Where's the river?" I began to hyperventilate.

Now Duffy was concerned. He took my pack and we walked together, slowly, in search of shade. The best we could find was a scraggly, gnarled bush. Scrambling under the thorny branches I huddled near the trunk, trying to take maximum advantage of the patchy shade, hiding from the sun as if it were rain. Low lying prickles snagged my hair and clothes. Flies buzzed in my ears and ants crawled up my legs, but I didn't have the energy to swat them away. Duffy gave me his water and I finished the last tepid gulps. Then, leaving his pack behind, he walked off with our empty bottles in search of water. I was left to ruminate on the sordid story of Kodikian and Coughlin.

When he returned he was blissfully wet. "You won't believe it," he gasped as he slumped down beside me and handed me a cold water bottle. "You can lay in it." And clearly he had. We hadn't seen a body of water big enough to lie in since our first night, at Lake Morena.

The creek was half a mile away. When we got there we plopped down in its foot-deep flow, letting the cool water rush over our bodies. We floated there for nearly an hour, moving on only after we began to feel severely sunburned. Dragging our red bodies a little farther along the trail, we found Zach leaning against a rock face that provided about five feet of shade.

Zach would turn twenty-one on June 16 and was already planning a celebration. A woman friend, Summer, was going to pick him up at Kennedy Meadows (476 miles away) and take him to a Moontribe rave in the desert. Even as he told us this, Zach was intently scribbling a letter to Summer, creating a pile of long, cramped pages of torn notebook paper. Solo hiking can be lonely, and after just two meetings Zach seemed to have developed a kid-brother kind of affection for Duffy and a curiosity regarding me. He was flabbergasted when I told him I'd only backpacked one night before embarking on this 2,655-mile trek.

"What if you don't like it?" he asked.

"Doesn't matter," I replied. "I'm not going home we until reach Canada or I can't physically walk another step, whichever comes first."

Carrying a book, a pipe, his guidebook section, his letters to Summer, a sleeping bag, and a homemade alcohol stove, Zach's sneaker-clad feet carried him northward quickly and easily. When he hiked, he went light and fast. But when he was off-trail, he could linger under a tree whittling a pipe all afternoon. He made it all look effortless—but still, I could tell that he wished he had someone to hike with. As evening approached, Zach strode off across the burning white sand, alone. I watched ripples of heat envelop him until he disappeared into the shimmering air.

X ▪ ▪ ▪ ▪ X

"We should get going," Duffy said, rousing me from my musings.

"What's your watch say?" I asked. We'd set it down in the shade to record the temperature.

"Hundred and eight . . . at six o'clock. Unbelievable." Duffy stood up to put on his pack.

As the sun set, cooler temperatures would hopefully arrive. We hiked to the top of a ridge and along its narrow spine until dark. Then we laid our space blanket and sleeping bag out under the night sky. Often, the desert night was cold enough that we preferred to be in our tent, but this night was balmy (probably because it had been 108 degrees at six in the evening). The stars shone like candles, and we could see the twinkling lights of Palm Springs, only 400 feet above sea level, to the east and the silhouette of 10,805-foot Mount San Jacinto to the south.

There are lots of reasons why sex on the trail can be unappealing—dirt, sweat, exhaustion, aching muscles, and cramped tents, to name a few. But none of them seemed to be able to take the romance out of that night. Under the stars, with an aria of coyotes in the background, all the day's troubles were forgotten and we made love. For the time being at least, we were enraptured by everything—each other, the night sky, the smell of sun-baked sagebrush, and coyote songs.

The next morning I was simultaneously euphoric and lethargic. Mentally, I was revitalized, but physically I continued to feel weak. There was good news, though; we were moving into the San Bernardino Mountains and from stubby brush to massive pines. As we hiked toward Big Bear City (where we would pick up our re-supply box and wait for the arrival of Duffy's brother, Chris, and our two friends, Lisa and Pete), I breathed deeply. The mountain air felt fresh and I could see laughter in Duffy's eyes. Mountains, I'd already discovered, brought out the little boy in him. At Onyx Summit (mile 254), he startled me with boyish excitement.

"It's the grizz!" He jogged to a chain-link fence separating the trail from an animal farm. In nearby cages, big cats—a cougar and a tiger—paced, eyeing us hungrily. The bear lolled in a corner, unimpressed by our presence.

"Just like Meadow Ed said," we remarked, almost in unison, before taking a photo and moving on.

X ▪ ▪ ▪ ▪ X

"Milky Way."

"Mr. Goodbar."

"Butterfinger."

My mind's eye sifted through a pile of trick-or-treat candy while Duffy, his brother Chris, my old college roommate Lisa, and another friend, Pete, awaited my answer.

"Strawberry Charleston Chew."

"Ohhhh, good one, good one."

Another narrow escape from Candy Bar Game humiliation. Pete's family must have taken lots of road trips, or he must have spent many rainy summer days as a camp counselor trying to keep cranky Blue Birds and Little Warriors from feuding. Either way, he grew up to be an excellent guide to the land of good, clean, mile-eating fun.

"Excuse me while I engage in some self-aggrandization. . . . "

"Such a fixation fills me with trepidation. . . ."

"I'm not sure I like your insinuation. . . ."

These snippets of nonsense were all successful plays in another of Pete's time-killers—the Radiation Game. Animation, flirtation, excommunication, even breast augmentation. We must have covered six miles with such "ations." It was great to have guests.

We met Chris, Lisa, and Pete in Big Bear, and they hiked with us for three days—covering twenty-four miles. That's right, a mere eight miles a day. The leisurely pace and fresh blood was a life- and hike–saver. After surviving heat and dehydration, we needed to have some fun. The best thing about having friends from home hike with you is how they change your routine and per-spective. We'd been working so hard to make the miles that we hadn't had time to sunbathe (a whole different way of perceiving the sun), nap, play Kick the Cone (the au naturel version of Kick the Can) or pinecone softball. With our friends around, we did all those things and more. We paused to listen to birds, watched pine boughs dance in the wind, made our first campfire, roasted turkey-dogs, concocted monster s'mores, and shared a few beers. Trail pur-ists may cringe at the thought of lugging such luxuries into the wilderness, but the company was cause for celebration. And beyond the bad jokes told by moonlight, trail games, siestas, tuneless renditions of "Puff the Magic Dragon" (later to become "Duff the Magic Dragon"), and the mesmerizing sparks of the fire, time with Chris, Lisa, and Pete helped us remember why we loved spending time in the outdoors. We were reminded that not everything about hiking the PCT needed to be a test of our relationship, stamina, or determina-tion. Hiking and camping were fun! If only we could have hung on to that feeling for a little longer.

We dawdled while our friends were with us and enjoyed every minute of it, but as soon as they left we felt the pressure again. Compelled to make up for lost time with fast miles, we set our sites on Agua Dulce, our next major re-supply point and home of the archangel among trail angels, Donna. To catch up to our itinerary, we'd have to make good time through Section D and the San Gabriel Mountains.

There are four things I remember distinctly about this 110-mile stretch of trail. The first is the hummingbirds in the morning, zooming by our tent with intricate aerial maneuvers. The second remembrance is much less pleasant—the yellow smog that hung in the valley below the mountains like a drop ceiling. Third, I recall the charred landscape left by a forest fire started by a hiker burning toilet paper three years prior. And finally, I remember an un-pleasant altercation between Duffy and our confounded stove.

On our twenty-fifth day on the PCT, at Messenger Flats Campground (mile 431), our MSR Internationale sputtered out. It was unfortunate timing; we were still twenty-five miles from Agua Dulce and out of food, aside from some uncooked macaroni. Duffy took out the stove maintenance kit and we patiently read all the instructions and followed them step by step. In the process, we managed to take the stove completely apart. It now looked like one of those wire puzzles where you twist and turn each individual piece in an attempt to get them all free. Trouble was, we couldn't get our pieces apart *or* back together.

It appeared that there wouldn't be any macaroni that afternoon—especially not after Duffy threw the stove against a stately ponderosa pine. Hitting the orange-brown bark, it collapsed in a heap on a bed of long yellow-green needles. On a warm day, the ponderosa oozes sap that smells like vanilla, a natural aphrodisiac and calming agent. This pine, however, was having no such effect on Duffy. He jumped up, ran toward the tree, picked up our mangled appliance, and threw it again—harder this time so that it made a satisfying clatter. "We'll return it to the store when we get home," I said, trying to at least soothe his wallet, since satisfying his stomach wouldn't be possible.

Eleven discouraged miles later, we came to the North Fork Ranger Station. A large, wolflike white dog barked as we approached the garage. While we filled our water bottles from a hose, a man emerged from the station and introduced himself as Todd. His dog's name was Dakota. He invited us in to use the station's showers and gave us clean towels. Throughout our hike, we eagerly anticipated getting to town so we could bathe. In keeping with this, we couldn't wait to get to Agua Dulce the next day—but now here we were, in the wilderness taking a surprise shower. It was a luxurious treat, but looking down at my sudsed-up belly, I couldn't help but notice it was caving in. We needed to eat.

After our showers, we headed to the ranger station's barbecue pit to build a fire and make dinner. Boiling water over a barbecue isn't very efficient, and we wasted a lot of time. The flames roared around our pot so high that we couldn't open it to stir the macaroni, and as the pot blackened, I knew our dinner inside was doing the same. Balancing the scalding-hot titanium pot on sticks, we managed to get it off the fire and onto a picnic table. Duffy burned his finger trying to remove the lid. Inside, our dinner was charbroiled around the edges and a soupy, porridgelike consistency in the middle. It reminded me of the first time I'd made pasta on our MSR, months ago in Philadelphia, in Duffy's driveway. We gulped the burnt, lumpy mess down hungrily at first, but soon began to feel nauseated. It was going to be a long sixteen miles to Agua Dulce.

Eager to get a head start, we declined Todd's invitation to stay the night and put in another three miles. Hiking down into a canyon, we camped at Mattox Creek. The next day, we awoke to the rumble of each other's hunger pangs and prickly, goosebump-covered skin. We packed up quickly and then Duffy was off like a rocket—he wanted to get to Agua Dulce as fast as possible. I followed close behind, eagerly anticipating an early morning snack at the trailer park on Soledad Canyon Road.

By eight in the morning we were hiking through the rows of mobile homes. We searched in vain for a vending or soda machine. Finally, we spotted an elderly gentleman cleaning the park's pool. He told us that the snack bar had closed years ago and the nearest store was in Acton, eleven miles away.

"What kind of thing ya looking for?" he asked.

"Anything to fill our bellies," Duffy responded, "bread, cereal, whatever."

"Why don't you go over to trailer sixty-seven and get my wife Jenny to fix up something? Just tell her Pete sent ya."

"Oh no, we don't want to put you out," I said. "Maybe we could just buy some bread."

Pete was insistent. I approached the trailer alone, hoping to diminish the initial shock of the early morning request. I knocked shyly several times. Nearly a minute later, an elderly woman in a flowered housedress and shower cap opened the door. She apologized; she'd been "on the can." I was so embarrassed I almost turned and walked away, but instead explained that Pete had said she might be able to give us some food.

"But we don't want to be any trouble," I stammered, "and we have money. Could we maybe just buy some bread and peanut butter or cheese?" Jenny would hear nothing of that and invited me in. She'd make us bacon and eggs, she said, as soon as she finished up with her previous business. While she attended to this, Duffy arrived and we made ourselves comfortable.

A few minutes later we were watching perky morning shows on the television and listening to Jenny chat merrily while she cooked. Soon a fine feast of bacon, scrambled eggs, toast with blackberry jam, milk, and orange juice was laid before us.

Leaving the RV park, we crossed the Southern Pacific Railroad tracks and passed a three foot rock and concrete obelisk commemorating the PCT's completion ceremony, in June of 1993. It seemed a strange and unattractive place to celebrate a beautiful trail. Garbage, graffiti, old tires, and shopping carts littered the landscape. Quickly, though, the trail led us out of the canyon and onto a brushy hillside. In the distance, we could see the pinkish rocks known as the Vasquez Formation. These weird conglomerates of igneous and metamorphic cobbles and coral pink siltstone looked flabby, like rolls of fat on a chubby belly. My energy had spiked shortly after our hearty breakfast, but now, as the sun's rays beat down on my bandanna-covered head, I started to crash. Duffy was speeding off ahead and I was struggling to keep up. It was becoming the same old story and I sank into a sulky sadness.

After we passed through a tunnel under Antelope Valley Freeway 14, we lost the trail. This was the straw that broke the Chigger's back, and I started to cry. Duffy glanced at my tearful face briefly, but having located the trail (after about ten minutes of searching), walked on. We were entering the Vasquez Rocks County Park, named for the famed outlaw Tiburcio Vasquez, who used the caves, nooks, and crannies of the large outcroppings as hideouts during the 1850s. The landscape is so bizarre and surreal that a number of sci-fi movies have been filmed there, including episodes of *Star Trek* and scenes from *Bill and Ted's Excellent Adventure.*

Soon we were involved in our own surreal scene. One minute we were snapping pictures of me cozying up to what Duffy called "Jabba the Rock," and the next we were arguing. I'm not sure how it started. I think Duffy asked me if I could "please smile . . . for once." His tone was aggravated and condescending.

"Of course I can smile," I said. "I just don't feel like it."

"You never feel like it. I'm sick of turning around and seeing you being miserable. I feel like I'm making you do something you don't want to do. If you don't want to be here, maybe we should just go home."

"Lately I feel like I might as well be out here alone," I replied in between sobs. "It's like you don't even notice me." I was exhausted and hysterical—quite the stereotypical girl. Duffy's accusations and ultimatum didn't help one bit. I needed some sympathy and positive reinforcement; encouraging words like "You're doing a good job," or "I know this is hard, but it's going to get better," and "It won't always be hot and dry like this."

"I don't want to go home and I don't want to quit," I said. "But I need you to slow down, cut me some slack, and stop being such a slave-driver. Could you just acknowledge that this is hard instead of walking stoically onward all the time? When did you become the iceman?"

Perhaps Duffy was partially right and I wasn't savoring our desert experience. But I didn't say that, and Duffy didn't apologize for acting like a drill sergeant. Back home, during our pre-PCT training, we joked about "Ballard Boot Camp," but lately it seemed all too real and not at all funny.

Despite the harsh words and bitter feelings, however, we still had common ground—neither of us wanted to go home, and we both wanted to get to Agua Dulce for food, Gatorade, and rest.

"I need to rehydrate and sleep," I said. "I think it's the sun." Duffy's response was as dry as the sand around us, pretty much par for the PCT course, so far.

We left Vasquez Rocks in silence. Now, instead of sulking I was fuming.

Suddenly it seemed that not only did I have to prove to the hiking community that I could make it to Canada, but I also had to prove it to Duffy, while smiling like a beauty queen. Miles ago I'd acknowledged that we, as a team, were in competition (albeit unspoken and hopefully healthy) with our thru-hiking peers; now it seemed we were also in competition with one another.

[6]

Saufley Electric and Ballard Gas

UNDER BRIGHT MIDAFTERNOON SKIES, we walked up Escondido Canyon Road into Agua Dulce. All was silent except the sound of trekking poles on pavement and the growl of an occasional passing vehicle. After the flurry of verbal fireworks at Vasquez Rocks, Angela and I hadn't had anything to say to each other. We were both brooding and sulking, and there wasn't much scenery to distract us from our ruminations. I hoped that a stop in Agua Dulce would help assuage the tension—we'd heard many hikers talk with excitement about the town's trail angel, Donna, and her home, "Hiker's Haven."

"Hiker's Haven had better live up to the hype," I thought. This was a fragile moment; another obstacle, no matter how small, could easily set off a domino effect and land us on a plane back home. I loved Angela very much, but hiking with her wasn't always easy. I knew she felt the same about me. With our recent battle fresh in my mind, it occurred to me that this hike was rapidly transforming us from honeymooners into bickering spouses. She wanted positive reinforcement, reassurance that she was doing well and that I was proud of her. She *was* doing well and I was *extremely* proud of her, but it was difficult for me to consistently express this. I didn't want to be a cheerleader, and I don't think she wanted that, either. Besides, most of the time I was too exhausted and tired to cheer. I tried my best to maintain a smile and a chuckle, and I didn't think it was too much to ask her to do the same. Otherwise, what was the point of being out here? This was supposed to be fun—a twisted and masochistic type of fun, but fun nevertheless.

96

My thoughts were interrupted by our arrival at Agua Dulce's downtown plaza. Agua Dulce is a small ranching town, and I was able to quickly process all of the options—three restaurants, a hardware store, and the Agua Dulce Market, with a post office inside. A large laminated sign in front of the market announced "Welcome PCT Hikers." The sight of the sign and a well-stocked store resurrected my mood, and in a flash I was inside procuring cold beverages. I delivered a Squirt to my little squirt and instructed her to rest outside while I retrieved our re-supply package. I also half-jokingly suggested that she consider working on an attitude readjustment. She looked at me sullenly.

We were sitting outside the supermarket ripping at our huge box when a man with a two-pronged goatee and a scraggly bushel of blond hair approached. I would have thought him a PCT hiker but for his shirt—dark blue cotton (*gasp!*) with white lettering on the front.

"Thru-hikers?" He asked.

We nodded our heads. He introduced himself as Tweedle. Tweedle's freshly sculpted facial hair indicated that he was "town clean." He looked like a man who'd know how to find Hiker's Haven.

"Hiker's Haven? No problem, dudes. We're about to head back there in Donna's car." Tweedle gestured at a dusty Jeep Cherokee.

"Yippee!" exclaimed Angela, her face reanimated. We picked up our packs and forty-pound re-supply box and walked toward the Jeep. As we did so, a team of scraggly hikers emerged from the nearby pizza parlor. They were wearing blue shirts like Tweedle's, and as one of them turned his back, I noted the imprint—"Saufley Electric." Very odd—a band of rogue electricians roaming the PCT. We all packed into the Cherokee and headed to Hiker's Haven.

Situated on the dusty outskirts of Agua Dulce, Donna's house and one-and-a-third-acre lot was a thru-hiker's delight. Behind a comfortable, one-story home was a well-tended lawn filled with lounge chairs, picnic tables, inflatable mattresses, five dogs, and a frenzy of hiker gear. Adjacent to the lawn was a long, rectangular guesthouse and a retired RV, both of which functioned as auxiliary accommodations. There were hikers everywhere—sorting through re-supply boxes, soaking feet in Epsom salts, coating umbrellas with Mylar, playing cards, and stuffing food into their mouths. And they were all wearing dark blue "Saufley Electric" shirts. A tall woman with buoyant blond hair greeted us. Everything about her screamed "Mom."

"Welcome! I'm Donna Saufley. You guys look like you need a shower."

I nearly exclaimed, "I love you, Mom!" but controlled myself enough to utter just a guttural "Yes, please."

"Okay, here's the deal . . . take the hamper, go inside the guesthouse, and take a left. The bathroom is down the hall, on the right. Dump your dirty stuff in the hamper and after you wash up, throw on some clean clothes from the closet."

"Ahh," I thought, "the blue shirt mystery is solved."

"Then you can get settled in the master suite. We don't have too many couples here now, so you guys lucked out."

Amen to that. Not only were we given the guesthouse master suite, but we also had access to the full range of Hiker's Haven services—phone, TV and VCR, an extensive PCT library, Internet access, and a tightly stacked, fully stocked refrigerator. To top it all off, those nasty clothes we dumped in the hamper, well—Donna washed the heck out of 'em. She delivered them to our suite and, with an unbelievable flourish, took a large whiff of my socks to demonstrate her cleaning prowess. What a brave soul. A few hours earlier and such bravado might have caused her to asphyxiate. And no band of rogue electricians could have saved her from that.

Not surprisingly, Hiker's Haven was a popular place. Over the course of our long weekend at Donna's, we met about twenty other hikers. There were some familiar faces, including Zach, Chris, and Stacey, but mostly there were strange, scruffy ones. Many we would come to know by nickname ("trail name")—Hawkeye, Tweedle, Fish, Pansy Ass, Aussie Crawl, Tye-Dye, Bald Eagle, Nokona, Madame Butterfly, Improv, Sunrise, and Mirage.

Some hikers, mostly PCT or AT veterans, began their hikes with trail names already in place. Others were urged to develop them as they went. Invariably, each had its own unique story. Surgical treatment for gastric cancer had left "Gutless" with only one-tenth of his stomach, necessitating small, frequent meals but also providing excellent nickname fodder. Then there was "Just Mike," a military man of well-chosen words. When asked his name, he'd reply "Mike."

If urged to reveal his trail name, he'd offer the practical response, "Just Mike."

On our second night at Donna's, we had a titanic barbecue. Casey and Toby, college-age buddies from Seattle, organized the event. Casey, a slightly chubby guy with bleached hair and melancholy green eyes, was known by the trail name "Crazy Legs." Apparently when Crazy Legs walked on narrow stretches of sandy trail, his aggressive stride sometimes collapsed its lateral edges, sending him on chaparral-infested detours. A crisscross of scars across both of his meaty calves validated this story.

Casey had spent the previous summer serving booze to tourists on an Alaskan tourist train. He was disorderly, gregarious, and unpredictable. In contrast, Toby was the organizational glue that kept the duo on the trail. He'd started the hike with the trail name "Major Major," a reference to a character in Joseph Heller's *Catch-22*, but this name proved too obscure, so he'd changed it to "Catch-23." Toby explained the provenance of his name by putting a twist on Heller's famous "catch."

"Given the dangers and discomfort, both real and immediate, of thru-hiking," he said without emotion, "one must conclude that it is crazy to hike the Pacific Crest Trail. But once you have started and gotten this far, to quit would also be crazy. So there you go, Catch-23."

"That's some catch, that Catch-23," Casey chortled in response.

"It's the best there is, Crazy Legs, the best there is" Toby sat back and scratched his short, bristly beard.

Toby had been planning to hike the PCT since he was eight years old. Casey, his childhood friend, had decided on a whim to accompany him, but only if they thru-hiked *their* way, the *fun* way.

"Casey and I," Toby said, "have defined our hike as a continuous walk from Mexico to Canada on or very near to the Pacific Crest Trail while maintaining a drunken state at least one percent of the time."

While the barbecue provided a perfect medium for Casey and Toby to make progress toward their one percent drunkenness quota, I was extremely content to sit at the picnic table and attack a plateful of ribs. Meanwhile, Angela's attention was focused on Ed, an "organic" farmer from Humboldt County. Ed, a vegetarian for over fifteen years, had decided that his rapidly emaciating body could no longer be separated from meat. So there he was, gorging on animal fat and protein hand-over-fist, trying to make up for as much lost time as possible. Although Ed wasn't exactly sure what type of meat he was eating (he kept asking, "What's this? What's that?"), he sure liked how it tasted. I wouldn't have wanted to be a well-fed squirrel or less-than-agile pigeon around a guy like Ed that night.

"No vegetarian can survive this trail," Casey said, and it made sense. A thru-hiker's body is subject to such constant assault that without consistent protein intake, it is almost impossible to maintain muscle and body mass.

Later, as the crowd gathered over bottles of beer and trail stories, Donna and her husband Jeff emerged from the main house. Rumor was that there was a funny story behind the inception of their trail angeling careers.

"Story! Story!" Crazy Legs chanted, echoing the group sentiment.

Somewhat reluctantly, Donna launched into the tale. On a Saturday night in the summer of 1997, Jeff went out for a friend's bachelor party and wasn't expected back until morning. Donna, with visions of lusty strippers and rowdy male behavior gyrating in her head, drove to the pizza parlor to indulge. As she suffocated her worries with mozzarella, she noticed a table of dirty and disheveled young people filling water bottles from pitchers at a nearby table. Later, Donna ran into one of the female hikers in the bathroom. The woman had her foot in the sink and was scrubbing it vigorously. Shocked but intrigued, Donna asked what she and her friends were up to. The woman explained that they were PCT hikers re-supplying in Agua Dulce. Because Agua Dulce didn't have any motels, they were going to walk a couple miles down the road and sleep on a church's lawn. Well, this was too much for Donna's motherly instincts. Before long she'd gathered up the motley group and arranged them comfortably on the couches of her guesthouse. Satisfied with her altruistic act but not completely at ease, she returned to the main house and proceeded to lock all the doors and windows.

At this point in the story Jeff broke in. He had been out with the guys, having a good time, but as the night wore on he became awash in drunken regret. He missed his wife terribly, so he convinced a buddy to drive him home. He arrived at his front door to find the house in total lock-down. He tried the doors, he tried the windows, he rang the doorbell, and he banged with his fists. Meanwhile, Donna, lying in supine paralysis, was afraid that the hiker riffraff were attempting to break in. Jeff finally gave up, assuming that Donna was pissed at him for returning home drunk and resigned himself to a night of punishment on the guesthouse couch. He stumbled in without flipping on the lights, and was about to lie down when he noticed a figure in the darkness.

"What the. . . . Who the *hell* are you?" he exclaimed.

An equally startled voice replied, "What! Who the *hell* are you?"

Eventually this real-life version of a *Three's Company* episode got straightened out, and everyone shared laughs over omelets the next morning. And so was born a tradition of hospitality at Hiker's Haven. "All we ask in return is that you write in our scrapbook," concluded Donna.

We'd only planned to stay at Donna's for two days, but the comforts created powerful inertia. Plus there were errands to run, most importantly an excursion to the Sports Chalet in Rancho Santa Clarita to purchase a new stove. We found a propane-powered stove to replace our broken, battered, and utterly useless one. Back at Donna's, Angela tested our new stove while I played cards and drank beer with Casey, Toby, and two newcomers, Fish and Ryan, from Tampa, Florida. Fish, a furry, barrel-chested veteran of the AT, was full of stories and tidbits of trail wisdom. He worked as a computer salesman for eight months of the year and then took off summers to hike. He struck me as an excellent salesman, engaging and jovial. Ryan was a hiking novice whom Fish had "sold" on the idea of a PCT thru-hike. At home he was a carpenter, one with a strong dislike of electricians—an exposed wire on the job had nearly electrocuted him. And while Ryan stubbornly refused to wear a "Saufley Electric" tee shirt, in all other respects he seemed to be a mellow guy with a clear determination to keep up with Fish. Like Casey, Toby, and me, Fish and Ryan relished a good beer or two with their re-supply stops, and thus it wasn't difficult for us to waste away the afternoon in Donna's backyard.

Our card game ended when Fish excused himself to address a burgeoning project. Daris (Pansy Ass) was a twentyish Canadian solo-hiker. As one of just a handful of single women on the trail, she received plenty of attention and enjoyed every minute of it. With dark, flouncy hair and a pleasantly round face, she was attractive in a crunchy sort of way. This made her even more of a rare commodity. Besides Pansy Ass and my own Chigger, I hadn't noticed many other attractive women hikers. Not surprising, I suppose, since dirt, blisters, and sunburns aren't typically associated with beauty.

Fish had been hiking long enough to know a good catch when he saw one and was laying the groundwork for another successful sale. Personally, I couldn't believe he had the energy to try. My sex drive had been jammed in neutral for the good part of the last several weeks. Angela and I had made up after our Vasquez Rocks blowout, but my libido continued to be beaten down by grime and fatigue. The first night at Donna's we'd vowed to be more receptive to each other's physical and emotional needs, but at this point in our trip regular sex was not one of them.

X ▪ ▪ ▪ X

On June 5, after three luxurious days, we reluctantly left Hiker's Haven. Actually, it was I who was reluctant; Angela was rejuvenated and feeling the itinerant itch. I felt ill—feverish, weak, and queasy. But Chris and Stacey were long gone, Casey and Toby had left the night before, and we didn't want to break the record for the longest stay at the Haven (apparently over a week). Donna dropped us off at the northern edge of town and we resumed our chaparral-dominated trek, now through Mint Canyon. It wasn't long before we encountered Casey. He was in the middle of the trail, kneeling on his waffle pad with gear scattered around him, stuffing his sleeping bag. His blond hair was an eddy of misdirected waves and his face was glazed.

"Good morning!" chirped Angela.

"Rotten morning," Casey replied. "Never should have left Donna's. Now I gotta go catch Gimpy." Toby had been nursing a sore knee since Idyllwild and had acquired yet another trail name.

"Good thing you got a head start last night." I couldn't resist.

"Morning is not my time."

We continued on, leaving Casey on schedule for a nine o'clock departure, or, as he said, "a right-on-time departure." As we started a several mile climb to Sierra Pelona Ridge, my nausea increased and my hip belt seemed to tighten its grip on my midsection. As we approached the ridge, Crazy Legs stormed up on us from behind. We hiked together for a while and Casey described his thru-hiking inspiration; Brad Pitt's portrayal of Austrian mountaineer Heinrich Harrer in *Seven Years in Tibet*. With yellowish scruff sprouting on his face, Casey looked somewhat like the unshaven Pitt in the movie. Later, I watched the film for a second time and was struck by a line from a letter Harrer wrote to his son. In Tibet, Harrer said, "People believe that if they walk long distances to holy places it purifies the bad deeds they've committed. They believe that the more difficult the journey, the greater the depth of purification." Perhaps this line captured a quiet agenda for not only Casey but all of us aspiring thru-hikers. Of course, Casey would never have admitted that thru-hiking could have such a philosophical purpose; he was too much of a joker. Instead, he probably would've morphed the quote into something like, "I believe that the more difficult the journey, the greater the required depth of intoxication."

At the gusty exposed ridge of Sierra Pelona, I started to experience some gusts of my own. My stomach was perfectly executing the quadruple lutz over and over again. Swallowing some pride, I told Casey to move on ahead and begged Angela for a break. She sat, guidebook in hand, and read, "From here we have a view south to the Vasquez Rocks and east to Mount Gleason, Williamson, and Baden-Powell." All I wanted was a view of the ground. I tried to rally myself for the descent, but a quarter of a mile in, I was figuratively out of gas while literally full of it. We laid our space blanket underneath the shade of a manzanita and I collapsed in a heap of fatigue and bloating. Angela wasn't sure what to do. Most of the time I was the one pushing us along; now the roles were reversed. She seemed very concerned, and I loved her for that. Feebly, I told her to go ahead. She looked at me, incredulous, and informed me that there was no way she was going to leave me here in the center of the trail—to die.

Two hours later, I awoke to find her sitting cross-legged above me reading a section of *Zen and the Art of Motorcycle Maintenance*. I was feeling marginally better, but the rapidly inflating gas bubble in my gastrointestinal tract was troubling my every movement and I was in need of some maintenance of my own. By this time my diagnosis was becoming clear. My mind flashed back to our hellish trek up Whitewater Canyon to cow-dung-riddled Whitewater Creek. There I was, lying in a foot and a half of water, gulping it by the mouthful. I was fully clothed, boots and all, and cool water was soothing my dusty throat while our PUR-Hiker water filter laid useless on the shore. Now it looked like I was paying the price for my indiscretion.

I rummaged through Big Red for the med kit and found what I hoped would be the remedy. I gulped down two Flagyl tablets and we moved on. I was pretty sure that I'd contracted giardiasis, and feared that the worst, and runniest, was still to come.

Giardia lamblia is a teardrop-shaped unicellular creature that alternates between two forms, trophozoite and cyst. The trophozoite is the active side of this schizophrenic beast. It uses five flagella to locomote through the small intestine of its host and to attach to the bowel wall. Under the microscope, the two nuclei of trophozoite sit adjacent to each other and resemble two large eyes. Once these quick and crafty creatures have set up camp in the intestine, they begin to reproduce like crazy, splitting into two *Giardia lamblia* over and over again. The newborns are released back into the bowel and as they move through it, they undergo a dramatic personality change. The flagella retract and they develop an environmentally resistant exterior. Transformed into sedentary cysts, they passively follow the path of crap and water until they can find another small intestine to awaken in. As cysts, *Giardia* can survive for weeks to months in water of just about any temperature, patiently awaiting ingestion by an unsuspecting bovine, beaver, bear, or backpacker. *Giardia lamblia* doesn't seem to bother the other critters, but for some backpackers the result, one to three weeks later, is *boom*, and *toot*, and uh-oh, "beaver fever." Fevers and fatigue are common early symptoms in those affected by giardiasis, although in some people there is no warning at all. Cramps, sulfuric burps, and explosive vomiting and diarrhea come on suddenly.

Apparently this was how Fish manifested his infection, sitting up in the tent in the middle of the night and barely peeking his head outside before a disastrous two-pronged explosion. We heard the story the next day in Lake Hughes from poor Ryan, Fish's tent-mate. I would have liked to ask Fish about it himself, but he was too preoccupied in a hotel bathroom. I left a several-day supply of Flagyl with Ryan and we wished them the best.

A significant percentage of people—at least fifty percent—are immune to *Giardia* infection. That is, they may swallow the cysts and the trophozoites may stick to their bowel wall, but this process does not trigger any remarkable symptoms. It was possible that Angela was immune, or more likely just smarter about her drinking water choices. Anyway, she stayed healthy throughout my bout with giardiasis.

I somehow managed to drag myself behind Angela to the Green Valley Ranger Station, a nearly twenty-three-mile day. By the next morning, after a couple more doses of Flagyl, I was feeling more energetic. My appetite, however, had deserted me and I found myself making frequent trail detours with trowel in hand—so frequent that Angela started calling me a trail name that I had, at one time, found amusing.

"There goes my Trowel Boy . . . again," she'd say.

"So funny it makes me runny," I'd reply.

From the small community of Lake Hughes we detoured from the trail for a surreal twenty-mile road-walk across the Mojave Desert. This route, which cut off twenty-seven nearly waterless miles, had been well publicized at Hiker's Haven and most of the hikers staying there had opted for it. While the official trail skirted the edge of the Tehachapi Mountains to avoid private land, we went straight up the gut of the Mojave. Starting in the evening to avoid the worst of the heat, we took Lake View Road past Fairmont Reservoir to the L.A. Aqueduct, a concrete conduit that takes water 338 miles from the Sierra to the lawns of Los Angelites. After filling our water bottles at an open section of the aqueduct, we dropped into the valley of the Mojave, weaving our way through a scorched landscape to 170th Street. We trudged along this unlit road in the darkness, occasionally taking refuge on the shoulder as a lone pair of headlights sped by. Finally, at about one in the morning, we pitched camp just feet from the road. I popped two Imodium tablets and hoped that I would last through the night.

A Blistered Kind of Love

When I awoke and peeked outside the tent, I was startled by the beauty of the desert morning. It was refreshingly cool, and long shadows and Joshua tree silhouettes accentuated the starkness of the landscape. These "trees," with their contorted, scaly trunks and yucca spike flowers, jabbed up and out of the surrounding sand, brush, and tumbleweeds. Joshua trees, named as such by the Mormons because they conjured up images of Joshua pointing toward the Promised Land, are the aesthetically dominating flora of the Mojave Desert. But as we abandoned the road in favor of the nearly dry bed of Cottonwood Creek, I found that there was much more to appreciate. Spring wildflowers dotted our path and lizards, antelope ground squirrels, and jackrabbits scurried and bounded. Three pristine snow owls were spooked by our approach and lifted off from a cottonwood tree, soaring up canyon.

At the bridge over Cottonwood Creek we were reunited with some familiar sights—the PCT, the L.A. Aqueduct, and the boys from Seattle. Over a short break, I tossed a Nerf football with Casey and Toby while they peppered me with medical questions. Toby asked about proper rattlesnake bite care, the utility of the Sawyer extractor, and the type and number of antibiotics I was carrying. Casey just wanted to know if I could write him a prescription for Percocet (a potent painkiller).

We also spoke of boredom on the trail. "Do you remember Dunbar, from _Catch-22?_" asked Catch-23. "His sole goal in life was to cultivate boredom, so that his life would seem longer. He didn't want to do anything interesting or exciting, otherwise life would go by too quickly."

"He would have liked thru-hiking," remarked Angela.

"Exactly what I was thinking. Hiking the PCT is all about spectacular monotony," said Toby.

Over the next couple days we made our way through the Tehachapi Mountains toward the town of Tehachapi. As we rose above 6,000 feet for the first time since the San Gabriel Mountains, we entered what some call the southern edge of the Sierra Nevada. The surrounding habitat looked far from alpine, however—Joshua trees, junipers, sagebrush scrub, and dirt bike marks filled our landscape, and there were no serrated, snow-capped peaks in sight. As we descended from our brief stay in the Tehachapis, a barrage of wind

106

buffeted us, the likes of which not even my giardia-infested intestines could replicate.

Tehachapi Pass is renowned for its nearly incessant wind and extreme weather patterns caused by cool, marine air coming from the west and hitting hot, dry air rising off the desert. As we raced past a windmill farm, I noticed black clouds hovering ominously ahead. These, combined with the constant and eerie whir of wind turbines, made me feel like I was in a Hitchcock film. Angela looked ill at ease, and I shared her sentiment. We descended rapidly under darkening skies to Tehachapi–Willow Springs Road. Within minutes a BLM Jeep pulled over, and we gladly accepted a ride from three jovial rangers. Nine miles later, we were safely deposited in the town of Tehachapi.

Our re-supply in Tehachapi started with a fierce thunderstorm that forced us to spend two hours in a vinyl booth at a fine eatery by the name of Denny's. By this time I'd recovered from the acute phase of giardiasis but still had little appetite. I stared forlornly at half of a Super Bird sandwich before passing it to Angela.

"The Mojave was everything we *didn't* expect," Angela remarked, munching on my Super Bird and sipping her sixth glass of Sprite. She was referring to the generally less-than-steamy temperatures, absence of rattlesnakes, and current rainy conditions.

Aside from Denny's, our most notable excursion in Tehachapi was to Kmart, where we purchased palm-size AM/FM radios. Initially, we'd been hesitant to bring radios, fearing that reception would be horrible and they would detract from our enjoyment of the trail. But after many, many, many hours of listening to nature's orchestra, we were ready for a distraction. Casey and Toby (among others) were battling the trail's spectacular monotony with radios and reported that the reception was not too bad. These important acquisitions promised not only to enhance my ability to keep up with the NBA Finals but also to provide Angela an opportunity to learn some manners from AM radio's doctor of ethics and etiquette, Laura Schlessinger (Dr. Laura).

As we resumed our trek after a day's layover, we stood at thirty-three days and 555 miles into our journey, a little over one-fifth of the way to Manning Park. At the time, though, we weren't thinking in terms of getting to Canada.

Instead, we were primarily interested in covering the remaining 145 miles to Kennedy Meadows, the PCT's gateway to the Sierra Nevada Mountains. Our conversations now began to center on topics such as snowy passes and spring run-off, and names like Adams, Donner, and Muir.

No discussion of the Sierra Nevada would be complete without a quote or two from the great John Muir, the patriarch of man's appreciation of the Sierra Nevada. Given our mountainous preoccupation at the time, let's start with, "Climb the mountains and get their good tidings. Nature's peace will flow into you as sunshine flows into trees." Yes, I was ready to feel the flow of nature's peace; I was ready to climb into some real mountains, *The* Mountains. Spanish missionary Pedro Font, when he first gazed upon *The* Mountains, described them as *"un gran sierra nevada,"* or "the great snowy range." At four hundred miles long, sixty miles wide, and with a peak elevation of 14,491 feet, they are not only that but much more.

I'd been eagerly anticipating this portion of trail since long before we'd left Campo. As a teenager I'd spent part of several summers in the Sierra, and experienced the pristine beauty of Muir's "Range of Light." I knew that *The* Mountains sure as hell beat the coyote scat out of the desert. Angela had never been in the Sierra before and didn't know the difference; as far as I could tell she still considered her conquest of Turkey Mountain a monumental event. So for the first 555 miles of trail, I'd tried to convince her that she should be juiced to get to *The* Mountains. For every twenty-mile piece of waterless trail we'd suffered, I promised, "Water is ubiquitous in the Sierra." For every cow-patty-infested trickle that we found to relieve our thirsts, I told her, "Just wait until you see the clear, cold streams and lakes of the Sierra." Every time we'd walked on or along paved roads for miles at a time, I reminded her, "In the Sierra, we won't see a single stinkin' road for two hundred miles." And every time she complained about having to go days without an ice-cold brew, I reminded her of my intention to "tap the Sierra . . . Nevada" just for her. Okay, maybe a tap or two for me, too.

Our goal was to make Kennedy Meadows by June 15, or "Ray Day," as Meadow Ed and others referred to it. June 15 is the key date used in all of Ray Jardine's itineraries for reaching the Sierra. Jardine believes that starting on this day allows hikers the best chance of avoiding major snow obstacles while plowing through the mountains. So, like long-distance runners catching a second wind as they sense the finish line, we busted ass through the Piute Mountains and Walker Pass.

As we rushed the last fifty miles toward the gateway to the Sierra, we were not alone in eager anticipation. Crazy Legs and Catch-23 continued their own unconventional ramble toward the Sierra. These two were consistently proving that one didn't need to follow the textbook to have long-distancing hiking success. Quite a few hikers we met along the way ascribed to some degree to a Jardinite, cookbooklike approach to hiking: minimize weight, rise early and hike until dark, avoid alcohol, caffeine, and unhealthy foods. But Casey and Toby wanted nothing to do with the cookbook. Their pattern of sleeping late and hiking late into the night continued, being more pronounced in Casey's case. On several occasions he snuck up on us from behind at a near sprint, pack bouncing from side to side as he raced to catch Catch-23. Casey and Toby retained as many civilized luxuries as possible—Walkmans, airplane-size miniature rum bottles in their re-supply packages, and nightly rounds of "Who Wants to Be a Millionaire," from Crazy Legs' trivia paperback. All in all, they were, as Toby said, "Trying to keep it real on the PCT."

X ▪ ″ ▪ X

On the morning of June 15 I was so excited I could hardly stand it. I made the descent from Lamont Peak to Canebrake Road at a full trot, reminding myself to stop every once in a while so that Angela could catch up. By midafternoon we'd covered more than twenty miles, and as I rounded a dusty corner with trekking poles flying and radio blaring I caught sight of an unbelievable thing: a deep blue-green, twenty-foot-wide moving body of water—the Kern River—the first significant water source on the PCT since Big Bear Lake. I waited for Angela before diving into the Sierra snowmelt; this was too precious a moment to enjoy alone. The river, warmed by its long course through *The* Mountains, was a perfect temperature, and it washed miles and miles of dust off of me. Lying on a flat slab of granite near the river's edge I sighed deeply, wishing I never had to move, ever again. Angela looked content, not to mention sexy, lying on her own granite bed.

We'd made it to *The* Mountains. Soon, we'd be hiking at 10,000 feet, with fresh cold air filling our lungs; looking up at weather-molded peaks and down on glacier-carved valleys and brilliant green meadows; resting under gnarled pines—whitebark, foxtail, and lodgepole; and sniffing the spring flowers—Sierra penstemon and primrose. We'd be out of the desert, away from roads, and in John Muir's world. I hoped Angela liked it, because if not I might be in trouble. I didn't need to be reminded of one of the oldest rules of courtship: "Don't promise a woman jewelry . . . and give her a chunk of cow patty."

[7]

Lost in Wonderland

WITH MY FEET STILL DANGLING in the cool water of the Kern River, I stretched my dripping body over as much of the sun-baked granite slab as I could. "This is what it must feel like to be a lizard," I thought as I pressed my fingers against the lichen-speckled mass below me. The rock seemed warm enough to be alive, and for perhaps the first time since our journey began, I felt like a natural complement to my surroundings. I looked over at Duffy; he swooned in a similarly indolent pose. Gazing upward, I watched wispy clouds disintegrate and coalesce again in the bright blue sky. It was the kind of blue I longed for in my crayon box back in first grade, a shade I thought existed only in my imagination. Dragonflies darted, zoomed, and hovered overhead. In their wings I caught glimpses of rainbows.

We could easily have lounged on the banks of the Kern River for hours, but the belly rumblings that started off faintly soon turned into tumultuous, demanding roars. There was a deep crevasse where Duffy's abdominal six-pack had once been. He'd probably lost ten pounds since Campo. Dinner in Kennedy Meadows called. Walking the last few miles to town, we meandered our way amidst willows and wild-rose tangles.

By the time we reached the steps of the Kennedy Meadows General Store, it was 8:30 in the evening. We'd expected a welcoming committee of trail friends, but the place was deserted. Hikers had been here, there was glaring evidence of that: half-empty packs, water and Gatorade bottles, and gutted re-supply boxes. But it was as if an apocalypse had struck the long red porch. A hand-painted sign by the dirt road indicated that "Real Hollywood Movies" were shown in the store's amphitheater every Saturday night, but it was only Wednesday. We had just decided to walk the two and a half miles to the Kennedy Meadows Campground when a large pickup with an open-topped cattle car on the back came barreling down the road. Nearly every available space on the truck was crammed with bodies—dirty, ragged, grinning bodies—a veritable sea of happy hiker trash. They were just returning from dinner at the Grumpy Bear restaurant and now were on their way to the campground.

We climbed into the back of the truck (which we later learned was owned by the proprietor of the Grumpy Bear) and found a small crack of railing to cling to. All around us hikers sat on benches and green deck chairs that were nailed to the truck's floor. As we rumbled into the campground a glaringly white, shiny mass appeared on the horizon. No, not the long awaited snowy peaks of *"un gran sierra nevada,"* but rather Meadow Ed's ass, in full moon. I'd been anxiously awaiting our reunion with Ed. I'd never properly thanked him for all the instruction he'd given us at Kamp Anza and (more importantly) I wanted to see the expression on his face when we arrived—still together, umbilical cord and all. Well, here it was—wrong end, but adequately expressive nonetheless.

Upon disembarking from the thru-hiker truck, we made straight for Meadow Ed's campsite. He pulled up his purple trousers and greeted us with a moustache-covered grin. "Duffy-me-boy!" he exclaimed.

"Did you eat? Didn't get to town early enough, huh?" Ed had to get a little jab in before showing his innate generosity. "There's turkey, roast beef, cheese, tortillas, and cookies. Dig in, you two." I was surprised. Last time we'd been with Ed he'd talked mainly to Duffy, and now, within thirty seconds, he'd already addressed me, albeit indirectly. Perhaps by making it this far I'd earned something. This was progress and I accepted it as such, along with the makings of a hefty sandwich and a beer from Zach.

We hadn't seen Zach since he strode off into the heated haze of Whitewater Canyon eighteen days ago, but immediately he picked up the conversation where we'd left it. "Summer is coming tomorrow," he said excitedly, "then we're going to Moontribe in Death Valley. You guys in?"

Every month, to celebrate the full moon, an enigmatic, anonymous group called the Moontribe throws a rave in a secret outdoor location. Duffy and I were intrigued. Neither of us had been to a rave before and it sounded like a unique experience—sort of the Generation X version of a Grateful Dead concert. Since our pilgrimage was all about discovering America, nature, and ourselves (not necessarily in that order), we rationalized that a Moontribe event fit right in.

"Maybe we can go," Duffy responded, shooting me a playful glance, "but we've got to see how much logistical stuff we can get done tomorrow." Ahh, the carrot had been positioned perfectly. Duffy knew me too well. Being a chronic procrastinator, I was apt to let much of a town day go by without sorting through my pack, organizing the food from our re-supply box, doing laundry, or updating my journal. But with a deadline or reward—or in this case both—I could be spurred into rapid, efficient action.

Bright and early on June 15 ("Ray Day"), we hitched a ride to the General Store. Here, at the "gateway to the Sierra Nevada," there were over thirty other hikers all making the necessary mountain preparations—strapping ice axes to packs and talking snow depth. "This feels like the end of the beginning," Toby said. With twenty-five percent of the trail behind us, all the hikers who'd made it this far were giddy with nervous excitement.

The first order of business was to collect our re-supply box from the small warehouse in the back. It contained the usual stuff—trash bags, film, ibuprofen, vitamins, toiletries, batteries, energy bars, and freeze-dried meals. It also contained some mountain-specific gear—ice axes, in-step crampons (which we promptly sent back home again because, we told ourselves, low snow levels made them superfluous—but really it was because we had no idea how to use them), a fleece blanket, and hats covered with mosquito netting.

The plan was to carry enough food to make it from Kennedy Meadows to Vermilion Valley Resort, 171 miles away. We hoped to cover this stretch in nine days, which, given that we each needed about a pound and a half of food per day, meant we'd have to haul a total of twenty-seven edible pounds (twelve more than we were used to) over six mountain passes—each more than 10,900 feet in elevation. Factoring in the additional weight of our cold-weather equipment, it was clear that pack weight was going to be an issue.

I'd grown pretty comfortable with the weight of my desert gear and wasn't eager to up the ante, so I borrowed a pair of scissors and employed Ray Jardine's "cut and whack" system.

First to go was the comfy mesh lining on my rain jacket. Next, I sliced my quick-drying "pack" towel and our new fleece blanket in half. My sun hat, the bag that once held our cooking utensils, our potholder, "town" toiletries, and a long-sleeved shirt were put in our "float" box and mailed ahead to South Lake Tahoe. Satisfied with my demolition, I went to take my two-dollar out-door shower. Afterward, I rejoined the throng on the porch.

Sitting on a hard wooden bench, I read photocopied pages from a moun-taineering tome to remind myself of proper ice-axe self-arrest technique. Meanwhile, Toby was holding a self-arrest crash course in the corner. It seemed as if he was the only one among us who'd ever actually practiced it. Trying to be coy, I scanned the porch and scrutinized the collection of ice axes. They all shared the same basic design and looked brand-spanking new. Chris and Stacy's axes were the talk of the ultralight crowd. They'd drilled holes in the shafts to eliminate a few fractions of an ounce each. I hoped they never needed to find out what such drilling did to an axe's lifesaving capabilities. "All for the sake of saving less than the weight of a full PEZ candy dispenser," groaned Casey.

When evening arrived, a large crew—including Chris and Stacey, Fish and Ryan, Casey and Toby, and Duffy and I—piled into the two-cab pickup and rumbled to the Grumpy Bear for dinner. "I think I figured out why the bear's so grumpy," Stacey, one of the few surviving vegetarians on the trail, muttered. "There's only swine for dinner." The menu consisted of pork burritos, pork chops, and macaroni and cheese with ham. While we sat at checkered-tablecloth-covered booths, our designated driver parked himself at the bar to drink with a couple of cowboys who were coincidentally seated under a sign reading, "If you ain't a cowboy, you ain't shit." Nearby hung yel-lowed photographs of Native Americans and some skins—including that of a five-foot-long rattlesnake. Sundry decapitated heads also peered at us from around the room—bear, boar, and deer. In the corner was a photo of a man baring his chest to show off a set of raw gashes, courtesy of what must have been a large bruin. The caption read, "Bear encounter at Kennedy Meadows Campground"—our home for the night.

X ◾ ▪ ▪ ◾ X

Fortunately, we didn't have any bear encounters in the campground that night, and the next day we found ourselves bumping down dirt roads on the back seat of Summer's rusty car heading toward Death Valley National Park. Somewhere within the valley's 3.3 million acres, the Moontribe was preparing for its weekend-long desert rave.

Death Valley receives less than two inches of rainfall a year, making it one of the driest places on earth. While that's enough to warrant the moniker "Death Valley," there's more. Back when miners and settlers were traveling to join the California Gold Rush, so many died while crossing Death Valley that it seemed an appropriate name. As if the name Death Valley weren't grim enough, sites within the park carry equally morbid titles, including Funeral Mountains, Coffin Peak, Dante's View, Badwater, Hell's Gate, Starvation Canyon, and Dead Man Pass. In 1900, a writer for the *New York World* declared Death Valley to be "the loneliest, the hottest, the most deadly and dangerous spot in the United States." Arguably, it's all those things, but mostly it's hot. From May to September, temperatures in the valley can be expected to be in the triple digits. In July, the daytime average is 116 degrees. The record high (noted on July 10, 1913) stands at 134 degrees. On that day a local rancher is reported to have said, "I thought the world was going to come to an end. Swallows in full flight fell to the ground dead."

After numerous hours of driving and half a dozen pay phone stops, Zach finally got specific directions and led us across the desert, first on a nicely paved road and then onto one nameless dirt road after another. Eventually, the dirt roads gave way to a two-laned track meandering across a sea of tumbleweeds. In the distance we spotted large water trucks and a dusty makeshift parking lot. The air shimmered with heat in a rhythm not unlike that of the music already booming from the huge speakers positioned amidst the rocks.

On the hillside a colony was forming in front of my eyes. Multicolored tents, tarps, and tapestries were going up, many connected by brightly hued fabric tunnels so that the inhabitants could go from tent to tent without stepping into the sun. The surrounding landscape was still and desolate. We set up our tents away from the densest population—in the suburbs, you might say—and tried to nap. It would be hours before the real party began.

When we awoke, the sun had set and the moon was making its way up into the sky. Hundreds of pairs of headlights were streaming across the plains in a straight, slow line. The colony below had burgeoned and the music was pulsing. Zach and pixie-haired Summer were a few yards away watching two female fire dancers. They swung long ropes with balls of flame on both ends over their heads, around their waists, and through their legs. As one of the dancers slowed, Zach spoke into her ear and moments later he was performing his own pyro routine.

The rest of the night was a blur of glow sticks and dance music. We wandered the rave amazed at the hundreds—perhaps a thousand—people who had traveled to Death Valley to celebrate the moon.

I'm not sure how long we stared at the scene unfolding around us. The rising sun and the setting moon shared an azure sky. I could hear a beat but wasn't sure whether it was emanating from the speakers below or my own heart as I gazed at the rough, gray hills and rainbow of tents. Suddenly, Summer was pouring milky, cool sunblock onto my palms which I watched drip down my elbows before slapping it on my face. Summer's sea-green eyes seemed to swirl and widen. I touched her spiky auburn hair; it was soft, like rabbit's fur. Zach appeared and gave me a bear hug. The scratchiness of his goatee on my shoulder sent shudders down my spine. Duffy then had me in his embrace and I soaked in the heat of his chest. "How do you guys feel about public displays of affection?" Summer murmured. I didn't get it and started jabbering away about how much Duffy and I were in love. Duffy, on the other hand, read the message loud and clear and led me off into the undulating, mine-riddled hills, abandoning Zach and Summer to themselves.

Later, I was shocked, yet weirdly flattered, when I realized that Zach and Summer may have been propositioning us for amorous relations—group amorous relations. Considering how sporadic sleeping-bag friskiness with my boyfriend had become, perhaps I should have taken them up on it. In October of 2002, *Backpacker* magazine published the results of a poll that asked readers whether they'd ever had sex with a stranger on the trail. Eleven percent said yes. Others responded with sentiments I could easily relate to: "If anybody can walk twenty miles, cook, eat, wash up, and still have desires other than sleep, I'd like to shake your hand." Amen to that. There were also responses that Duffy particularly appreciated: "Yes and the darn bear is still calling me for a date." But one made me realize that Duffy and I were kind of lucky to have received an offer: "No, but I'm reasonably good-looking and legally available, and after many months on the AT, I should at least have liked to have been asked."

At about noon, we packed up our stuff to leave. In the midday sun, the rest of the crowd kept dancing, refreshed by periodic showers from the water truck. Clambering over the surrounding hillsides and in and out of mine shafts were semiclad people. They looked like ants. In the distance, cars were still streaming across the desert, and as we pulled away we were driving against the grain. The party would go on for another twenty-four hours, but we'd had enough. The obligations of a thru-hike pulled us back to the PCT.

$$X \cdot {}^{\blacksquare \ \blacksquare} \cdot X$$

Back at our campsite in Kennedy Meadows, we lazed under pinyon pines on the banks of the Kern River and watched beavers swim and scurry about their work. As we napped, Meadow Ed came by to see if we ever planned on leaving. We assured him that we did, and on June 18 we were good to our word. As we left the campground, I felt a bounce in my step, despite the extra weight on my back.

For the next three hours we weaved among yellow monkey flowers, mountain mahogany, bitterbrush, willows, and wild roses as we headed consistently, albeit moderately, upward toward Monache Meadows, the largest meadow in the Sierra. From there we hoped for our first clear view of Mount Whitney, the highest peak in the lower forty-eight. After a couple days of rest and recreation we felt refreshed, energized, and even ebullient. "I've got mountain madness!" Duffy screamed as he charged ahead, as if trying to conquer the entire Sierra all at once.

Cresting a hill, I eyed another rocky climb straight ahead while, to my surprise, Duffy (with his headphones blaring ESPN Gameday) nodded toward a trail branching to the right. "Is that the trail?" I hollered, trying to be heard over a discussion of Tiger Woods' domination of the U.S. Open. I got a nod in response and then my long-legged hiking partner was off, striding up a steep, boulder-strewn path. A brownish-yellow sign nailed to a tree read "37E01." Duffy was already fifty yards ahead of me. I braced myself against my trekking poles, gave my legs a pep talk, and started dragging myself up the hill.

After a hefty climb, the trail skirted a sun-filled meadow. Before us swished a sea of green feathery silk. The blades of grass were as fine as a toddler's hair and I bent down to run my fingers through them. Our path through this lushness was faint. We didn't mind, though; it seemed appropriate to tread lightly on such a delicate carpet. Soon we came upon a rusty cattle gate that put up a big fight, but after some struggling (and relief that we'd both had our tetanus shots) we got it open. The altimeter on Duffy's watch read a few hundred feet above the elevation for Beck Meadows (a finger of Monache Meadows) stated in our guidebook. The watch, however, had been wrong on many previous occasions, so we trekked on toward the South Fork of the Kern River.

I got into a groove as I glided through the meadow grasses. The walking was easy and while my body trucked on autopilot, my mind tried to articulate the surroundings, soaking in juxtapositions between boulders, flowers, toppled pines, and the close, rich mountain sky. Soon we were descending sharply and I could almost smell the river. My stomach rumbled in anticipation of the waterside bagel and cheese lunch we'd planned. We expected Fish, Ryan, Zach, and others to be there ahead of us, but as I crashed through a thicket I found only Duffy.

He looked perplexed. "There's supposed to be a bridge here." He shook his head and half-scratched, half-rubbed his scalp.

"Huh?"

"I said there's supposed to be a bridge here, but we must be too far down the river."

I looked up and down the rocky shores. There was no bridge in sight. My heart sank. I knew exactly where we'd gone wrong.

"The sign said 'South Fork Kern River' this way," Duffy explained. I hadn't seen that sign, but what I had seen, we both now realized, was the PCT veering off in the opposite direction.

If only we'd referred to our guidebook earlier, we'd have read about " . . . a T junction with Haiwee Trail 37E01, which follows an ancient Indian path east to the river and through Haiwee Pass to Owens Valley—a route that almost became the eastern leg of a trans-Sierra highway." We were heading east, toward Kansas, rather than north, toward Canada. We ate lunch in silence. Our foray into the Sierra was off to a misdirected start.

We knew the PCT crossed the river upstream somewhere, so if we followed the river's bank we should eventually find it. Well, that worked for about two hundred yards, until a faint riverside trail petered out and we were forced to scramble through thorny shrubs, crawl over wet boulders, and slosh in cold pools.

Still optimistic and determined not to backtrack (when you're walking to Canada, forward momentum is everything), we struggled along through heavy brush. Soon it became impossible to continue; the thick brambles, roaring torrent, and slick rocks were impassable. The only acceptable way out was up—two hundred feet up. Looming above us was a massive pile of granite, but beyond that was a tree-lined precipice, taunting us with flat earth.

Without packs, I suppose the rock climb would have been enough to get the adrenaline pumping, nothing more. Maybe the tomboy kid I once was would have loved the knee scrapes and tinge of danger. But the woman with the forty-something pounds on her back did not. Duffy had it worse; his pack was pushing fifty-five pounds. About fifteen feet from the top we hit a wall, literally—a six-foot, smooth face of rock with just the tiniest gravelly crack as a foothold. Duffy took off his pack and while perched with one foot wedged in the narrow crack and one hand clinging to the top ledge, hoisted Big Red over his head and onto the shelf above. Next went my pack, then Duffy, then—with a few heart palpitations—me. The final few feet up brought more of the same, but we made it, and celebrated our mountaineering skills with some deep sighs and gulps of Tang.

No longer game for bushwhacking, we decided to follow a whisper of a trail up a number of steep switchbacks. Finally, on top of a ridge, we plopped down, exhausted. Admitting defeat, we pulled out our compass (for only the second time in forty-two days) and learned that we were still traveling east. As luck would have it, our map showed an unnamed trail heading northwest and connecting the Haiwee Trail with the Olancha Pass Trail, which in turn came to a junction with the PCT. We changed course in the hopes of finding it and within a half mile had discovered a faded path—this one heading in the right direction.

Three-thirty in the afternoon found us thrashing through brush, constantly losing and regaining our little trail as it rocketed up and down every hill in sight. As the afternoon slipped away from us, so did our hopes of getting back on the crest before dark. We pitched our tent on a tiny patch of rock- and brush-free soil. I think I can safely say that no one had ever camped in that exact spot before, but while I could appreciate the beauty of our pristine surroundings, being so far off-course overnight made me nervous.

"What if we never see the PCT again?" I thought. "No one will ever find us out here. No one even knows we're here. What if we run out of food, or a bear steals it?"

The next morning we jumped out of the tent at six o'clock, eager and determined to find our way back to the PCT. At nine that morning we came to the junction with the Olancha Pass Trail, and an hour later we hit the PCT. Finally! Duffy fell to his knees and kissed the tread. I plopped down and ate a Snickers. Our celebration was short-lived, however. We'd covered just fifteen PCT miles since leaving Kennedy Meadows the previous morning, and our carefully planned itinerary of miles and food per day had been disrupted. At the very least we'd face twelve provisionless hours at the end of the 171-mile stretch to Vermilion Valley Resort. As we continued to climb into *The* Mountains, it seemed that we were also climbing toward greater and greater adversity.

While we knew there'd be problems (and empty stomachs) ahead, we weren't about to turn back, not when what also lay ahead, in the words of John Muir, was "a glory day of admission into a new realm of wonders as if Nature had wooingly whispered, 'Come higher.'"

As we climbed to more than 10,000 feet over the course of the next twenty-five miles, we thought about the six high passes we'd soon be tackling. Ranging in elevation from 10,900 to 13,180 feet, each would be a quad-burning, back-crushing, and often snow-covered, feet-freezing experience. Every day in our foreseeable future would treat us to a 3,000- to 4,000-foot ascent over half a dozen miles and then an extended descent down a snowy mountainside.

In an effort to prepare myself for the challenge, I memorized the name and elevation of each pass: Forester, 13,180 feet; Glen, 11,978 feet; Pinchot, 12,130 feet; Mather, 12,100 feet; Muir, 11,955 feet; and Selden, 10,900 feet. There would be more high passes after Vermilion, but there were only so many physical hurdles I could contemplate at one time.

I didn't ruminate on these painful Stairmasterlike workouts for too long. More pleasant things soon distracted me. Everywhere I looked there was a new delight—yellow evening primrose, corn lilies, buttercups, mountain bluebells, and groves of my favorite tree, the foxtail pine. The foxtail lives only in the sandy soil found just below timberline, thriving where other trees wither. The tree's needles grow in clusters, and at the end of each branch is a bristle that looks like (you guessed it) a fox's tail. Illuminating the foxtails was sunlight like I'd never seen before, crisp and bright as if God had placed this realm in his own private spotlight. Climbing still higher, we veered off-trail slightly for lunch and a dip in Chicken Lake, a glacial pool filled with water so cold it should have been ice. As we ate we noticed a hush, as if we'd entered a temple. We weren't sure where the High Sierra officially began, but we felt like we'd made it.

I'd been hearing about how beautiful the High Sierra was since day one. But still, when we finally arrived—well, I couldn't believe my eyes.

Picture lush green meadows, a green only clear snowmelt could inspire. Sprinkle the grasses with buttercups, scarlet Indian paintbrushes, and blue bugles. Send a stream rushing, snaking, and pouring around and over boulders of granite twinkling with quartz crystals. Make the granite so white you might mistake it for snow. Surround the meadows and rock gardens with forests of pine and creamy-barked aspen. As a backdrop, insert snowcapped peaks, kissed by bright afternoon sunshine, glowing in warm twilight, and looming ominously when shrouded in thunderclouds. Nature's cathedrals, the bare summits reaching toward heaven, double-dare you to be unimpressed. And, of course, don't neglect the frosty alpine lakes, rimmed with turquoise ice, clear as fine crystal, and still as mirrors.

Next up on our wonderland tour was Sequoia National Park. The park greeted us with a sign reading "No pets, weapons. No grazing." Good-bye cow poop, hello big trees. Sequoia National Park is home to the giant sequoia, the largest living organisms on dry land (some whales are bigger). General Sherman is the king of these giants. Discovered in 1879 by a veteran of the civil war, the General Sherman tree boasts 47,450 cubic feet of lumber, is 275 feet tall, has a girth of 102 feet at its base, and weighs more than 1,385 tons.

As we trekked through Sequoia National Park, my eyes were wide, trying to absorb every iota of magnificence. A steep climb brought us to Crabtree Meadows and a junction with the John Muir Trail (JMT), leading to 14,491-foot Mount Whitney. We hadn't planned or provisioned for this side trip, but as we stood looking up at Whitney we realized that we couldn't walk past the highest peak in the contiguous U.S. without climbing it first. The detour would mean that we wouldn't be able to get to Vermilion Valley Resort without heading out of the mountains to re-supply nearly 100 miles early, in Independence. But given that we'd already gotten lost and that our food supply was rapidly dwindling, an early exit was probably inevitable anyway.

Following the John Muir Trail, we hiked to Guitar Lake, five miles below Whitney's summit. It was midafternoon and although there was plenty of daylight left, we didn't dare make an evening assault of the mountain. Whitney, while not a technical climb, is still a powerful peak, with a tendency to attract equally powerful afternoon thunderstorms.

For safety's sake we camped early. Nestled in an ice-carved canyon, Guitar Lake's still waters were surrounded by a sea of sparkling snow patches and boulders, home to both pink rockfringe flowers and mischievous marmots. About the size of raccoons and the largest members of the squirrel family, marmots seemed as common in the High Sierra as pigeons in the city. They paused their grazing only long enough to glance quizzically at us and let out an occasional whistle.

As we set up our tent, a stiff, cold breeze came down off the mountain, bringing large pellets of rain. The storm quickly intensified and the rain transformed into grape-size balls of hail. We hid in our tent and in the distance watched a string of six people descending switchbacks cut into the mountain's face. They were running, and even though they were still far away we urged them on. This was no time to be on the exposed flanks of Whitney and definitely no time to be exposing one's own flanks. But that wasn't stopping Fish, Ryan, Pansy Ass, Madame Butterfly, Improv, and Amigo from celebrating "Naked Hiker Day." As each red, birthday suit-clad hiker rushed by our tent, we handed them a spoonful of hot mashed potatoes and wished them luck. The storm was getting worse and they needed to get to shelter (and into some clothing), fast.

Just as we handed out our last spoonful of spuds, thunder began to crash directly above us. They were the loudest, deepest, most teeth-chattering claps of thunder I'd ever heard. The mountain's wrath was descending upon our tent in its entirety. Black clouds transformed the afternoon into the pitch of night, but only temporarily. Soon, the darkness was splintered by a strobe light-like flash of lightning, and then another. The bolts were coming down around us like raindrops. Lightning storms, I'd read, reach a high degree of savagery on mountaintops—a savagery which we were now witnessing and which has been known to kill at least one hiker per year on top of Whitney. We weren't at Whitney's apex, but we were close enough to be scared, and the fact that Duffy was now busy reading "Chapter 6: Lightning Injuries" in his wilderness medicine book didn't help.

"Although the chances of being struck by lightning are minimal," he recited, "two-hundred to four-hundred persons die of strikes in the United States

123

each year. Lightning is the electrical discharge associated with thunderstorms, and an initial stroke can measure thirty million volts."

"Is this supposed to make me feel better?" I asked. "How about something useful? Like where are we supposed to be during a lightning storm?"

"Anywhere but in a tent, which attracts lightning," he replied. "Really, we should be out there." He gestured toward the boulder field now being pelted by rain, sleet, and hail. "But then we risk getting cold and wet. Just stay away from the tent's poles." Reflexively, I curled my toes toward the soles of my feet and pulled my knees toward my chest. "There's only a short interval between the thunder and lightning," Duffy continued, "which means the storm's right above us. Hopefully it'll pass soon."

We cowered in the center of our tent for the next few minutes while thunder, lightning, and precipitation waged war outside. I hugged Duffy close. If we were going to be struck, I figured we might as well do it together. Finally, the thunder peals softened and the flashes of electricity became less frequent. Peeking outside, we saw the sky brighten and breathed a sigh of relief.

Inspired by the previous evening's vicious display, we got up at sunrise to start our ascent of the nine long switchbacks that wind up Whitney's rocky slopes. For speed's sake we left our tent and other nonessentials behind. Cold wind blasted our faces. The only sound was the gritty churning of our trekking poles. Soon, the crunch of snow underfoot and our labored breaths were added to the orchestra. The path ahead was largely gray and white except for small patches of blue flowers tucked into rocky crannies.

Atop Whitney, at 14,491 feet, the world seemed like an ocean of granite and snowy peaks. Layers and layers of mountains spread into the horizon. And the air, in the words of Mark Twain, "the air up there . . . is very pure and fine, bracing and delicious. And why shouldn't it be? It is the same the angels breathe."

The photographs we have from that day are among my favorites. Grinning from ear to ear, Duffy and I stand with our arms wrapped around one another on the precipice of the earth. Behind, like a timeline, sprawls the crest we'd already traversed. Bright-eyed, we look onward—to Canada.

To celebrate the moment, Duffy pulled our Nerf football out of his pack.

We were going to play the highest game of catch in the continental U.S. For the past 761 miles, we'd received some funny looks whenever we brought out that football. It was a luxury, but in the words of a four-year-old (quoted in *Backpacker* magazine after completing a hike in the Grand Canyon), "If you don't bring toys, all you'll have to play with is rocks and sticks." After a few passes, however, our recess was cut short by the sight of clouds looming over Mount Russell (a nearby 14,000-foot peak). Not wanting to risk getting caught in lightning, we began a rapid five-mile descent. As the sky turned black we bumped into Just Mike, still on his way up and determined to reach the summit no matter what.

"That your blue tent down there?" He asked in curt military fashion.

"Yes, sir," I answered.

"There're marmots clambering all over it. Sure hope you didn't leave any food in there. Those critters'll chew through cement."

"Yeah, one of 'em already got a strap on my pack." I'd left my pack a thousand feet from the summit at the junction with the Mount Whitney Trail. When we descended from the peak, I found my sternum strap gnawed in half. A fat, white-whiskered marmot sat on a nearby rock looking pleased with himself. Marmots often chew hikers' clothing and backpacks because they like the salt left by perspiration. As we hurried down the mountain, I worried about all the trail sweat we'd brought into our tent.

Thankfully, we made it back to Guitar Lake before the foul weather caught us and in time to save our gear from sharp marmot teeth. We packed up quickly and scurried back to the PCT.

Our next mission was to conquer 13,180-foot Forester Pass, the highest point on the trail. After spending the night at Tyndall Creek (which was the first of many formidable and frigid fords), we approached Forester in the morning, when the snow was still firm. Ahead of us, a wall of granite jutted toward the sky. Somehow the trail would lead us up and over it. We reached switchbacks, chiseled into the rock, which led to the pass—a small notch in an otherwise solid gray fortress. Laboring and lumbering, we ultimately reached the PCT's apex. We took the requisite photos and began a tradition of eating a snack in every major mountain pass. I quickly discovered that Snickers are

particularly delicious when eaten while looking back on a successfully completed 4,000-foot climb and ahead into a lake-speckled valley.

After successfully going up and over Forester, we set our sights on the
town of Independence for food, fuel, and a rest. Reaching Independence required branching onto a trail that led nine miles over Kearsarge Pass and down
to the Onion Valley trailhead. From there we caught a ride down to the hot
valley floor, where we found hiker-friendly lodging at the Independence Court-
house Motel. Fish and Ryan were already there, hosting Chris and Stacey
(who'd set up camp in a nearby park) for the afternoon. Fish had purchased
a Wiffle bat at the local market, and it wasn't long before we'd started up a
spirited game in the motel parking lot. After I struck out for about the tenth
time, I called it quits and jogged over to the post office.

Even though Independence wasn't a planned re-supply stop, I hoped to
find a card from my mother. At each of our re-supply points (planned and
otherwise) thus far, I'd found her cards waiting for me—colorful cards with
pretty French sentiments printed on the front. And inside, in her neat script,
were inspiring, encouraging notes from my mom. Given the tension prior to
my departure, these nurturing messages meant a lot to me. Even though she
didn't agree with what I was doing, the cards showed that my mother was
reaching out, giving me support. But there was no mail for us, just Meadow
Ed, checking up on who'd signed the trail register.

"No mail, huh?" he said.

"Nope, not today. But we hadn't planned on stopping here, so I shouldn't
really have been expecting anything," I responded, feeling a little stupid.

"Lotsa folks think they can get from Kennedy Meadows to Vermilion in
one shot, but not many do. It's a shame; now you'll have to make the climb
back up to Kearsarge."

X ▪ ▪ ▪ ▪ X

The steep climb over Kearsarge Pass to rejoin the PCT was just as difficult as
Meadow Ed had predicted. But our radios were getting clear signals, so we
passed the time and miles by yelling station numbers to each other and sing-

ing along to the songs, which included the appropriately titled "Higher," by Creed.

With Whitney and Forester behind us, we felt quite accomplished, but really we'd only just begun. We had five more high passes to go before our next re-supply. That day we tackled the rocky flanks of Glen Pass and camped at the emerald-green Rae Lakes with Fish and Ryan. The mosquitoes were swarm-ing, and despite slathering ourselves with the potent (and potentially toxic) repellent DEET, they engulfed us, flying in our ears, up our noses, and even deep into our throats. Duffy swatted himself mercilessly, yelling *"Yes!"* when-ever he killed one of the "blood-sucking bastards." In desperation, I put on my rain pants, jacket, and mosquito-netting hood. I sweated profusely as a result but at least was able to stall the buggy onslaught. Duffy tried another tactic. While Fish, Ryan, and I were cooking dinner, we heard hollers and then a large splash.

"He didn't just do that," Ryan said, incredulous.

"That's one crazy son-of-a-bitch." Fish looked out into the darkness to-ward the lakes.

The water in Rae Lakes was fresh from the snowy peaks and the coldest thing this side of the North Pole. Duffy's evening swim did ward off the mos-quitoes temporarily, but its more lasting effect was to leave him shivering like an outboard motor for most of the night.

The next morning we were back at it again, continuing our new routine—climb up to a high pass all morning and then embark on a long afternoon descent. Interspersed were numerous icy stream crossings that were both nerve-wracking and aggravating. The mosquitoes seemed to take our slow crossings (via logs or rocks, and sometimes wading) as invitations to snack.

While the mosquitoes tested our patience and all of the high passes tested our endurance, Muir Pass, with its elusive summit and snow-covered trail, taxed us the most—both mentally and physically. It took us six hours to cover six miles, and I think I can remember every labored movement. With each step, my foot crashed through crusty ice, crystals scrapping and burning my bare legs, then I'd wobble to the left and wobble to the right before submerg-ing a trekking pole into the snow to catch my balance. When we reached snow-free ground on the other side of Muir Pass, we dropped to our knees and lay on our packs, unable to find even enough energy to eat an energy bar. But the endurance test wasn't yet complete. We still had Selden Pass to tackle before the much-anticipated Vermilion Valley.

Targeting this 10,900-foot pass, we charged ahead, with five miles ahead of us to reach the top and then thirteen miles to Edison Lake and the ferry across to Vermilion. We'd have to move quickly if we wanted to be there in time for the boat's final afternoon trip.

At first we made good progress, but in midmorning we were abruptly blocked by a wide, swift expanse of frigid water—Bear Creek. Fear washed over me like snowmelt over rock. The memory of our difficult crossing of Evolution Creek just the day before was still unnervingly fresh in my mind.

When we'd arrived at Evolution early the previous afternoon, we found a note left by another hiker. "BE CAREFUL," we read. "Water chest-high. Current strong. Find a better crossing." Heeding the advice, we headed upstream to look for shallower water. A quarter of a mile up we thought we found a good spot and began to ford arm in arm. The bed of the stream was a solid sheet of slippery rock, but we located a long crack and, step by step, wedged our feet into it. The water wrapped around my ankles and thighs and tugged like an army of small hands. While deliberately sliding my feet along the crack, I tried to ignore the mosquitoes that were feasting on my arms. I didn't dare let go of Duffy to slap at them. If I fell, I'd either break my ankle or be washed downstream toward the rapids. We made painstaking progress through the bitterly cold water until, at last, we were safely on the opposite shore. Creek fords can be the most dangerous aspect of hiking through the Sierra.

Now we were faced with another, deeper and scarier, creek ford. After some discussion, Duffy decided to go across the creek first without his pack, in an attempt to gauge its depth and find a safe route. The floor of Bear Creek was a tangled mess of slick rocks, and as Duffy crossed he stumbled like a college kid leaving a keg party. Once safely on the other side, he crossed back over, grabbed his pack and my arm, and we stepped into the torrent together. The water reached up to my waist and sent its freezing fingers through my entire body. My hands rapidly turned white-blue and my feet felt wooden. Within seconds I was having one of the most severe Raynaud's attacks of my life. Given the depth of the water, we'd decided that I should cross the stream packless, hoping that without its extra weight I'd be able to fight the strong current. This meant that Duffy would have to cross for a third time. When we made it ashore, I jumped around to warm up while Duffy strode back into the creek to retrieve my pack from the other side. While I watched him wobble his way across Bear Creek for the final time, I realized that I wouldn't have been able to safely cross without him. He wasn't always the most attentive boyfriend, but challenges like Bear Creek seemed to bring out the protective and valorous side of him. I envied his strength, but more importantly, I loved him for it.

After the delay, we really had to move to make the Edison Lake ferry. Duffy, spurred by the thought of the "first beer free" policy at the Vermilion Valley Resort, led at a trot. We cruised along Bear Ridge through a hailstorm and then started down fifty-three pine-sheltered switchbacks. Glancing at his watch, Duffy broke into a gallop and I kept up as best I could. We had to make that ferry; if we didn't, we'd have to walk an extra six miles around Edison Lake. The High Sierra had been wondrous, but we were spent—so spent that the idea of six extra miles sent us into a frantic race against time. As we glimpsed the lake, we sprinted over rocks and roots. We were going to get that boat or break a limb trying.

[8]

Wounded Knee Walker

 FOR AS MUCH AS WE'D FRETTED about the possibility of needing to perform ice-axe self-arrest in the Sierra, in reality my axe had pretty much been deadweight. Lashed to the back of Big Red, spike jutting toward the heavens, the green chunk of aluminum had traveled hundreds of miles through *The Mountains*, but I'd only unstrapped it once, on the downhill traverse of Forester Pass. This wasn't due to safety concerns—the snow was soft and the steps deep—but rather for a photo opportunity. We needed at least one mountaineer-esque shot for our scrapbook, and I needed to put that axe to some use. After all, I hadn't used it to dig fire pits, fight off bears, or even to hunt wild marmot. So far, the only useful thing that axe had done was allow me to wrap some extra Duct tape around it.

Now, let me emphasize two things: An ice axe *can* save your life, and some years it *is* an essential piece of thru-hiking gear. Who knows, Dr. John Lowder might still be alive if he'd been carrying an axe in June of 1999. We'd been fortunate, however, catching the Sierra in a low snow year (around seventy-five percent of normal) and following in the footsteps of dozens of other hikers up and over six high passes. For us, late in an anomalous snow season, axes had been extraneous. But regardless of our experience, I wouldn't recommend that aspiring thru-hikers spurn the ice axe. Fish, on the other hand, wasn't convinced.

"Useless. Utterly useless piece of equipment. That Ray Jardine is full of shit. I traded mine for a Wiffle bat."

X ▪ ▪ ▪ ▪ X

We sat around a crowded table at the Vermilion Valley Resort (VVR) enjoying steak sandwich dinners. Angela and I traded joyful banter with Fish, Ryan,
and Daris (Pansy Ass)–banter about the Whitney summit and "Naked Hiker
Day," the difficult and ice-cold creek fords, the surreal beauty of the High Sierra during snow melt, and the day's race to Edison Lake.

"I was sure you guys wouldn't make it," Fish said. "We hadn't seen you in
days, not since Mather Pass. Then, 'poof,' you appear from the woods as the
ferry is taking off."

By catching the last ferry of the day across Edison Lake we'd avoided the
six-mile side trail around the lake to the VVR. I'd run the last quarter of a
mile, the sound of a primed engine spurring me on, screaming the whole way,
"Hold the boat! Hold that boat!"

"I tell ya, the Fish should learn not to count people out." Fish often spoke
in the third person.

Our dinner-table discussion abruptly changed course when the waitress
appeared with pie à la mode. The Vermilion Valley Resort was famous for its
pie—apple, cherry, and boysenberry, baked fresh each day by co-owner Peggy
Wiggs. Peggy and her husband Butch had owned the VVR since 1996 and
continued a tradition of hiker-friendly services, including the much-anticipated
"first beer free" policy.

Like the Pink Motel, the Vermilion Valley Resort is somewhat of a mis-
nomer. While the concept of "resort" is a matter of perspective, the wacky
thru-hiker may be the only person liable to consider Vermillion Valley to
have actual "resortlike" facilities. A noisy electric generator supplies power,
phone service is only available via satellite, and two mildewed showers serve
the entire encampment. Hotel-style lodging is limited, so most hikers pitch
tents or sleep in the bunkhouse, choosing from a collection of stale mattresses. Perhaps not what Hugh Hefner would opt for, but to us a splendid
luxury.

After dinner, I struck a deal with Butch. In return for work in the kitchen (scrubbing pots and cleaning floors), he'd clear our tab and throw in a few beers. I considered this a fantastic coup, and happily listened to a broken stereo brutalize the Doors while sorting through a soup of dirty dishes. Angela, on the other hand, was not pleased. She'd been given the task of mopping the floors and was disgusted by the antique, grime-encrusted janitor's mop. Needless to say, she would have preferred to be socializing by the campfire. I love campfires, too, really I do, but I couldn't resist an opportunity to do something other than *spend* money. As a medical student with tens of thousands of dollars in loans wrapped around my future, I'd developed a severe case of financial guilt. And I was up for anything that could alleviate this guilt without having to sacrifice the trip in the process. In reality, our hiking budget was not all that tight—Angela had saved money from her salary, my parents had made numerous contributions, and I'd taken out an extra Stafford loan. By comparison, Chris and Stacey were struggling for every noodle and hot chocolate packet. At Independence, their re-supply box was once again missing in action. This was the third time that their Pittsburgh re-supply headquarters had botched a delivery and they had to spend an extra day in town, scrounging supplies from the hikers box and soliciting donations from fellow hikers. We gave them a few of our brick-weighted MREs and some of Angela's stale (not to mention bland) gorp. I told Chris that these "gifts" were our belated revenge for their water-hoarding back at Scissors Crossing.

Our work detail lasted an hour, and then we headed toward the campfire. On the way, I assured Angela that I wasn't really a cheap bastard; it was just that I was somewhat spending-impaired. People like me needed help and understanding from our loved ones, not to mention blank checks and gift certificates.

In front of a raging fire, a ring of about twenty people surrounded a hiker strumming the guitar. Peggy sang along to "Bye-bye, Miss American Pie" and Butch, a stocky guy with a thick mustache and beard, sported a wide smile. His noggin, with trademark cowboy hat, swayed back and forth and he tapped his leather boots to the rhythm. I put my arm around Angela and felt her tension melt. We became lost in the music and the clear mountain night.

X ▪ ▪ ▪ ▪ X

There was another communal campfire the next night, this one at Pocket Meadow, a three-mile hike from Vermilion Valley. Angela boiled water for our freeze-dried dinner while I envied Fish and Ryan's feast—deep-dish apple pies from the VVR. It was Ryan's first time in *The* Mountains, and he was glowing nearly as brightly as the fire's embers. "You haven't lived until you have been in the High Sierra" he exalted. The High Sierra had also invigorated Angela; despite the long, tough miles, the look of wonder never dimmed in her round brown eyes. All my desert promises had been fulfilled, and then some.

As dinner wound down, I asked Fish about the genesis of his trail name.

"So, it's April of ninety-eight and the Fish is on the AT." Fish adjusted his seat on a boulder, leaning in to tell the story. "I was hiking in the North Carolina Mountains at about 5,000 feet. Being from Tampa and not owning a winter jacket, the possibility of cold weather hadn't occurred to me. So I'm rolling along, eating up miles. Suddenly, this white stuff, cold white stuff, starts falling from the sky. Now, remember, I'm from Tampa. I've never seen snow before—never. This white stuff sure looks like it could be snow, but I'm not sure. So, I stop this south-bounder and ask him. He nearly coughs up a lung laughing. 'Yeah, it's snow.' he says."

"What else could it be?" exclaimed Daris between giggles.

"Well, mystery solved, right?" Fish continued. "So I keep rolling in my tee shirt and shorts and this darn snow stuff gets colder and wetter and colder and wetter until I don't feel the cold anymore. After ten miles of this, I start to realize that I'm in deep shit. So I stop at the next shelter, but it's totally packed. Twenty-four people in a seven-person shelter. So now I have to pitch my tent without being able to feel my fingers. Probably took half an hour to get it up. I don't even remember crawling in. Must have just passed out. Next thing I know, it's the middle of the night and I'm shivering like crazy and racked with nausea. So I light my stove in the tent to try and warm up."

"Why didn't you wake up someone in the shelter?" Angela asked.

"The Fish was too proud to wake up other hikers. . . . In the morning, my tent is completely covered with snow and ice, inches of the stuff. And right about then I'm hating snow. Some guys eventually come over from the shelter to check on me, and I tell them I'm not going anywhere until all the snow is gone. I don't think they realized how serious I was, they just kept asking if I was okay, if I felt all right. 'I'm fine,' I said to them, 'but you know what, I'd rather be fishing.' That's how I became Fish."

Later, we sat tossing twigs into the settling remnants of our fire, discussing upcoming plans. Fish, Ryan, and Daris were debating whether or not to catch the bus into Mammoth from Reds Meadow (about twenty-seven miles up-trail) for an unscheduled stop. I wasn't sure how much the burgeoning tryst between Fish and Daris played into this; I surmised that Fish was anxious to find a cozy room where he could fondle Daris' pansy ass. As tempted as we were to join them and observe the progression of this romance, we were determined to continue on to Yosemite and Tuolumne Meadows. We hoped to get there before the July Fourth holiday; maybe we'd even find Catch-23 and ol' Crazy Legs there.

On the first day of July, our fifty-fifth on the PCT, we woke early and were soon greeted with a ford across Mono Creek's swift-moving current. I stepped into the unbelievably cold water and maneuvered around the frothy rocks, nearly losing my balance several times. Safely on the other side and jogging in place to warm my numb and achy legs, I yelled words of caution to Angela. She was midstream and looked up fearfully to acknowledge me before stepping forward. Abruptly, she lurched sideways into the current, submerging herself to chest level. She yelped and grimaced. For a moment I thought she was going to be washed away, but she quickly righted herself. She scowled down at the rocks beneath her and (quite uncharacteristically) uttered a loud profanity.

"I crunched my knee, bad," she said once on dry land. "Wrenched it." There was a superficial cut and an area of redness around her left knee.

"Yeah, you have a lot of erythema," I noted.

"Ery—what? Sounds serious. Think you'll need to amputate?" She was joking, so I knew it couldn't be too bad. I gave her knee a kiss and covered the wound with antibiotic ointment and a bandage before we hiked on.

Two days later that knee bump was no longer a laughing matter. We were camped above Thousand Island Lake in the Ansel Adams Wilderness. The lake is an aptly named narrow expanse of water dotted with thousands of granite outgrowths, some bare, some decorated with trees or tundralike growth. Lying in our tent, sheltered from the wind by granite on both sides with a brilliant view of the sunset reflected in the patchwork lake, we had every right to be optimistic. The toughest sections of the Sierra were behind us and we were twenty miles from Tuolumne Meadows and only eighty or so from the thousand-mile mark. The only problem was that Chigger's knee wasn't co-operating. Hiking, especially downhill, had become painful, and she now walked with a distinct limp. Angela was not one to complain about physical pain (her focus usually centered on emotional aches and general fatigue), but she was clearly hurting, and I worried that she'd suffered a ligament or carti-lage injury, or perhaps was developing patellar (knee cap) irritation. Even excessive doses of ibuprofen, or Vitamin I as we called it, weren't helping. Angela had been popping them like jellybeans all day but still grimaced with pain at nearly every step.

Things were no better in the morning as we tackled the arduous climb up to Donahue Pass and into Yosemite National Park. The descent was treacher-ous, featuring unsure and unkind footing. Angela was struggling but stoically picked her way down the trail. Our pace had slowed to just faster than a crawl and after a brief discussion we decided that I would hike ahead to grab our re-supply package from the Tuolumne Meadows post office before it closed for the July Fourth holiday.

With 13,000-foot Mount Lyell towering over me, I strode purposefully through Lyell Meadow and along the west bank of the Tuolumne River. The river flowed down a series of peaceful curves, gently gliding its way north through green fields. The trail's tread, however, was not peaceful; there were multiple paths, many of them wet and muddied as repeat foot travel eroded them below the water table. Sierra meadows, I'd learned from the guidebook, had started as lakes left by receding glaciers. Slowly, over thousands of years, silt and rock from surrounding mountainsides filled the lakes, eventually creating lush meadows. This meadow, however, hadn't completely evolved—with my every step ancient lake water oozed above ground.

Eventually I reached drier ground and kicked into a hip-swaying speed walk that would have made Richard Simmons proud. I arrived at the Tuolumne Meadows General Store with ten minutes to spare. By 4:20 that afternoon I was sitting at a picnic bench adjacent to the General Store, sorting through our re-supply box. Chris and Stacey relaxed nearby, mixing rum and Coke. Chris, with an extremely earnest face, provided an extended dissertation on the cost-effectiveness of hard liquor versus beer.

"Rum and Coke—just can't beat it, man. Most buzz for the money. Beer can't compete, fizzy water with no kick."

Normally I would have jumped to the defense of barley and hops, but right then I was preoccupied with the whereabouts of Wounded Knee Walker. About fifteen minutes later, as I began to re-pack my gear, she appeared, still grimacing and with a slow and deliberate limp. I was ecstatic to see her and very proud. She'd handled this better than I would have, I was sure of that. At the same time, I was afraid that this might be it; our trip could be over. Done, kaput, finito, stick a fork in us. I knew that by this stage in a thru-hiking endeavor, chronic-use injuries more than anything else forced hikers off the trail. And Angela, possibly initiated by her fall at Mono Creek, appeared to have developed a painful chronic-use injury.

Remarkably, she was in a good mood as we set up our tent in the Tuolumne Meadows Campground. Perhaps it was because she finally had an ailment that commanded my full sympathetic attention. While she rested, iced, and elevated her knee, I toured the campground looking for firewood, without much success. Instead, I discovered a fascinating fireside lecture by a park ranger on the deadly mountain carnivore, the *ochleratatus tahoensis* mosquito. I only planned on staying for a minute but was sucked in. I returned to the tent with a barrage of mosquito facts.

"Hey, Chiggy, did you know that it is only the female mosquito that bites humans?"

"Yeah, that's because we girls are dangerous," she said, baring her choppers.

"Okay, but did you know that their saliva has both a painkiller and a blood thinner? That's why you don't always feel the bite, and that's why they can suck up a bunch of blood without it clotting. It's also why you get a bump . . . the anticoagulant proteins trigger an immune response."

"Ohh." She pretended to be impressed.

"And," I said with a flourish, "the female can only lay eggs after sucking blood, and the more the better, so that's why those blood-sucking bitches will sit there with their proboscis imbedded in ya until completely full . . . if you let them, that is."

"Gross! To think that I had all of those probe-thingees in me when we crossed Evolution Creek."

"You think that's gross, they once did a study in the Alaskan tundra where they videotaped a man standing outside for a full minute, completely nude. They watched the tape and counted the bites. Over one million!"

"Can we talk about something else? Like you finding me some more ice for my knee?"

Later that night we were awakened by a horrible ruckus. Air-horns, shouts, a bottle rocket, and then more shouts. A cruisin' bruin! Yosemite bears are notorious campground scavengers, habituated from years and years and millions and millions of careless tourists. Nowadays, some are so bold that they will run up and grab a PB&J sandwich out of your hand in broad daylight. Wisely, we'd stored all of our food and gear in the sturdy bear lockers of Tuolumne Meadows Campground, and without food, humans are of little interest to most bears. Besides, the events of the previous summer suggested that in Yosemite, one is at greater risk from fellow humans than hungry bears.

During the summer of 1999, the brutal slayings of three Yosemite tourists and a naturalist by handyman Carl Stayner had terrified visitors to national parks throughout the country. They had terrified me as well. Bears were in many ways predictable and avoidable; wackos with internal voices urging them to kill were not.

Having made it through the night unscathed by man or beast, we greeted July Fourth without much excitement. Back home, friends were preparing for beer-b-cues and fireworks. At Tuolumne Meadows, all we were preparing for was potential disappointment. Angela's knee felt somewhat better, and equipped with a new elastic knee brace she was able to move around. Still, a return to the trail anytime in the near future seemed unlikely. I was reminded of that ominous PCT fact—even in the best of years, only one out of four thru-hikers would make it from border to border. Were we soon to be added to the growing list of thru-hiking casualties?

Bald Eagle and Nokona, AT veterans we first met in Agua Dulce, had driven through Tuolumne the day before in a blue rental car to pick up their re-supply box. They were heading home and trying to scavenge a few important items from boxes up and down the California PCT. After being plagued by deep blisters, body-covering poison oak, toothaches, and shin splints, they'd finally thrown in the towel at Independence after Nokona developed severe altitude sickness. They both looked dejected. Nokona, wearing dark sunglasses, stood silently at a distance. Bald Eagle vowed they'd be back another year, but I wasn't convinced.

Aussie Crawl had become another victim of *The* Mountains: He was air-lifted out of an area called Death Canyon with severe vertigo. Word was that he was also on his way home. There'd been no sign of Ricky Rose (although this bothered no one), and Zach hadn't been spotted since Lone Pine. Casey and Toby were still on the trail; their frequent and amusing notes in the trail registers were proof of that. In fact, we'd only missed them at Tuolumne by a few hours. But it didn't appear that we'd be catching them anytime soon.

$$X \bullet \bullet \bullet X$$

From Tuolumne Meadows, the PCT reclaims its independence from the John Muir Trail. While the JMT continues west for twenty-seven miles to Yosemite Valley, the PCT enters a difficult but spectacular section of glacier-carved wilderness. Chris and Stacey had decided to follow the JMT to Yosemite Valley, where a ranger friend offered them an empty house and fully stocked fridge for the weekend. I'd never seen them so excited. We were excited in our own right, but cautious. Angela's knee was feeling much better, but while I wondered whether this was because it was completely numb from forty-eight hours of icing, she was anxious to test it on the trail. This was risky. We didn't have another re-supply scheduled until Echo Lake, 150 miles and at least six days away. We struggled with the decision, recognizing the risk, but one does not finish the PCT by being risk-averse. So we decided to set off again toward Canada, knowing that at any moment we might be forced to turn back.

Our first stop was at Soda Springs, where carbonated spring water actually bubbles from the ground. Mixed with Tang, this minor miracle of nature made for a delicious trail soda. Our first six miles out of Tuolumne were easy walking. The only disadvantage of the gentle grade was that it allowed for a large collection of sun-hat and white tenny-clad tourists. After months of solitude on the trail, their presence made me feel like I was in a shopping mall rather than protected wilderness. And given our hulking packs and trekking poles, I wasn't so sure that we ourselves weren't part of the attraction. Catch-23 wrote about this phenomenon in his trail memoir:

"All day we got inquisitive looks from Japanese tourists and old people in motor homes; it was pretty funny, being a tourist attraction and all. We joked about tour bus narrators giving a speech over the intercom: 'Ok folks, if you be real quiet we might just catch a glimpse of The Western Long Distance Hiker, they're known to frequent these parts. Let's try their mating call, *Buffet! Buffet! All you can eat!* Look folks! There's one now on the left side of the coach. Excuse me, sir, in the back, please do not feed the distance hiker.'"

After passing Glen Aulin, the trail reverted to its familiar roller coaster pattern and the tourists were suddenly, magically, gone. Even though we'd started well after ten in the morning, we covered nearly twenty miles that day with nary a whimper from the Wounded Knee Walker. Miraculously, over the next several days, Angela's knee remained relatively pain free, and we made good progress toward Sonora Pass. On July 7 we crossed a steel bridge over the West Walker River and continued several miles to Kennedy Canyon. This was just another small stretch in a thirteen-hour hiking day, but it contained an important landmark: one thousand trail miles, Campo to

Kennedy Canyon. I recalled the words of Fish at Mono Creek, "Once you've made it a thousand miles, that's it, you're done. You've made it. Nothing will stop you." I didn't feel that we had quite "made it," but the sense of accomplishment was palpable. Somewhere out there Meadow Ed was scratching his bald head; he'd lost his bet on us weeks ago.

The next morning I was up before seven, creating a photo op by drawing a large 1-0-0-0 in the dirt in front of our tent. I was about to snap the shot when the Moaks, Fallingwater and Drip, came charging by, waving cheerfully. This had become a morning ritual ever since we'd left Tuolumne. Fallingwater (city name Ron) and Drip (city name Brandon) were a father and son duo that we'd met at Kennedy Meadows. Fallingwater, a distant veteran of the AT, was, after a prolonged battle with cancer (somewhere in his back) and years of desk-side atrophy, engaging in a Bill Bryson-esque attempt at youthful revival. Drip, sixteen, was joining his dad for part of the trail while on summer vacation.

Fallingwater had a rough time in Southern California—he struggled with excess waistline and painful blisters—but by the time Drip joined him, he'd shed some weight and rediscovered his long-lost trail legs. Now, this father and son team was flying. For the past few days we'd been playing leapfrog with the Moaks. They would whiz by us at an ungodly hour of the morning while I was still wrapped in a cocoon of all available clothing. Later in the day, though, we would inevitably find them resting up against some rocks, cooking or lounging with their diaries. On we would plow, hiking until near darkness, leaving ourselves just enough time to set up camp before the night sky became complete.

X ▪ ▀ ▪ X

From Kennedy Canyon we climbed up over exposed slopes toward the crest above Sonora Pass, passing into and out of the Emigrant Wilderness. The change in mountain landscape was striking: We were now on the volcanic slopes of the Northern Sierra. Glacier-carved, glowing-white granite walls were replaced by gentler but more barren brownish-black slopes. Winds blasted us from the west as we walked the panoramic crest alongside Leavitt Peak. We could see the Moaks several hundred yards ahead of us, also buffeted by wind.

The 1,200-foot vertical descent to Sonora Pass and Highway 108 was initially steep and snowbound. Deep steps were already in place, but it was slow going. Soon, the trail became a meandering series of switchbacks through groves of lodgepole pine—twisted and turned like tree Gumbys. From above I could see the Moaks taking the turn of a long switchback. Directly ahead of me was a split in the trail with a less-established tread heading due north. It looked, smelled, and tasted like a perfect shortcut. I have to admit it; I'd grown to relish shortcuts, especially if they involved cutting switchbacks. Cutting a switchback could be pretty exhilarating sometimes.

I know what you're thinking—that this is a violation of trail ethics—and you're right. But on some occasions, I just couldn't understand the utility of the switchbacks we encountered. Recently, the trail had led us on numerous switchbacks across pure granite slabs—the only trail markings being stones placed in curves across the rock. I'd often cut across these curves, figuring that my steps posed no real threat of erosion. I suppose that over millions of years we hikers could wear down those granite slabs, but by then a big old McDonalds will be sitting there anyway.

There was certainly no threat of erosion at this junction; ahead lay a direct and defined alternative trail. "Ahh," I thought, "we'll beat those Moaks to Sonora Pass." So down the path I went, and Angela, not really paying attention, followed along. Soon our "shortcut" steepened, and we were standing on top of a precipitous 100-foot glacierlike snowfield. Straight ahead the snow pack leveled where it met a flat volcanic ridge, but to the left it continued down a steep canyon. It looked like we'd have to glissade down.

Well, Angela didn't like this suggestion, not one bit; her nose wrinkled and her eyes tightened as they often did whenever we discussed an alternative route. Ever since we'd taken that misdirected and adventurous path from the Kern River to the Olancha Pass Trail, she'd suffered from a severe allergy to my creative shortcuts. But I was not to be denied and slid rapidly down the snowfield. It was quick and fun, like a cheap amusement-park ride, and I hit the lip straight on, gliding to a stop well before a collection of rocks. It seemed easy enough, so I gave Angela the "okay" sign and shouted lots of encouragement. It occurred to me that an ice axe would be a useful adjunct to this slide, but since we'd just sent them home from Tuolumne Meadows, that wasn't an option.

Angela apprehensively sat down, inched her way to the edge of the slope, and after a long pause pushed off. Immediately, she did two things. First, she screamed, and second, she dropped one of her trekking poles. Down she came, making no attempt to direct herself. Soon it became apparent that she was heading for the leftward canyon.

"What the hell? Where is she going?" I thought, and then, "Uh-oh. Why did I make her do this? And without an axe . . . oh, crap." She was still barreling along to the left and nearing the end of the snowy slide. I took a step and jumped at her, grabbing her pack and trying to pull her toward safety. She dug her remaining pole into the ice and we tumbled to a stop.

We were both a little scared but unharmed. We could see the rest of our descent to Highway 108, and there were no more snowfields in our way. There was just the matter of an abandoned trekking pole. Back up I went, taking three steps forward and sliding back two until I reached the pole. Then I glissaded down again, staying well away from the treacherous canyon to my left.

The Moaks had barely beaten us to Highway 108 and looked relieved to see us.

"Are you guys okay?" asked Drip.

"Fine, just tried a little shortcut."

"We heard Angela screaming and looked over to see you jump at her, and then you both disappeared from sight. We were worried." Ron was still concerned

"Yeah, another one of Duffy's little side routes gone awry," Angela said. "I didn't even realize he'd tricked me until it was too late."

We sat with the Moaks for a while by the side of the road. Why the side of the road, you ask, with all of this gorgeous wilderness north and south of us? Well, we were secretly hoping that a good-hearted car camper would gift us a beverage or two, and indeed, Ron was able to "yogi" several beers for us and a soda for Drip. It was about two in the afternoon, and having finished our drinks we were preparing to tackle the climb out of Sonora Pass when we saw Fish, at a full trot, Wiffle bat strapped to his pack, covering the last hundred yards to Highway 108.

"What time is it? What time is it?" he asked urgently. His face glistened with perspiration.

"Fourteen-hundred." Drip was eager to please.

"Shit, I'm early. Grandpa won't be here for another hour. Fish be flying, baby."

Fish had covered over twenty-five miles that day, before two. His grandfather was picking him up at three for some R&R, and he didn't want to be late. Ryan and Daris were somewhere behind. We didn't have the time to wait and see how far.

Energized from our roadside break, we wound our way up to a saddle high above Wolf Creek canyon. Here, at 10,500 feet, we took our last footsteps above 10,000 feet on the PCT. We were 1,016 miles into our journey, 73 miles from Echo Lake, and 1,643 from the Canadian border. The hiking terrain was becoming noticeably easier, and the miles passed quickly as we continued our cat-and-mouse game of "I'll catch you, can you catch me?" with the Moaks. It looked as though we would make it to Carson Pass, just twelve miles from Echo Lake, by the night of July 10.

But as evening approached on the tenth, I stupidly took us down a wrong trail. Again. This trail wasn't an ancient Indian route or a steep icy slope. It began innocently as a rather gentle descent over an exposed mountainside. But as we descended toward a forested canyon, overgrowth began to snare and punish us, and I realized that I'd made a mistake. I optimistically pushed forward, confident that I could figure out a way for us to jump back onto the PCT without backtracking. We lost three hours, six miles, and 1,000 precious feet in elevation before I finally acquiesced to Angela's repeated, near-tearful, pleas that we turn around.

I was extremely frustrated. I'd let my competitive spirit get out of hand and led us down an easily avoidable detour. If only I'd taken two minutes to consult the guidebook I would have seen that this was the Summit City Canyon Trail, not our beloved PCT. Weeks before I'd vowed not to fall into another speed trap, but clearly I had. I sat, head in hands, on a boulder and nearly burst into tears. Just in time, I remembered Meadow Ed's words at Kamp Anza, "You'll cry . . . you both will." I wasn't willing to give him the satisfaction of being right—at least not yet—and not over such a stupid mistake. The only option was to get up, change directions, and keep walking.

X ▪ ▪ ▪ ▪ X

Early the next morning, my Rockport boots were bothering me. They'd developed the traction of bowling shoes and I kept slipping on the gravelly trail. When we finally made it to Carson Pass, I jettisoned them into a trashcan and donned my Teva sandals for the last sixteen miles to town. Having carried me over 1,000 miles of tortuous terrain, my Rockports probably deserved a more proper burial, but if they weren't going to be of use, there was no reason to carry them. The sandals were a marked improvement, and we cruised into the Echo Lake Chalet at two that afternoon. The Moaks had beaten us again and seemed proud. I tried not to let it bother me.

Our arrival at Echo Lake filled me with mixed emotions. I was happy that we'd soon be frolicking in Lake Tahoe and ecstatic that Wounded Knee Walker had managed a tough stretch of trail so ably. I was melancholy, though, about our impending departure from *The* Mountains. There was a lot more trail left before Canada, but I didn't expect any of it to match what we'd already seen.

[9]

Food Fight

SITTING ON A TREE STUMP in front of the Echo Lake Chalet, I peeled off my once-white, now brownish-gray knee brace. When we'd left Tuolomne Meadows six days earlier I'd taken five ibuprofen tablets with breakfast, popping them in my mouth while Duffy wasn't looking. Being a medical student, Duffy exhibited some concern for my stomach and kidneys whenever I went overboard on Vitamin I. But I was more concerned about being able to walk and didn't want to bicker about it—hence the surreptitious self-medicating. Besides, I was pretty confident that my internal organs could handle the pharmaceutical strain. During my college days, a field hockey opponent relocated my nose to the right side of my face, I fractured my tibias and a metatarsal by running too much, and broke my cheekbone in three places—so I was no stranger to pain or its companion analgesics. But back then, I only had to "play through" injuries for two-hour practices or hour-long games; hiking with an injury for twelve to thirteen hours a day, day after day, was another story.

Despite my best efforts to grin and bear it, I'd found myself limping and slipping farther and farther behind with every passing mile, until finally Duffy had to sprint ahead without me in order to retrieve our re-supply box from the Tuolumne Meadows post office. That's when it crossed my mind that maybe it was over. Walking into Tuolumne Meadows, I'd covered only one and a half miles an hour. At that rate we'd be lucky if we made it to Canada by Easter. Deep down, I guess I never really believed I could walk 2,655 miles anyway.

During the ensuing two days I tried to mentally prepare myself for going home a failure. Duffy and I didn't talk about it, but I knew he was scared. Like me, he feared that my bum knee signaled the beginning of the end.

As if my newly acquired limp wasn't enough of a bad omen, our arrival at Tuolumne Meadows was perfectly timed to witness the final hours of Bald Eagle and Nokona's hike. After sixty-seven days, 784 miles, and a cornucopia of lesions and afflictions, these AT veterans were going home. I'd shared only a few words with Nokona and knew little about her other than her trail travails, but still my heart ached for her. Physical misfortunes had ended not only her hike but her boyfriend's as well. Later, I read Nokona's Internet diary and was further moved by the details of her summer of injuries and illness. This girl had sampled liberally from the all-you-can-suffer buffet.

In the beginning, she was optimistic in the face of adversity, writing, "One great thing about being ill or injured and off the trail, is that it gives you a greater appreciation of how lucky you are when you finally return." But as the maladies mounted, the couple was forced to skip trail and spend more and more time resting in motels. Soon, injured egos and bitterness were added to their list of woes. "I know some people think we're planning on getting off the trail," wrote Nokona, "but we won't let it beat us." That was before an incessant hacking cough, suffocating congestion, and a strange tingling in her face, hands, and feet robbed her of the ability to hike and carry a pack at the same time.

As Nokona cried on the other end of the phone, an emergency room physician told her that her hike was over. Given her symptoms, it seemed likely she had mild pulmonary edema, which meant fluid was collecting in her lungs and preventing her body from getting enough oxygen. At high altitudes, where the air is thin, pulmonary edema equals suffocation—hence the tingling feeling. The only treatment is rehydration and resting at sea level for six to eight weeks. If she returned to high elevations, she would run the risk of more serious—possibly fatal—health problems.

Seeing Nokona in those dark sunglasses, sitting alone in the front seat of a rental car, depressed me profoundly. It appeared that the PCT had dampened her spirit and destroyed her pride. Wasn't this supposed to be an uplifting experience? I grieved the death of her dream while feeling a dark shadow pass over mine. I did not want to be the one donning those sunglasses. Not here in Tuolumne Meadows—not anywhere. Gulping down more ibuprofen, I put a fresh ice pack on my already red and purple mottled knee and propped it up on a picnic table. Bald Eagle and Nokona drove away, leaving a heavy silence.

For the next forty-eight hours I vigorously iced, elevated, and rested my wounded knee. Vigorously resting is an oxymoron, I know, but my reclined pose was more tense than restful; my mind was at work, simultaneously worrying and willing my body to heal.

Remarkably, unbelievably, it worked. When, on July 5, we began walking again, my pain had eased from a nine out of ten to a four out of ten (Duffy insisted that I quantify pain in this fashion), and by lunch it was nothing more than an annoying twang. It was magical, and Duffy, despite his medical training, couldn't offer an explanation. I like to think that the soothing medicine of mountain scenery played a role. And later I convinced Duffy of such by reading him the results of a medical study suggesting that mountain landscapes can ease pain. In the study, researchers from the Johns Hopkins University School of Medicine found that scenes of mountains and sounds of babbling brooks cut patients' pain in half during unpleasant medical procedures. The scientists call the phenomenon "biophilia" and hypothesize that it works by distracting the part of the brain that interprets pain and, in essence, taking the mind's focus off the discomfort and putting it on something pleasant instead. So, perhaps getting back on the trail (in combination with massive doses of ibuprofen and hours of icing) was just what my knee needed. And, thankfully, for the next six days and 154 miles, that mountain medicine kept right on working, allowing me to hike resolutely to our next re-supply at Echo Lake Resort. From Echo Lake we hitchhiked ten or so miles to the glitzy, neon-lit banks of South Lake Tahoe.

We spent two and a half days in South Lake Tahoe, surrounded by a muralscape of ivory-faced peaks and pine-covered slopes. While North Lake Tahoe is home to the rich, lakeside mansion crowd, South Lake offers strip malls, condos, and, across the state line into Nevada, casinos. It's also the largest, most cosmopolitan town within ten miles of the PCT, which means that few thru-hikers can resist the lure of its beaches and cheap eats. I for one had been dreaming of dessert buffets for days.

Once settled in our $32-a-night motel (a short walk from the state line), we peppered our usual errands with big-town excitement. For the first time since leaving the East Coast, we went to a genuine, elephantine supermarket. The selection was as enormous as our appetites, and we spent over an hour filling our cart. We wore our (empty) packs to carry our groceries in, and I proudly sported a new red sundress. I'd bought it so I had something respectable to wear while I did the laundry; I was tired of wearing nothing but Gore-Tex while in town and longed to feel like a girl again Duffy steadfastly refused to purchase anything non-essential and had to wait in our motel room in his birthday suit until the wash was done.

That night we headed to a $10.99 all-you-can-eat buffet at Harvey's Casino, where, after about four plates of food and two desserts, I slipped into a food coma. To revive me, Duffy whispered "movie," and soon we were in the Horizon Casino Cinemas watching a Jim Carrey flick, which I swear was the funniest, most entertaining two hours of my life. I'd never before found Jim Carrey to be the least bit funny. Of course, I was high on sugar and seriously Hollywood deprived, so perhaps my opinion should not to be trusted. After the movie, Duffy lost $150 on blackjack (his frugality, it seems, does not apply to gambling), I broke even at the roulette table, and we walked back to the motel.

The next day, Duffy waited in the park while I called my parents from the McDonald's payphone. As my father and I talked, I thought I heard enthusiasm in his voice and soon, while watching the traffic whiz by on Highway 50, I was happily reliving our Sierra adventures, from the Guitar Lake hailstorm to the hairy stream crossings and glacier traverses. Just days before our hike began I'd promised my parents that I'd call them from every town to let them know that I was safe. This was my ninth such call and each time the knot in my stomach loosened. Duffy and I had hiked 1,089 miles without serious illness or injury. I hoped that meant my parents would worry less and begin to see the bright side of the journey. Certainly I was worrying less, especially compared with the weeks after first telling my parents of our plans. Back then, I lived in fear that maybe I was doing the wrong thing. But now, with each step north I was more secure in my decisions.

"*Salvitur Ambulando*," I told myself, "'walking solves all things,'" and I tried to believe it. It was a bright, sunny, warm day, and I jogged down the sidewalk to my rendezvous with Duffy.

As I neared our meeting place, I was startled by the sight of a man's bare back. He was sitting on a bench reading the newspaper, and I could see each of his ribs, along with the knobs of the individual vertebrae. It was like I was watching a PBS special on war refugees, but in actuality I was watching my boyfriend slowly waste away.

Ever since his bout with giardia, Duffy had been fighting a losing battle with weight loss. To understand this, you must know that Duffy is naturally tall and thin, like a beanpole. He didn't have much excess body fat to rely on when he became sick. And although Duffy was barely eating, he continued to hike, burning thousands of calories a day. By the time we reached Kennedy Meadows, his appetite had returned but any hint of body fat had disappeared. Through the Sierra, climbing a high mountain pass per day, he continued to lose body mass until his legs looked like toothpicks. At this rate, he'd be invisible by the time we reached Washington.

Many hikers underestimate the amount of food they'll need on the trail. A man sitting on the couch watching football all day will burn 2,000 calories. But a man carrying thirty pounds over uneven terrain will burn approximately 512 calories per hour—in ten hours of hiking, that's an *additional* 5,000 calories. Of course, calorie usage varies with body weight, hiking conditions, and other factors, but a male thru-hiker's approximate daily caloric requirement is 7,000 calories, the equivalent of ten Sourdough Jack burgers, twenty-five Snickers bars, or thirty-eight root beer sodas.

The hiker who isn't ingesting as many calories as he burns will quickly run into trouble. First, he'll have less energy for the day's hike, making it feel more arduous. Second, to compensate for lack of energy, his body will metabolize fat and, in the absence of fat, muscle. This in turn makes him even weaker. It's a hungry and insidious spiral. Fortunately, most of us have spare tires and love handles to turn to for emergency energy. But when all that body fat has been used up, a race against time ensues. Duffy was already at that critical juncture, and we still had 1,566 miles to go. He'd have to make a concerted effort to eat more or else it wouldn't be my knee sending us home, but his skin and bones.

In her book *Woman's Guide: Backpacking,* Adrienne Hall states that male long-distance hikers are at greater risk for weight loss than their female counterparts because they have a lower fat-to-muscle ratio. On Hall's Appalachian Trail thru-hike, she lost eight pounds while her husband (who'd even tried to fatten up prior to the trek) sacrificed thirty. I could see a similar equation playing out before my eyes—while I'd probably dropped ten pounds Duffy was well on his way to losing twenty-five.

When I broached the subject of his new starvation look, Duffy became defensive. "Maybe if you didn't eat so darn fast I wouldn't be burning up all my muscle."

Whoa. Granted, we shared our dinner out of the same pot, and I do eat fast, but it never occurred to me that Duffy didn't think he was getting his fair share. Now it was my turn to be defensive.

"We're both hungry and losing weight," I said. My voice got higher in pitch and I waved my spindly arm in his face for effect. "But if you think you're not getting enough to eat, we should carry some extra peanut butter or something, just for you. Don't blame it all on me; we need to be carrying more food, that's all." But Duffy was hesitant to add much more weight to our packs. He wanted to stop splitting the food fifty-fifty.

"I'm bigger than you and carry a heavier pack. I need more calories," he stated with a hint of resentment.

This was my worst fear. Resentment is an ugly, gnawing scourge of an emotion. I knew that all too well because it was already scratching at the back door of my mind. I resented the fact that Duffy could walk so quickly and so far without needing a rest, and that our hike seemed to be more physically and emotionally demanding on me than it was on him.

I'd expected to see bitterness in Duffy's eyes at some point, but I thought its source would be my hiking pace and stamina (or comparative lack thereof). The fact that his unhappiness centered on how we shared our food was shocking and humiliating. No one wants to be known as a greedy pig, and for a woman, that's an especially stinging slap in the face. But here I was, with my lover telling me that I was eating too much and that he was falling ill as a result. Could I feel lower? I rubbed my protruding collarbone and pulled my knobby knees toward my chest.

It seemed ironic that we'd be having this food fight in town, not long after visiting the supermarket. But on the trail, there was little energy for fighting. In town, with full bellies and a good night of sleep behind us, our animal survival instincts belatedly kicked in. Before we went for each other's throats with gnashing teeth, I was determined to come up with a solution. "Fine," I said, "from now on, you get more of the food. You can have a big bite of every Snickers, energy bar, and cookie before I eat it. At dinner, you use the ladle and I'll use the little spoon."

"That'll only work if you stop shoveling so fast." Duffy was not fully satisfied.

"I'll go bite for bite with you. And when we have peanut butter and crackers, I'll give you two for every one of mine. Deal?" At this point I'd have done anything to make Duffy happy and forestall an anorexia-induced collapse.

The seemingly logical solution to all this was to just carry more food. We weren't hiking through a famine-ravished nation and had an abundance of nutritious and delicious items at our disposal. But we feared that by carrying much more food we would just trade one discomfort for another—heavier packs instead of gnawing hunger pains. For better or for worse, we chose hunger.

Even though we'd come to a fragile food distribution compromise, the sunny afternoon in town seemed to dull and we became restless. There just didn't seem to be much to talk about anymore. It was time to start hiking again.

X ▪ ▪ ▪ ▪ X

We took a taxi from the town of South Lake Tahoe back to Echo Lake, where we rejoined the trail and entered the Desolation Wilderness, so named for its dearth of trees. When glaciers carved this sixty-thousand-acre region they left a layer of rocky soil too unstable to support the root systems of many trees. The result is subalpine terrain with many characteristics of higher elevations, including wide-open views of granitic peaks and numerous rockbound, glassy lakes and tarns. In sum, it's a backpacker's playground, just a few minutes from the bustling shores of Lake Tahoe and only hours from San Francisco. Which is why the Desolation Wilderness is far from desolate—it boasts the highest density of hikers per square mile of any roadless area in California.

As the blue waters of Echo Lake faded in the distance, we climbed along wildflower-blanketed slopes, passing side trails leading to Triangle Lake, Tamarack Lake, Lake of the Woods, Lake Margery, and Lake Lucille. After six miles we came upon Lake Aloha and its open, white granite shores. The water was wind-rippled, speckled with barren islets and pierced by gray, weathered lodgepole snags. On the opposite shore, rising out of the stillness stood Pyramid Peak, delicately laced with snow. The scene was stunningly beautiful, and we approached Aloha's waters slowly, as if advancing toward an altar. After soaking the scene in for a few minutes, we reluctantly moved on.

We camped at a delightful tarn that night—one with long, spindly grass growing out of it. As the sun set, it bathed the rock face behind the tarn in warm pink light. The foul aura of our food fight dissipated as we wrapped our skinny, shivering limbs around each other for warmth.

Over the next several days we continued to descend out of the glaciated Sierra and into the volcanic Cascades. While traversing a four-mile ridge we peered down slope toward the Alpine Meadows and Squaw Valley (site of the 1960 winter Olympics) ski areas. Spidery chair lifts were strung overhead like mountain swing sets.

Cruising along Tinker Knob we had dramatic 360-degree panoramic views of the Tahoe area. Tahoe, in the Native American Washoe language, means "water," and with an average depth of 989 feet and a circumference of seventy-one miles, Lake Tahoe certainly holds a lot of that. Lake Tahoe's maximum depth is 1,645 feet, which makes it the tenth deepest lake in the world and the second deepest lake in the country (Crater Lake in Oregon is deeper). From our mountain vantage point, however, the lake looked like a large rain puddle, perfect for splashing in with a new pair of rubber boots.

Mark Twain wrote of Lake Tahoe, "I thought it must surely be the fairest picture the whole earth affords." And even after all the eye-numbingly exquisite vistas I'd seen over the past sixty-nine days, I had to agree—this was up there. As we sat on a ledge for a photograph (taken by an obliging day hiker), the lake and its forests spread out below. My legs dangled off the edge, and it seemed like if I just stretched a little farther, I could dip my big toe in the cool blue water.

Lake Tahoe is arguably Northern California's favorite getaway, offering skiing, snowboarding, snowshoeing, and sledding in the winter and hiking, biking, boating, and swimming in the summer. The lake, once known for its crystal clear, deep blue waters, is now paying the price for its popularity. Construction and overuse have caused the slopes around the lake to erode, sending sediment into the waters, increasing the growth of algae and generally mucking everything up, to a point where the lake's clarity has been reduced by twenty-five percent. By all accounts, Tahoe is still gorgeous but perhaps a little less so, which has plenty of people concerned. If you've ever driven around Northern California, you've certainly seen the bumper stickers that read "Keep Tahoe Blue."

I'm sure that if Tahoe Tessie could (or should I say "would"?) speak, she'd plead for Tahoe's blueness as well. Since the time of the Washoe Indians, there have been reports of a monster in the lake. Even today, fishermen report that "something big down there" straightens their hooks and breaks their lines. This "something," known as Tahoe Tessie, is reported to be ten to fifteen feet long. Every year about half a dozen Tahoe Basin residents and tourists say they see her—albeit briefly—before she disappears into the lake's depths. Jacques Cousteau headed an expedition to the lake's bottom in search of Tessie, but never revealed his findings or film footage to the public, reportedly saying, "The world isn't ready." But I was pretty darn ready and had the Lake Tahoe Monster Museum's hotline number in my pack, in case I needed to report a long-distance sighting.

Leaving our scenic lookout, we returned to our daily rituals—hike, eat, hike some more, admire the scenery, eat again, hike again, and so on until sundown. As we neared the cannibalistically infamous Donner summit and Highway 80, however, our predictable pattern was disrupted. Suddenly, instead of admiring the serenity of the scenery, we found ourselves people-watching and counting articles of trash. Tufts of toilet paper peeked out from under leaves and rocks (clearly not buried in the requisite six-inch-deep cat hole), while candy bar wrappers, soda cans, and used Band-Aids lay alongside the trail. I'd heard an occasional thru-hiker admit in a whisper of feeling excited at the sight of trail trash, because it meant civilization, junk food, and a can of beer (or two) was only a few miles away. I couldn't subscribe to that; I love a beer as much as the next girl, but those tufts of toilet paper made me gag. I couldn't be too high and mighty about the issue, however; unless my own trash bag was within convenient reach, I rarely picked up litter. Not like Amigo (one of the Naked Hiker Day participants), who claimed to regularly hike out other people's used toilet paper. Now there's a man who stands by his convictions.

Although our trip to Donner summit led through pine-scented forests, meadows drizzled with flowering lupine, phlox, alpine everlasting, and daisy, and past igneous rock blanketed with red lichen, my most vivid memories are of trash and people—lots of people: trail runners, dog walkers, Boy Scouts, church groups, families, tourists with expensive cameras, solo-hikers, hikers from all walks of life. And then the unmistakable roar of traffic.

Interstate 80 is the only four-lane road to cross the four-hundred-mile-long Sierra Nevada Mountains. Here in the mountains we found a maze of exit ramps, train tracks, and traffic lanes. To bypass the four lanes of rumbling, roaring, thundering freeway we used a dank, graffiti-inscribed tunnel.

Safely on the other side, I stopped to cook dinner under a canopy of pines while Duffy ran to the trucker's stop to use the rest room and check our handheld email device.

It started to rain, and I tried to protect our chicken and broccoli Lipton noodles from dime-size droplets. I also tried desperately to refrain from eating it. I must have stared at the creamy pot of starch for ten minutes, stirring it with a big spoon as it bubbled on our stove. "What the hell is he doing over there?" I thought. "Either we got a lot of email or he's doing something unspeakable to that toilet." Despite that unpleasant thought, my stomach continued to roar and churn with vehemence. But after our recent food fight I didn't dare sneak a mouthful. Eventually, I walked away from the noodles and paced the trail, trying not to look like a starved dog doing laps in his kennel. The minutes leading up to Duffy's return were interminable, and when he finally arrived I thrust the pot and ladle into his hand saying, "Dinner's served—let's eat!"

After dinner, we continued four miles into the evening, climbing away from the din of the freeway, the trash, and the crowds. As we climbed, the forest grew dark. Long shadows of white fir intersected our path. We were finishing up the twenty-fourth mile of the day and beginning a descent to a grassy meadow when we spotted a shingle and stone cabin behind a row of trees. As we neared it, we realized it must be the Sierra Club cabin mentioned in our guidebook, one of the few backcountry shelters available to hikers along the PCT. Curious, we pushed open the creaky wooden door that led into a cluttered room. Empty wine bottles held half melted candles. Sinister-looking hooks dangled from the ceiling, which, judging from the trails of mouse droppings over the wooden countertop, were used to keep the rodents from stealing food. I climbed up a ladder to a loft, where musty mattresses were stored overhead on exposed ceiling beams. Downstairs, Duffy tinkered with the wood-burning stove.

The dark, musky smell gave me the creeps, and I went outside for fresh air. A carved wooden sign labeled the rustic shelter as the "Peter Grubb Hut," built in memory of a man who died at the age of eighteen from sunstroke. Duffy's head appeared out the second floor window. "Let's stay here tonight," he suggested eagerly. "We'll sleep on the mattresses and won't have a lot to pack up in the morning. We can get an early start." The stained mattresses were a little ill-used and institutional for my taste, but I was too tired to argue—or to hike the additional miles to make not staying in the hut worth it. Duffy must have sensed my disgust. "I'll find clean ones," he said, referring to the mattresses. "I promise."

Back in the dusty darkness, I lit some candles, hung my pack from a ceiling hook, and then sat down at the wooden table to sign and read the hut's journal. A note from Crazy Legs caught my eye.

"Y'all better hurry up because it's getting lonely up here. Stop reading and start walking."

I missed those guys and wondered whether we'd ever catch up to them. One of the difficult aspects of being part of the thru-hiking community was that after you made friends, your footsteps usually dragged you apart, some going faster, others slower, until what seemed like an unbridgeable distance grew between you.

"Chiggy, come to bed." Duffy was already nestled under our green sleeping bag and brown fleece blanket on a mildewed mattress upstairs. I barely slept a wink that night as scratching and scurrying noises emanated from every corner.

X ▪ ▪ ▪ ▪ X

To math teachers across the nation, thirty is just another number. But to many of us trapped in the ethos of a youth-centric culture, thirty comes on like a death sentence. Rational minds recognize that not much changes between twenty-nine and thirty, but it's a turning point nonetheless. No more excuses— when you hit thirty, it's for real.

I'd been wary of thirty. I wasn't sure that I was ready. Was I strong enough? Would the burden overwhelm me? How much of the journey would show in my face? Would a thirty's-worth of sun, wind, sweat, and dirt age me?

But then again, thirty is an achievement. And no true achievement is made without a little pain. You can run from it, hide from it, or deny it, but really, as a thru-hiker as in "real life," you haven't reached maturity until you get there.

At the time, I was still four years away from turning thirty years old. But on the seventy-first day of our journey, I struggled with a similar milestone—the thirty-mile day—and let me tell you, it hurt like hell. But I became a stronger hiker for it, and all subsequent thirty-mile days, like birthdays, were a little less painful—and a little less celebrated as well.

We hadn't planned on doing a thirty that day. Sierra City was thirty-four miles away and we figured we'd be there for breakfast the following day, perhaps after a ten-mile morning hike. But by noon we'd cranked out twelve miles and the thoughts of cold beer, a shower, and a bed lured us onward.

Our descent toward Sierra City was steep. I knew that every step we climbed down would be matched by a more arduous climb up the Sierra Buttes on the other side. Bulging out of the mass of deep green trees across the valley, the Sierra Buttes looked like the naked humps of camels.

Contrasting with the green horizon, the ground beneath my feet was brown, covered in pine needles and cones. Occasionally an oak sapling pierced through the deep duff as it struggled skyward. Soon the trail turned from dirt to jagged dark rocks, which sounded like chips of pottery as my feet skidded over them. Evening was approaching, but the ambient air remained hot—hot enough that the pine needles were baking, filling my nostrils with sweetness.

The thirty-miler, I learned, is not only a physical test but also a mind game. To keep thoughts of quitting, insecurities, and fears at bay for thirty exhausting miles takes mental stamina and somehow, when physical energy wanes, cerebral energy does, too. I'd recently heard (on my portable radio) that as survivors of the Holocaust get older, their ability to bury painful memories weakens to the point where many find themselves reliving events they'd hidden deep in their subconscious. I found it interesting that the physical changes of aging affect selective memory. I think that a thirty-mile day can do something similar to the mind, bringing to the fore things you'd rather not think about because you don't have the energy to hold them back.

That evening, while Duffy strode a hundred yards ahead of me, my mind was besieged by worries big and small. I worried about my credit card bill. I worried whether the extra jar of peanut butter we purchased in South Lake Tahoe would be enough food to stave off Duffy's starvation. I worried about whether I was making my parents sad. I worried about what I'd do with my life after the hike was over. I worried about whether Duffy and I could survive the trials of the trail ahead. I worried about whether I was a good person or not, and I worried about the forest around me and about the greater Western wilderness it represented. Would it still be here for the next generation? I worried so much my head ached as much as my feet.

X ▪ ▪ ▪ ▪ X

From Jackson Meadows to Milton Creek, the PCT meanders across 2,880 acres owned by the largest private landowner in the state of California—the Sierra Pacific Industries (SPI) timber company. Growing on this private land are the biggest and oldest Douglas fir trees in the Tahoe National Forest. Remnants of old growth forest, some of these trees are six hundred to eight hundred years old. Regardless, the Milton Creek area could be logged by SPI at any time. Still, I harbored hope that SPI would protect the old growth trees and the aesthetic continuity of the PCT because it was the "right" thing to do. But such protection isn't guaranteed, especially given the fact that the language granting the PCT an easement through SPI property preserves the company's right to grow and harvest future forest crops. No one, according to Tim Feller, a district manager for Anderson, California-based SPI, said it would be a pristine trail from Mexico to Canada. Indeed, logging near Milton Creek began in 2002.

As we hiked in SPI territory, we passed many old growth trees. They were drenched in lime-green wolf lichen. Adrenaline and peanut butter carried us down to a green bridge over the creek. At about 8:30 that evening we crossed over that bridge and into long-distance hiking adulthood. We'd done our first thirty-mile day, but we didn't linger.

With Sierra City so close, we decided to push another four miles. During those last four miles, my feet throbbed like they did on our first day. My hamstrings tightened like rubber bands stretched near breaking point, and my hands grew cramped around my trekking poles. The sun went down as we passed through the Wild Plum Campground and then the surrounding residential neighborhood. Dogs barked when they heard me stumbling over broken pavement, and Duffy glanced back to make sure I was still standing.

Finally, at 9:30, we reached the center of town, which consisted of a post office, a general store, and a few motels. We didn't have energy for bargain-hunting, so we stopped at the first motel we saw, the Sierra Buttes Inn. We celebrated our first thirty-miler with a beer, lukewarm showers, and a soft bed, where I elevated my swollen feet and rested my weary, worried head.

[10]

Kicking Buttes

 BY THE END OF JULY 17, our seventy-first day on the PCT, Angela and I had ample reason to be bursting with pride. We'd just walked thirty-four miles in one day, an effort that would legitimize us in the eyes of even the most hard-core long-distance hikers. Thirty-four miles, with oversized packs and medium-light technique—that was legitimate, all right. Thirty-four legitimate miles.

We should have been swollen and engorged with self-worth. The only problem was that I was too tired to feel anything—too tired to tell if my feet were throbbing or my shoulders screaming. Lying on our saggy bed at the Sierra Buttes Inn, I was too exhausted at first to even care that the kids next door were being utterly obnoxious, as only prepubescent boys can be. First, there was the running and bouncing around the room as if they were playing a game of duck-duck-goose. Then came the fake farts—a lyrical series of dry farts, explosive farts, fat and juicy farts. It was too much. I was forced to mobilize the only muscles I had that weren't shut down with fatigue—those in my throat.

"Stop farting!" I shouted. "Stop right now or I'll come over there and fart in your little faces!" Sweet silence, but for the scattered "Shh!" "Be *quiet*," and "Shut up!" from next door. I blissfully sank back into a near sensationless state.

The human body is not designed to walk thirty-something miles in a day with a forty-to-fifty pound load. Such activity induces exhaustion, pain, and injury. We saw it frequently, hikers driven by re-supply schedules and competitive spirit to go beyond their physical limits. The first thirty-miler was always the most exhausting. Ron "Fallingwater" Moak, who'd recovered from cancer to hike the PCT, described his experience in this way:

"When I did my first 30-mile day I finished it in extreme pain with a body racked by waves of cramps. I didn't boast of my accomplishments; I was too busy trying to keep from crying out and disturbing everyone else's sleep. Nevertheless, I was indeed proud. I was proud I was still alive. I was proud my body had recovered from cancer enough to carry me that far. I was proud that I pushed when I felt like giving up. I was proud because I knew that only a few short years ago hiking a few short miles was a major accomplishment. And I'd covered 33 in a single day."

Given my fatigue the night of our thirty-four-miler, I would have never guessed that thirty-plus-mile days would soon become unremarkable occurrences, each becoming just another piece in our walk-to-Canada puzzle, our bodies adapting and responding to the crazy demands our minds had concocted. But, eventually and inevitably, the question would arise: How much punishment could we absorb?

A day after covering thirty-four miles we hiked a leisurely fifteen into the spires of the Sierra Buttes. Ahead was Mount Lassen, the first in a string of fifteen volcanoes that marked the remainder of our trek to Canada. We hiked through diverse country, moving high above the Lakes Basin, and were tempted with views of abundant lakes—Upper and Lower Sardine Lake, Packer Lake, Salmon Lake, and Gold Lake.

Gold Lake, which sits a few miles east of the PCT, draws its name from one of the biggest hoaxes of the California Gold Rush. Back in 1849, long before the 49ers won their first five NFL titles, thousands flocked to the Sierra Nevada Mountains looking for super bowls of gold. In this frenzied, get-rich-quick environment, rumors swirled of a magnificent lake with banks of gold flecks, speckles, and nuggets. The rumors began with a mysterious man known as Stoddard, who claimed to have found a "golden" lake somewhere in the Feather River Canyon. He'd been scared off by Indians before he could cash in, but now he was organizing a return expedition out of Deer Creek Dry Diggins mining camp. He gathered a group of five hundred men, promising wealth, riches, and early retirement. All that he asked for in return was a guide fee.

The expedition meandered the mountains for days without striking gold. Finally, the frustrated 'Niners gave Stoddard an ultimatum: show them Gold Lake in forty-eight hours or they would show him how to hang from a tree by a rope. But the miners were not the sharpest picks in the mountains; not only had they followed Stoddard into the hills, but then they let him escape quietly out of camp with their money, never to be heard from again.

X ▪ ▀ ▀ ▪ X

Miles were flying by so fast that scenery became a blur, an amalgamation of volcanic ridges and viewless forest. Our evolution into thirty-mile-a-day hikers was progressing rapidly, spurred on by mile-eating ambition. Two days after our thirty-four mile day we put in thirty to Black Rock Creek Road and now were on our way to another thirty-miler.

Toward midafternoon, our grumbling stomachs demanded that we detour to Lakeshore Resort at Buck's Lake for a restaurant meal. We humbly acquiesced and began a three and a half-mile road-walk into town. I initially hoped that we might catch a ride, but after two miles of walking, arm and thumb extended, with trucks blasting past, I gave up and put on my headphones to find a baseball game. Soon I was in a radio-entranced zone, far away at Pac Bell Park, the smell of Giants franks wafting through the air and the crack of the bat ringing in my ears—that is, until I caught a glimpse of something completely unexpected. Angela was waving at me from the passenger seat of a caramel Jeep while speeding past at forty miles an hour. I waved back, wondering if they planned on stopping for me.

"Well," I thought, "there she goes, left me for good . . . always finding a way to ruin a perfectly good ball game." As the Jeep finally pulled over a couple hundred yards up the road, I remembered how a high school friend of mine used to pull over in front of hitchhikers and then, once they started running toward the car, hit the gas and speed away. Thankfully, no such treachery was in the works, and I arrived at the Jeep to find Angela laughing and the driver, an older woman with startling hot-pink lipstick, smiling.

"I saw you two from my porch and said to my husband, 'Hmpf. He's not even walking with her. Maybe I should pick her up and teach that boy a lesson.' And so I did. Then I said to Angela here, 'Now, when we drive by, you just smile and wave.'"

"Very funny," I admitted. I didn't mind having a joke played on me if it meant we scored a ride to the restaurant. Safely in the car, we shared our story with the woman, Babs, who immediately offered us dinner and a place to stay for the night. Normally we'd have dropped our packs on the spot upon hearing such a hospitable offer, but an impending trip to Pasadena (596 road miles away) for a friend's wedding had put us on a tight schedule. We needed to be in Burney, 149 trail miles to the north, by July 26 in order to catch a flight out of San Francisco on the morning of the 28th. We'd struggled for weeks with the decision of whether or not to attend the wedding, but finally, at Lake Tahoe, we'd purchased airline tickets. It'd be unfortunate if the wedding caused us to miss miles, but we figured that we could always make them up some other year. We'd never have another chance to attend Tom and Belinda's wedding. To get to Pasadena in time, we'd have to average twenty-five miles a day over the next six days. There would be few opportunities to bail out. I already doubted whether we would be able to make our deadline, and we certainly couldn't afford an evening of indulgence at Bucks Lake. So we thanked Babs profusely for her gracious offer and settled for a bacon double-cheeseburger dinner at the Lakeshore resort.

After we'd each devoured a burger and fries, our waiter came by to ask if we'd like dessert. Why, yes we would. How about a grilled cheese sandwich with a side of Snickers for the lady and me? After polishing off our calorie-rich second course, we were back on the road to Buck's summit and then up the trail for eight energetic miles.

Our extra effort was rewarded the next morning with an easy fifteen-mile hike to Belden Town. It was nearly all downhill, with the last six miles dropping us 4,000 feet via dozens of Ponderosa-pine- and Douglas-fir-sheltered switchbacks. We wound our way down to the tracks of the Western Pacific railway and then on to Belden Town, a small remnant of a mining settlement that sits abreast the Feather River.

We'd planned on blowing in and out of Belden Town, but a mailing snafu forced us to modify the plan: Our re-supply box was missing. We replaced most of our provisions from the hiker box and added some from the Belden Town store but unfortunately couldn't completely replace our missing guide-book section. We discovered some torn-out pages of Section M in the hiker box, but after Burney, at mile 1,410, we would be guideless until we picked up our next box at the Lake of the Woods in Southern Oregon (mile 1,775).

By the time we'd figured out our re-supply situation and taken a dip in the inviting emerald waters of the Feather River, a sizable group of hikers had gathered at the Belden Saloon. The Moaks were there and so was Luke, also known as Amigo, a red, scruffy-bearded prankster from the Chico area. We'd admired Amigo's trail register cartoons lampooning ultralight gear, witnessed his antics on Naked Hiker Day, and heard of his admirable "You pack it in, I'll pack it out" approach to toilet paper on the trail, but we hadn't actually spent much time with the guy. With a round face that was a natural extension of his wide smile and eyes that laughed along with his mouth, Amigo sported a perfect visual complement to his collection of jokes and stories.

"What did Sushi A say to Sushi B? Wasabi!" Our table, including the Moaks and a bunch of newcomers from Washington, chuckled in appreciation.

Amigo continued, "So, there are these two trees growing in the woods, and this sapling grows up between them. The one tree asks the other, 'Is that the son of a *birch*?' 'No, it's the son of a *beeeeech*.' These two trees are debating back and forth like crazy until this woodpecker shows up. They ask him to settle the debate. So the woodpecker rocks over to the sapling and flies back a few minutes later. He says, 'You're both wrong. That's not the son of a *birch* or the son of a *beeeech*. That's the finest piece of *ash* I've ever had my pecker in.'" More chuckles intermixed with a few groans.

Someone asked Amigo how he'd received his trail name, and he immediately launched into the story.

"Okay, so I am at the Mexican border and surging with adrenalin. Not the quick surge, but the dose that keeps you rocking like crazy for . . . minutes. I'm belting out Lionel Richie, 'Oh, what a feeling . . . I'm dancing on the ceiling.' The first few moments on the trail were dreamy. The sun, the birds, the earth. Wow! And then I'm slammed out of my warm fuzzy moment by a piece of trash—just a quarter of a mile from the border. I pick up an empty water jug and then a discarded bread bag. 'How dare they trash my trail,' I'm thinking. And then it occurs to me that this isn't hiker trash, but illegal immigrant trash. But I pick it up nonetheless. Soon, I come across a greasy white tee shirt. It must have been dropped by an illegal who was either too hot or didn't want to be seen with a white tee shirt. Anyway, I pick it up and it says, 'YO SOY AMIGO DE LUCAS.'

"It means 'I'm Lucas' friend.' I have no idea who Lucas is, but still, it's a rockin' shirt. So I wash it at the kickoff party, and it becomes a big hit. My pal Hawkeye, the dude who used to be a prison guard, well, he starts calling me 'Amigo.' It stuck."

More trail name stories ensued, and as Angela and I emptied a series of tasty pints it became apparent that the climb out of Belden would have to wait until morning. Over the last eight days we'd covered 194 miles, in the order of 15, 28, 27, 34, 15, 30, 30, and 15, and we were due to let loose. We stumbled out of the saloon and threw down our mattresses on the first patch of ground we saw, not noticing the significant slant of our campsite or its proximity to the railroad tracks. Shortly after we fell asleep, the Western Pacific Railroad, which has been running trains through Belden Town since 1903, ran yet one more—*right* through our campsite. Well, at least that's what my confused mind thought. I awoke in a panic and jumped, on all fours, over Angela, like Spiderman ready to spring. How I planned to protect her from a hundred-ton train, I'm not sure. It was well past us before I relaxed my crouch, realizing that ten feet had spared me the messiness of a lopsided confrontation. Angela giggled drunkenly. For the rest of the night trains rumbled by every few hours, nearly imploding our eardrums with their *chooo-chooooooo's*.

We arose at the first hint of dawn, tired and dehydrated but ready to tackle the ascent out of Belden Town. As we sweated and strained our way up from the Feather River, we moved north of the geologic border of the Sierra and out of gold country. Not a big deal, really—I felt like we had left *The* Mountains miles ago, and I couldn't recall seeing anything gold all summer besides Sierra sunshine and Angela's fading highlights.

X ◾ ◾ ◾ ◾ X

As we continued our race to the Burney deadline, the miles peeled away, and Mount Lassen, the monolithic master of the Southern Cascades, grew closer. On the morning of July 23, we strolled through rather monotonous forest and our views of Lassen became obstructed by a canopy of ponderosa and sugar pine. The trail was silent but for distant birdcalls, the occasional crack of a falling branch, and the crunch of deadwood under foot. On both sides of us lay a graveyard of trees and tree parts—deadwood of all sizes and shapes, providing many nooks and crannies for spiders to spin their webs. The tread was relatively flat, and because I'd fallen into the soothing monotony of a thru-hiking groove, I barely noticed when, just past Ruffa Ridge, I passed a PCT emblem with "½" marked on it. It wasn't until a quarter of a mile later that the significance set in: We'd passed the halfway mark, 1327.5 miles to Canada, 1327.5 miles to Mexico. It wouldn't make much sense to turn around now.

Our trail continued on mostly level terrain, weaving in and out of parcels of national forest and private land. The scenery gradually took on a more volcanic character. Pockmarked, scarlet-tinted rocks and boulders mingled with bright white and pink wildflowers. The tread beneath my feet became reddish and dusty, engulfing my boots in a thick cloud with each step. We were drawing tangibly close to an active volcano, Mount Lassen, the "sweathouse of the gods." By the next afternoon we'd be there.

Our jaunt through Mount Lassen National Park was disappointing. We hiked rapidly through the park (our goal was a thirty-three-mile day, to Old Station), so we didn't have much time to stop and smell the sulfur. We were in and out of the moonscaped surroundings before I even had the chance to examine Lassen's famous mud pots—indentations of viscous mud emanating vapors and gurgles. The only thing that I remember clearly is the myriad signs that warned us how dangerous volcanic activity can be. As if I had any desire to jump into the steaming bowl of pale Easter egg-green soup called Boiling Springs Lake.

When we finally made it to the RV community of Old Station late that night, I was both exhausted and elated. We were going to make it. It was just thirty-eight miles to Burney, and we had a full day and a half to get there. I'm periodically amazed by the motivational power of a fixed deadline, and this was one of the more remarkable instances I've experienced. In eleven days, we covered 284 miles—without a single day of rest, without shortcuts, and with two overstuffed packs. For experienced long-distance hikers this was nothing special, but for neophytes like us it was unexpectedly prolific. The accelerated mileage had, however, come with a cost. We were two and a half months into our journey and halfway to Canada, and our bodies continued to rebel, feeding us a consistent menu of sores and chafing as well as emaciation. And we weren't alone.

We'd seen it firsthand, the toll that many hard miles can take: bodies treated like cheap rental cars, driven hard and fast without rest or proper maintenance. The complaints ran the gamut of discomfort: shin splints, plantar fasciitis, tendonitis, lower back pain, stress fractures, shoulder separation, backpack palsy, altitude sickness, vertigo, diarrhea, dehydration, heat illness, pneumonia, extreme weight loss, debilitating blisters. The results of overuse are unfortunate but not surprising. A 1993 survey of 178 successful AT hikers (134 thru-hikers and 44 section hikers) by B. J. Crouse and David Josephs (physicians from the University of Minnesota) found that eighty-two percent had suffered at least one significant illness or injury along the way. Sixty-two percent of hikers had experienced extremity or joint pain, twenty-two percent had gastrointestinal issues, and seven percent sustained fractures. One in four of these injuries required medical attention, and on average, the ailments resulted in 4.7 lost hiking days. And this was in the group that completed their hike; one would assume that "unsuccessful" hikers experienced an even higher prevalence of illness, injury, anguish, and grief.

Our problems hadn't quite reached the level of anguish and grief, but they were moving in that direction. Angela's knee was better; she only periodically experienced a twinge of pain going downhill, but there were new problems afoot—literally. She'd discarded her worn boots at Lake Tahoe, opting for a new waterproof model. Too watertight, perhaps, because she soon discovered that they didn't allow in enough fresh air. For the first time, Angela developed blisters—five of them. They were cute little things, red and inflamed, with pockets of serous fluid. Well, I found them cute; she just found them painful. Each morning I'd carve five moleskin doughnuts for her and then wrap her dust-coated toes in Duct tape. My feet and hands didn't look much better. Several painful blood blisters had formed in the crease of each palm. The culprit? My trekking poles were rubbing me raw.

The blood blisters hurt like hell, but in the big picture they were insignificant compared to my bony and hollowed frame. I'd started the trail thin, but with pockets of reserves. These pockets—a thin stripe below the umbilicus and two bulges on my thighs—were gone. Completely gone. So were the hint of love handles and pinch of flab under the triceps. Even worse, my receding hairline was quickly progressing to a chrome dome. I was shedding hair like a Siberian husky in Cancun. I could only assume that my dietary deficiencies were contributing to this troubling process.

I'd become stick man, the incredible shrinking man with the incredible sloughing scalp. No matter how much blubber I ate in town, I still got thinner and thinner and balder and balder. I'd started our hike a robust 185 pounds, but at last check I was down to 160. In their survey of AT hikers, Crouse and Josephs found that the average thru-hiker lost eighteen pounds. I'd already dropped twenty-five, and we were only halfway to Canada. It was too much; continuing at this pace I'd soon be skinnier than a Calvin Klein model.

What was to blame for my drastic downsizing? Well, the simple answer was a big fat calorie deficit. I estimated that I'd been consistently running a thousand-calorie deficit daily. Considering that fat is burned at a rate of 3,500 calories per pound, it doesn't take a mathematics degree to figure out that I'd long since burned through my fat reserves. But as much as I harassed Angela about her eating habits, food distribution was only a small part of the problem. The timing of my bout with giardia had been unfortunate; I lost my appetite at the very time when I needed it most, as we were tackling a long string of strenuous miles through the Sierra. And if we'd bothered to consult Ray Jardine, we'd have recognized additional culprits.

Our base pack-weights were high, so there wasn't much leeway for carrying extra food. This, according to Jardine, is ass backwards: "Even though reducing our pack weight is extremely beneficial, reducing food weight is entirely counterproductive." To make matters worse, our food choices were perhaps just as dangerous as the portions. Our diet was rich in foods that Jardine disdains—processed flour products such as bagels, crackers, Pop Tarts, and macaroni, as well as energy bars that Jardine considers no more than "high-priced candy bars." And freeze-dried meals—well, in Jardine's opinion, you might just as well be eating Styrofoam: "I suspect that those who eat freeze-dried foods are feeding, instead, on the reserves stored in the cells of their own bodies." He recommends products that are not only heavy, but also often difficult to obtain on the trail—fresh fruits and vegetables, whole grains, legumes and potatoes, seeds and nuts, eggs and cheese, meat and fish, and the incomparable power food, corn pasta.

Pretty much the only food group in our repertoire that Jardine would have approved of was the peanut. We did eat lots of peanuts. We never tired of the peanut or its offspring, and with each day they seemed to become a larger component of our diet, so much so that we sometimes joked that our trail names should be "The Peanuts"—"Skip" and "Jiffy," "Smooth" and "Crunchy," "Salted" and "Honey Roasted," or even "Snoopy" and "Linus." But even the mighty peanut could not hold off the evil forces of thinning, and so, as we neared Burney, I eagerly anticipated a week of buffet-style eating.

But before any buffets, we'd have to navigate the Hat Creek Rim, a notorious stretch of trail many hikers refer to as the *Hot* Creek Rim. Sitting just a few miles from Hat Creek and its verdant canyon, Hat Creek Rim promised thirty exposed, fire-marred, and waterless miles. This was the longest waterless stretch of the entire PCT. Luckily, our friend Amigo had arranged for a cache along this water-starved walk. Cache-22 he called it in his note at the Old Station Trail Register. Cache-22 would be of tremendous assistance; I'd learned that it didn't take much extra weight to make your pack feel awfully unwieldy. Yes, Big Red would be thankful, and so would Purple Precious—

she'd be spared three excess liters of water. Angela had started calling her pack "Purple Precious" a while back. I didn't find the name all that appropriate. First of all, the pack wasn't purple—never was purple. It was and is blue. Second, the only thing precious about it was how precious little it often carried.

Later that day, loaded light and loving it, we were off, inspired by Amigo's words in the trail register, "I had a dream and I lived it." Hat Creek Rim was indeed hot and dry, but not nearly as unpleasant as I'd expected. We had unobstructed views back to Lassen and forward to Mount Shasta. The sparse forest of ghost trees that populated the rim was unlike anything I'd seen before. The trees looked as if they had been attacked not only by a forest fire but also by a blender. Portions of them were chopped off at strange angles. With a bright pink sunset providing a glow to walk by, Angela and I excitedly discussed plans for the upcoming wedding. We were eagerly anticipating the opportunity to see friends, catch up, and tell stories. Several nights at a hotel, a steady diet of junk food, and maybe a movie or two—those were added bonuses.

Somewhere along the way, perhaps shortly after we were chased a hundred yards by a group of curious cattle, the tone of the conversation changed. We both had misgivings about leaving the trail, especially since we'd hit a nice groove. Angela, in particular, was scared. She'd decided to attend a second wedding after Pasadena, in Massachusetts. Amie was one of her best friends and Angela was her bridesmaid, so I fully supported her decision to go—I would have done the same thing. The conflict, though, revolved around my decision to return to the trail at Burney for a week of hiking without Angela. She was upset, partly because I wouldn't be going to the wedding with her, but primarily because I would be hiking a section of trail without her. She wanted to be with me for the *entire* trail, didn't want miss any part of it, didn't want to have her accomplishment the least bit diminished.

I understood her sentiment, but another tight deadline stared us in the face. We needed to be done by September 16, shelling out Canadian dollars for souvenirs and Molson Lights. As it was, we would probably have to skip a section, or at least a portion of one, in order for me to get back in time to resume medical school. My feeling was that if one of us were hiking a section, then at least we'd be minimizing what we both had to skip. We did, after all, aim to write a book about the experience. Our discussion never really came to a satisfactory resolution. It was a no-win situation. Our long-distance hike had already required many sacrifices and compromises. This was yet another one.

X ▪ ▀ ▪ ▪ X

In the morning all was forgotten, at least for the time being, as we wound along a gullied trail. The excitement of a real vacation was setting in and I found myself daydreaming of greeting old friends, pick-up basketball games, and late-night dancing to Kool & The Gang. My daydreams, however, were rudely, and nearly disastrously, interrupted by a sunrise skunk encounter. I luckily escaped, barely avoiding being sprayed with uniquely outdoorsy cologne.

Later that afternoon, after much dry and dusty hiking, we arrived in Burney and checked into the Charm Motel. It was an ironic name, considering that Burney itself lacks any recognizable charm. Basically, it's a strip-mall town along Highway 299. After settling in and checking bus schedules, we bummed a hitchhike the eight miles to Burney Falls State Park to retrieve our re-supply package.

Throughout our trip we seemed to get a disproportionate number of rides from people who were intoxicated in one way or another. We'd already risked our lives with Tim, the psychedelic in Julian, as well as the Twizzler-eating drunk girl in Idyllwild, and now we rolled the dice with a tipsy cowboy and his front-cab booze-mobile. I don't know whether our experience speaks more to our desperation to find a ride, or the fact that someone needs to be majorly buzzed to think that picking up two dirty, scraggly hikers is a good idea. Either way, this cowboy wasn't shy about his drinking. We'd been in the car all of three minutes before he pulled over to a mini-mart to grab a six-pack of Mike's Hard Lemonade for his thirteen-year-old son and a twelve-pack of Bud for himself. Thankfully, and graciously, they waited until after dropping us off at Burney Falls to resume their father–son bonding. In retrospect, I probably should have called the police on this guy the second we reached

Burney Falls, but we were appreciative of the ride, and given what we'd seen of Burney, for all we knew he could *be* the police. So instead, we stopped briefly to admire the 129-foot Burney waterfall cascading over moss and rock into a large blue-green pool and then proceeded to the camp store.

Seated on wooden picnic benches outside the store, surrounded by a forest of beer bottles, were Casey and Toby, Catch-23 and ol' Crazy Legs. Toby was sporting a long, thick beard that nearly engulfed his face. His hair was long and shaggy. Casey had thinned out considerably; his cheekbones were now prominent, enhancing the intensity of his green eyes. Only his calves, meaty as ever, had been unaffected by generalized trail thinning.

"Holy shit," said Casey when he saw us. "Where did you guys come from? Duffy, man, you are one skinny dude."

"I was just thinking the same about you."

[11]

Time-out

"I DON'T KNOW WHAT TO SAY, all I know is that the next few months are going to change my life." These words had been scratched with a hurried hand in the trail register at the Mexican border. I can't remember what I wrote in that first register (I'd been hurried, too), but that unknown hiker's entry remained with me as if imprinted on the insides of my eyelids, so that sometimes, when I laid down at night, it was the last thing I saw before drifting off into exhausted slumber.

My life *was* changed. I was changed, although I couldn't quite figure out how or when it had happened—or even exactly what it was that had happened. Perhaps I walked a little taller, and a little stronger. Thru-hiking hadn't turned me into an über-athlete or anything, but like my feet I was becoming tougher. I think I was also gaining a better perspective on my life, something fairly typical among long-distance hikers and anyone given nearly limitless time to ruminate.

I once read a newspaper article about thru-hikers in which a young man was quoted as saying, "Even if you are with your best friends on the trail, you are ultimately by yourself as you walk. Many hikers get homesick. But most grow into the mountain quiet, and as they walk, experience remarkable clarity, recognizing exactly what counts for them and what does not."

X ▪ ▪ ▪ ▪ X

A smoky haze blurred the neon lights. Fallingwater, Drip, Crazy Legs, Catch-23, Duffy, and I were bowling in Burney. In between turns, Fallingwater amused himself by picking out the spelling mistakes on the bowling alley's menu while Drip munched on "Bufalo" wings. Duffy grinned like an imp. The simple pleasure of playing a game seemed to bring out the children in all of us and we stayed as late as the establishment would allow, sharing trail stories and wondering what lay ahead. Interestingly, we never talked much about our "real" lives but rather left them to hover in the background like ghosts. Maybe this was because we didn't want to think about going back, or maybe it was because we were in the process of reinventing ourselves, and real life would never be the same anyway. Most likely, though, it was because our trail lives were so immediate. Our feet and the earth beneath them—these things bound us together and seemed so much more important than the identities we'd left behind.

I think this is part of the reason that long-distance hikers adopt trail names. So far from home, first and last names and the lives attached to them can seem distant and irrelevant. The trail is an equalizer such that it doesn't matter if someone is a minister or a stockbroker, a teacher, an engineer, or an artist. More important is your hiking style (fast, slow, gimpy, or agile), your gear (heavy or light, homemade or brand name), your sense of humor, your generosity of spirit, and identifying physical characteristics. Names like Cantaloupe (for the girl who ate a lot of them), Hazmat (for the guy whose rain suit made him look like he worked for the Department of Transportation's Office of Hazardous Materials Safety), Casino (who won big at roulette in South Lake Tahoe), Charity (for her effort to raise money for one), the Abominably Slow Man (which speaks for itself), and of course Crazy Legs, helped create community and showed a recognition of the fact that not only were our bodies in transit but so also were our souls.

"Hey Lodgepole, check out Drip's nasty gutter ball." Crazy Legs was shimmying in his bowling shoes as he laughed and pointed.

"Foxtail, if you finish those wings, you best be moving your tail to get some more." Duffy eyed the near empty basket of chicken in front of me.

Initially, Duffy and I had been uncomfortable with adopting trail names. In our minds, trail names were reserved for legitimate long-distance hikers. It took us close to a thousand miles to feel as if we might be worthy of them. Near Reds Meadow, we'd stumbled onto an "interpretive" side trail, where various trees were identified with placards. Duffy kneeled so I could take his picture with a fine lodgepole specimen, and as he did so a new trail name was born. It seemed appropriate—Duffy's parents had at one time planned on naming him "Big Tree," and as our hike progressed he appeared to grow taller and leaner—more and more like a lodgepole pine. If Duffy was going to be a pine tree, I'd better be one, too; that way we could call ourselves "The Pines." It would be fun to share a "last" name, sort of like playing house. I immediately knew which pine I wanted to be—the foxtail, because it's scrappy, living where no one would think it could. By becoming the Pines we tacitly accepted our trail life and the new identities that went along with it.

Crazy Legs and Catch-23 crashed on our motel room floor that night. The space was cramped and musky, the air scented with a mixture of earth, sweet and sour body odors, warm beer, and damp sleeping bags. In the morning we left the boys to the joys of television, doughnuts, and indoor plumbing as we headed to the supermarket parking lot to board a rural bus to Redding. It was approximately sixty miles to Redding; from there we'd catch a Greyhound bus to Sacramento, then another to San Francisco, and finally a plane to southern California for Tommy and Belinda's wedding.

Upon disembarking in Redding I had an epiphany: "This," I thought, "is the hottest place on earth." In retrospect, I was wrong. Forget earth; it's just not hot enough for an accurate comparison. Imagine a city on the planet Mercury instead. Temperatures in Redding during the summer months have been known to reach 115 to 118 degrees.

My sundress stuck to the skin on my back, which was dripping with sweat under the weight of my pack. Salty warm droplets ran down my arms. In the distance, the sidewalk shimmered. The air didn't move except to blow its scalding breath on my skin. We ducked into a bookstore for relief. The air conditioning was cranking but I continued to sweat.

After only ten minutes, I hated Redding. Everything about it depressed me—the blackened store fronts, empty streets, and dingy motels. Mostly I hated that it was my gateway back to the real world. It irked me that I was getting off the trail, and it irked me even more that I couldn't do it with complete satisfaction. I felt I was betraying my new self, my trail self, but I was going to do it anyway, because one of the things I'd decided was really important was friendship and being there for the people I cared about.

Poring over maps, calling bus companies, and jotting down timetables, Duffy and I made a plan. After the wedding in Pasadena, he'd return to the trail at Burney Falls and solo-hike for six days. I'd fly to Boston for Amie's wedding, playing the role of attentive bridesmaid. Then I'd fly back to San Francisco and take a Greyhound first to Redding and then Yreka. From Yreka, I'd take a rural bus to Etna, where we'd meet and get back on the trail. All told, I'd skip 180 miles of trail, a 6.8-percent hole in my 2,655-mile goal. Up until this point, Duffy and I had trekked 1,410 miles together, not hand in hand, but as a team. Now he'd be traveling without me, and in the end he would have hiked more of the PCT. I hated that idea. Suddenly I felt like a failure, and our trip wasn't even over yet. Could I still call myself a thru-hiker when this was all over? And what did it mean to be a *thru*-hiker, anyway?

In the long-distance hiking world, there are "purists," and then there's everybody else. For a purist, a successful thru-hike is defined as a hike along any of the nation's long trails during which the hiker walks every step of the distance, unassisted and in a single season—no alternate routes, hitchhiking ahead, or Sherpas allowed. And while a pure thru-hiker is permitted to hitch-hike into town, he or she must return to the same exact spot on the trail before resuming hiking. Duffy and I had joked many times about what the ultimate pure thru-hike might entail. What if you never, ever stepped off the PCT—always walked on it, ate on it, slept on it, and even pooped on it? Would that make you more of a thru-hiker?

When eighteen-year-old Eric Ryback set out on his own in 1970 to attempt the first PCT thru-hike, he scheduled just five re-supply stops at locations spaced 375 miles and twenty-two days apart. At the time, the Pacific

Crest Trail was more theoretical than tangible; for much of his trek Ryback relied on map, compass, and landmarks to help him stick to routes that existed only on paper. Soon after he completed his hike, Ryback was featured on the cover of *National Geographic* and credited with the first-ever PCT thru-hike—an accomplishment that helped the trail gain popularity and much-needed support. Still, purists (and others) discount his hike, asserting that he strayed off the trail and accepted rides for portions of it. The fact that there wasn't a physical trail for him to deviate from was apparently irrelevant. If a pioneer such as Ryback couldn't satisfy trail purists, I was pretty sure that we didn't stand a chance.

By purist standards, we were never, and never planned to be, thru-hikers. If an alternate route promised better scenery, precious water, or a chance to eat a cheeseburger, we were likely to take it. If we hitchhiked into the south end of a town, we might get back on the trail at the north end and miss several miles in between. But purism be damned, we still felt like thru-hikers. We were walking from Mexico to Canada. We slept on hard ground. We didn't shower for weeks at a time. We starved. We froze. We overheated. We limped. We even bled. And we called ourselves thru-hikers—well, aspiring thru-hikers.

On the PCT email digest, the following question was posed "When is a thru-hike no longer a thru-hike?" On the purist side of the fence responses were predictably literal: "I've always thought that a summit attempt that stopped short of the summit is unsuccessful."

More permissive points of view were exemplified with replies like, "I think the important thing is to get wherever you need to get to (this will likely be different from what you thought it was when you started). More important still is whether you became a better person for it."

Fallingwater chimed in. "Does hiking most, but not all, of the trail dilute the accomplishment? If so, then what really was the purpose of your hike? Was it to achieve some mystical glory heaped on by your peers? Most people hike for reasons they can barely comprehend. But glory is probably the least of them."

Jim Owen, who has thru-hiked the PCT, AT, and Continental Divide Trail, writes in his *Thru-hiking Papers*, "Five years after you've finished the trail it rarely, if ever, matters whether you did it as a purist or not. The bottom line is that when you finish you'll be different." There's that word again, different. Yes, for us, many things would be different.

X ▪ ▪ ▪ ▪ X

In San Francisco, Duffy walked me to the gate for my flight to Boston. As I handed my boarding pass to the smiling attendant, I realized that Duffy and I hadn't been separated for more than a couple of hours in nearly a hundred days. Saying good-bye felt like having my right hand twisted off.

Compared to the other people in the crowded waiting area, Duffy looked exaggeratedly sinewy, bordering on frail. Friends' voices rang in my ears. At Tommy and Belinda's wedding they'd called Duffy "Skeletor" and asked whether he'd been an extra in the movie *Schindler's List*. And I was leaving him alone? A heat wave had been predicted for northern California, so not only would Duffy face a continued fight with malnutrition but also a long, arid section of trail. I was worried. If anything happened. . . .

Getting off the plane in Boston I navigated the airport, a bus, and then the subway as I traveled to meet Amie and her mom. They were all laughter and questions. I was exhausted. Everything was so loud and fast. I thought I might short-circuit from sensory overload. The motion of the **T** and then the car made me nauseous. Traffic fumes made me gag. Constant noise gave me a headache. My body was in Boston, whisked there by a 747, but I felt like my soul, continuing to travel by foot, was still on the PCT. There was no telling when it would catch up and in the meantime, I was neither here nor there.

Writing about my "vacation from my vacation," years later, I find myself just as conflicted as I was then. Even now, those 180 missed miles loom long. My hiking hiatus did, however, help to recharge my energy stores and consider my hike from a new perspective. It was during my "time-out" that I remembered that hiking was a privilege. I didn't want to waste another minute of it.

As Amie's wedding night slipped by, I slipped away. Sitting in a rickety wooden phone booth, I tried calling the last number Duffy had left for me. The phone rang and rang. I envisioned an empty motel room with a broken air conditioner hanging precariously out the window and a brightly colored, shiny bedspread. I went back out to the caterer's tent in the garden, now illuminated by the glow of twinkling white lights. I was reminded of a recent morning on the trail and smiled.

A friend caught me. "What're you smirking for?"

"Nothing, really. Something about the light made me think of a morning on the trail."

"Yeah? Tell me."

It had been barely dawn. The sky over the Hat Creek Rim was still a deep bruiselike purple. The sun was just peeking out over the horizon, bathing the tallest of the scorched tree trunks in golden light. We stumbled onto the trail and were moving slowly. The muscles in the arches of my feet were tight and painful; they'd be that way for the next half an hour or so, until the steady pace forced them to relax. A few birds twittered, but otherwise there was silence. Like most mornings, we'd cover our first few miles without talking.

We'd slept under a deep green canopy of pine trees the previous night. I could still smell the needles' sweetness in my clothes as we passed out of forest and into a dry meadow. Fifty yards ahead Duffy loped along, wearing his purple fleece hat, a generously sized article that perched precariously on his ears. Suddenly, the quiet was destroyed by hooting, woo-wooing, and *whoas*. With his trekking poles flying in all directions, including straight up in the air and out to the sides, Duffy sprinted off directly perpendicular to the trail. He took Rumpelstiltskinlike high steps, bounding over scruffy bushes and charred tree trunks. Big Red bounced high off his shoulders and landed back against him with loud thuds. It all took only thirty seconds, but I doubled over in deep belly laughs. I laughed harder than I had in months, certainly since we'd left Campo. The air resounded with my howls of joy and Duffy's yelps of panic. Then I saw what the uproar was all about: Heading in the opposite direction, bobbing through the grass, was a fluffy

black and white tail—a skunk, nearly as panicked as my bounding boyfriend.

I don't think my friend found this story nearly as amusing as I did. I guess
you had to be there. Thankfully, *there* was where I'd soon be.

X ▪ ▪ ▪ ▪ X

My return trip to California was filled with crowded bus stations and air-
ports. Finally, in San Francisco, I stepped through diesel-laced fog to board
the bus that would take me back to Redding. Glancing at me, the bus driver
asked, "How ya doing today?"

"Good." I meant it. After all, I was now within 340 miles of my rendezvous
with Duffy.

"You can't be too good," he said, "if you're going to Redding."

I had to stay in Redding that night because I missed the last bus out of
town. I left the bus station at 10:30 in the evening and walked down Butte
Street toward a strip of cheesy motels. Wearing my purple pack (don't believe
Duffy when he says it's blue) and flowered dress, I stuck out like a redneck in
Manhattan. The streetlights were dim, and the air was irritatingly close and
searing, the kind of temperature that ignites tempers. I walked fast and tried
to look big and unafraid. I checked into a crumby motel, dumped my stuff,
and returned to the streets of Redding because I *needed* to eat. I'd passed a
Wendy's a few blocks away and jogged there to grab some dinner. On my
way out of the Wendy's parking lot a white pickup truck with three guys in
the front pulled up alongside me. The men leered and laughed. They called
me "baby" and other endearing names. I somehow managed to resist their
charms and strode briskly away, but as I turned a corner the pickup followed,
just a few yards behind me. I turned another corner in an attempt to lose
them, but they stayed on my tail. I ran across a grassy median and a parking
lot, taking a route to my hotel that would be difficult for an automobile to
follow. Sprinting with my room key clutched in my fist, I leaped over
flowerbeds and didn't look back.

During August of 2000, forty-eight violent crimes were committed in Redding. That's nothing compared to San Francisco, New York, or Philadelphia. But still, I shouldn't have been walking those streets, not in the dark and not alone.

Winded and scared, I jumped into my motel room and immediately deadbolted the door and locked the windows. It must have been ninety-five degrees in the room, and the AC made weak buzzing noises. Tomorrow I'd take a Greyhound to Yreka and then a rural bus to Etna, where I'd meet Duffy. The thought of seeing him made me feel safe again.

[12]

The Misadventures
of Solo-man

 IN JUNE 1990, AT THE AGE OF EIGHTEEN and a few days
from high school graduation, I embarked on a three-day
"vision quest" along the shores of Pyramid Lake in western Nevada. The trip, organized by my progressively minded school,
was based on the Native American tradition of sending young
boys near or at the age of puberty into a trial of meditation, fasting, and physical
challenge. To Native Americans, the details of the trip are unimportant; the
significance lies in creating a "period of solitude in which we seek an inner
revelation—a vision—which grants profound meaning and direction on our
life." In search of such profound meaning, twenty classmates and I fanned
out across the desert for three days of solitude. I fasted for two days, meandered for hours through the barren hills above the lake, wrote prolifically in
my journal, and tried to focus on achieving a better understanding of myself.

Much later, just before our PCT adventure, I looked back at my vision
quest journal, hoping that I'd written something substantive that would help
prepare me for our upcoming trek. My sixty pages of scribble began like this:

"I can hear a cricket chirping, he chirps ceaselessly. It is as though his whole
existence depends on the continuation of that one monotonous sound. Pyramid Lake is a spectacular place, especially in the late evening. They say the
sky often turns red, but it didn't tonight. I feel very much at peace here in the
desert."

And then, after several more pages of description and bland philosophy, I
found fifty-six and a half pages of rumination on one thing and one thing

182

only: girls. The girls I liked, the girls I dated, the many girls I attempted to date, on and on. Reading this, I was disappointed. I hadn't found any sort of divine truth on my vision quest; I'd merely spent the time plotting romantic strategy, a "girl quest," if you will. "Perhaps now," I thought, "ten years later, I'll find greater meaning in a trial of solitude."

For six days I'd travel alone north from Burney Falls as "Solo-man." I was excited to hike alone, to make each and every decision for myself, to walk at my natural pace without stopping to look back, and to have hours of time to myself. I was also scared—scared that I wouldn't like it, but mostly frightened of being frightened. It had been a long time since I had spent a night in the woods alone.

X ▪ ▪ ▪ ▪ X

Returning to the trail at Burney Falls, it turned out, was just as difficult as getting off of it—actually more so, because I didn't have Angela around to look cute and help get hitchhikes. By the time I'd negotiated the six steps required to get back to the trail—plane, shuttle, taxi, Greyhound bus, rural bus, and hitchhike—a full day and a half had gone by. But at least I had a guidebook section with me; I'd managed to photocopy Toby's Section O before we left Burney for the wedding.

Record heat was blasting the West, and wildfires and brownouts were plaguing California. My last night in civilization, low-lying Redding, had been so steamy that I'd pulled the mattress off the bed at the Econo Lodge and placed it right next to the econo air conditioning unit. And still I'd slept in a pool of my own sweat. It wasn't much cooler at Lake Britton, two miles from Burney Falls, when I headed uphill. My pack was feeling heavy and unwieldy due to an assortment of items taken from Angela's pack—sleeping bag, titanium pot, stove, and ground cloth. As I climbed 2,500 feet over dry and exposed trail, with just one water source along the way, I was miserable.

Over the past seven days, I'd physically and mentally atrophied from trail life; my back ached, hot spots rapidly formed on my pinky toes, and sweat dribbled down my forehead. Worst of all, I'd lost the mental edge. I thought about quitting, turning around and heading right back to Burney. It might take several days and a dozen modes of transportation, but I could find my way to SFO Airport and from there to Boston. I'd meet Angela in Andover, Massachusetts for Amie's wedding and afterward we would take Amtrak back to Philly. I'd have no trouble filling the rest of the summer with golf, pool parties, and barbecues, lots of barbecues. There'd be leisurely mornings with a couple cups of coffee, afternoons sunning myself by the pool, and big juicy chicken thighs on the grill. It was tempting, very tempting, but as my stomach screamed, "Chicken!" my legs stoically whispered, "Canada!" After nearly three months on the trail they knew no other direction, and by the end of the day they'd carried me fourteen miles, to Peavine Creek.

Still, the day's challenges weren't through. Now I had to make camp without Angela. After more than two trail months, I was habituated to our routine and our teamwork—I constructed the tent and inflated the ThermaRests while she set up the bedding and started making dinner, or, if we'd already eaten, a hot drink. I didn't have the tent with me, but I still faced a daunting number of tasks. I felt like an assembly line worker suddenly trying to integrate his task with those ahead and behind. I was lost. The simple decision of what to do first—prepare my bed, clean off, or make dinner—felt excessively difficult. I attacked the dilemma by completely unloading Big Red, an act usually reserved for town. By the time I was done, the basic camping tasks had taken three times as long as they should have, and I laid down on a soft grassy bed, completely exhausted.

I was just beginning to relax when a loud and grating noise exploded from a manzanita bush ten feet in front of me. *Click-grate, click-grate.* It was a cricket, chirping ceaselessly and with a poorly tuned voice.

"Ignore him," I said to myself. "Ignore and sleep."

Twenty minutes later: *click-grate, click-grate.* It was as if his whole life depended on the continuation of that immensely aggravating clicking. *Click-grate, click-grate, click-grate.* This had to stop. I felt to my right and grabbed my Nalgene bottle and hurled it at the bush.

Click-grate.

Next went the stove, then the propane container, and finally the pot.

Click-grate.

That persistent bugger. "How rude," I thought. "I'll shut him up." I dragged myself up and staggered forward. *Hssssssssssssssssss.* I relieved my bladder in the bushes.

Blissful silence.

I picked through the manzanita and ceanothus in the morning, retrieving wayward items. At least the cricket had distracted me from what I'd feared most about being alone—nighttime thoughts filled with spooks like bears, Bigfoot, and criminals.

I slowly refilled Big Red with dew-moistened items and hoisted it onto my back. Its weight pushed sharply on my shoulders. As I started climbing, the buzzing of chain saws frequently irritated my nerves. Since leaving the Sierra we'd seen numerous areas of clear-cut forest, but this was my first extended exposure to the blight brought on by the timber industry. Clear-cuts are never attractive, but when you've been walking through pristine wilderness for weeks on end, the visual impact of the destruction strikes home especially hard.

Two of the predominant victims of clear-cuts in northern California are the California red fir and a closely related hybrid, the Shasta red fir. The California red fir, *abies magnifica*, grows up to 250 feet tall with a diameter of two to five feet. It's named after the color of its bark—ashy white when young, but dark reddish brown and deeply furrowed when mature. Fluorescent-green Brillo-padlike moss called wolf lichen often circles its trunk, indicating the previous year's snow line. Some of the red fir's lower branches grow close and perpendicular to the trunk, giving the illusion of clouds pressed against a mountain peak. On steep slopes, its trunk curves up out of the ground like a swan's neck. Early morning in a grove of red fir can take on an enchanted aura, like a medieval fairy tale. *Abies magnifica* is indeed a magnificent and ethereal tree. It is also an easily harvested tree. The timber industry values the red fir not for its mysticism but for its sparse understory—it can be felled and harvested without the annoying chore of clearing deciduous undergrowth.

Now, I'm certainly no forestry expert, and I appreciate plywood and two-by-fours as much as the next guy, but these clear-cuts pissed me right off. I was angry like a rabid football fan wronged by an official's errant ruling. I tried to remind myself that the local economy and many families' livelihoods depended on harvesting the red fir. I attempted to summon feelings of gratitude for the timber industry. "We should raise the price of toilet paper a buck a roll," a Burney local had said to me, "so we'll all feel it in the ass." It didn't help; the artificial swath through the forest was too painful a reminder of man's worldwide assault on ecosystems and biodiversity. Having studied this issue extensively in college, I was well aware that on a region-by-region or forest-by-forest basis it was easy to rationalize habitat disruption and economic development over preservation. But in the big picture, we risked something much more important than job stability or affordable toilet paper.

In his book, *The Diversity of Life*, botanist E. O. Wilson likens the worldwide loss of habitat and biodiversity to a large experiment, one in which the entire planet is the subject. He speculates that we may some day reach a critical level of biodiversity loss beyond which the planet will not be able to sustain life, human or otherwise. A century and a half before, Chief Sealth had warned President Franklin Pierce, "Whatever befalls the Earth, befalls the sons of Earth. Man did not weave the web of life, he is merely a strand of it. Whatever he does to the earth, he does to himself." It seemed to me that in the face of global warming and epidemic levels of pollution-associated disease, these words were truer than ever.

X ■ ▪ ▪ ■ X

As I continued my stroll through the plywoods on a dusty and scorchingly hot day, my anger eventually gave way to fatigue and from fatigue it drifted to indifference. Worldwide appreciation of biodiversity would be great, but today I would settle for a trail that was reasonably free of debris. Section O had, over the last decade, gained the reputation as the most poorly maintained section of the PCT. Unattended tree blowdowns and trailside overgrowth had made this area a bush-whacking experience. The guidebook described backpacking through portions of Section O-vergrowth as being "little better than cross-country hiking." Because of this, it is common for PCT hikers to skip Section O-shit and walk on Highway 89 or Forest Service roads instead. While I found the trail conditions to be better than expected (thanks to volunteers from the previous summer), I was still grateful for the midday opportunity to jump onto Forest Service Road 38N10, which my map showed as paralleling the trail for twenty-three miles.

At least I thought it was Road 38N10, but I couldn't be completely sure. Forest Service personnel must have excellent memories, or maybe they just don't mind getting lost, because they rarely bother to label their roads. And, as I soon found out, there were lots of unlabeled dirt roads branching all over the place. After some time and several confusing intersections, it occurred to me that I was walking east–northeast rather than the correct north–northwest. Eight miles later I was greeted by the *whoosh* of vehicles traveling at great speeds. It was the always lovely and scenic Highway 89.

I spent a long, hot afternoon walking along the highway's four-foot shoulder. Trucks stacked a story high with fresh timber raced by at eighty miles an hour just feet from me; acres and acres of forest must have sped by that afternoon, all on the way to their destiny in an Ikea showroom. Each time a loaded truck passed me I ducked my head to avoid the ensuing dirt cloud and wind gust.

Kimmo and the other JourneyFilm Crew boys must have loved this. We'd been keeping up with the JourneyFilm Crew via their periodic web updates, and I'd recently seen that they'd embarked on an extended road walk, from Old Station (mile 1372) to ten miles south of Ashland (mile 1722). They'd started out along Highway 89 and finished on Interstate 5, all the while staying at hotels and traveling light, covering 350 serpentine trail miles in approximately 150 direct, point-A-to-point-B road ones. They'd apparently abandoned the notion of breaking Ray and Jenny Jardine's record, but Kimmo and J. B. continued to hike with speed and purpose. While Joe had dropped behind to savor the scenery, Kimmo was intent on pushing himself to the limit. Recently, he'd completed the "pyramid of death," a five-day, 190-mile endurance test that followed a 30-40-50-40-30 mile-per-day sequence. J. B. did his best to keep up, but did so with a different goal in mind. J. B. had left his sweetheart at home, thinking of his hike as a period of reflection and growth before taking the next romantic step. Now, it seemed, he was determined to finish as quickly as possible so that he could rediscover the comforts of female companionship. After only two days as Solo-man, I was quickly gaining appreciation for his perspective.

Following the JourneyFilm Crew's path on Highway 89, I was shocked to discover that by midafternoon I was only sixteen miles from McCloud and twenty-nine from Mount Shasta City. Not too shabby considering that Mount Shasta City is eighty-three trail miles from Burney Falls. Less than a mile later there was more good news: A 1970s-vintage road sign advertised Bartle Lodge, food, and cocktails.

Bartle Lodge was a logger's bar, and if this wasn't evident from the dirty hats, scruffy faces, and sap-smeared jeans of the clientele, the ornamentation on the wall erased all doubt: "Destroy our country—join an environmental group," and "Loggers pay taxes, owls don't." The bartender, Rufus, had white hair and a white beard and could have passed for Kenny Rogers if it weren't for the tube of styling gel that had attacked his white mane. Rufus wasn't particularly friendly, but he served me a beer and a 7-Up so I restrained myself from offering rebuttals to his bumper stickers, such as "Owls are loud, but loggers are loud *and* ugly," and "Destroy our race—reproduce with a logger."

It turned out to be a good thing that I kept my opinions to myself, because after a second soda and a heavier tip, Rufus warmed up and asked me what my story was. The offshoot of the conversation was that I discovered a more scenic (and less dangerous) way to travel the next fifteen miles. Two miles up, explained Rufus, was a paved road to a campground, and from there a trail branched along the McCloud River all the way to the town of McCloud.

Thanking Rufus heartily and trying to ignore the creeping suspicion that loggers could be good people too, I cruised those two miles and then set up camp on a patch of sand underneath a bridge. I slept well, despite the periodic pattering and scurrying of an unseen rodent and a strange drop of liquid that fell on my face in the middle of night.

The next morning I followed the McCloud River west. Ten soothing miles passed alongside a succession of inviting swimming holes. Eventually I reached a series of waterfalls, each tumbling into magnificent pools of clear blue water. I stopped at the Middle Falls, a seventy-by-seventy-foot cascade, and ate lunch on boulders adjacent to the pool. As I ate, I caught whiffs of the refreshing spray from the impact of water on water. Two pudgy young kids swam across the pool and stood on a ledge not far from the falls, holding fishing poles and looking intently into the blue-green water. I pondered whether they would actually eat anything they caught and whether such variation might throw off a finely tuned Taco Bell diet.

All too soon I was on Highway 89 again, being blown back and forth by logging trucks for the remaining seventeen miles to Mount Shasta City. I entertained myself during this monotonous trek by counting cars and trucks moving north and south. I wondered if Kimmo and J.B. had discovered this scintillating form of entertainment.

Things were much more civilized for Solo-man in the peaceful town of Mount Shasta City. Round Table Pizza and the Mount Shasta Inn saw to that. Lying on a queen-size bed with remote control in hand, I tried to call Angela but couldn't get through. I was lonely and missed her. Hiking solo was a fine novelty for several days, but without Angela I'd quickly lost interest. I'd assumed that I'd move faster without her, that the miles would fly by as I pushed myself to see how far and how fast I could go. But for the most part I'd dragged along. The crazy notion of thru-hiking seemed senseless without her there to share it. Together this hike had meaning; alone it didn't.

All this made me wonder about the motivational construct of solo-hikers. How does a guy like Brian Robinson, who hiked the Triple Crown (the three longest National Scenic Trails—the PCT, AT, and Continental Divide Trail) in the calendar year 2001, stay motivated? Robinson, a forty-one-year-old systems engineer known as "Flyin' Brian," hiked for 300 days and 7,400 miles, and did virtually all of it by his lonesome. During his ten-month Triple Crown, Flyin' Brian averaged more than thirty miles a day through twenty-two states. Along the way he went through seven pairs of running shoes, suffered from frostbite and Bell's Palsy (temporary facial paralysis), hiked through snow up to his hips, and climbed an estimated one million vertical feet. Why did he do it?

"I did it because I needed a challenge," Robinson says. "I wanted to do something I could be proud of for the rest of my life." I can identify with Brian's need to challenge himself and do something memorable. But the isolation? I couldn't handle it. It would be too lonely and the payoff wouldn't be great enough. Scaling Mount Whitney, dodging rattlesnakes, and running through hailstorms—all of those adventures would still be memorable if they were experienced on your own, but to me they were much more meaningful when shared.

While the appeal of solo-hiking had worn off, the reality was that I still had many solo miles to cover. My dilemma was this: My initial goal had been to hike the full length of Sections O and P (183 miles) before meeting Angela in Etna. But at this point to do so would require hiking a hundred miles in less than three days without a guidebook (I'd traveled out of range of the pages I'd photocopied from Toby), without motivation, and through an extended heat wave. It wasn't going to happen. I needed to find a map and design an alternate route.

In the morning, my first stop was the Mount Shasta City post office. The hiker box was virtually empty, but there was a message from Amigo in the trail register.

"Lodgepole, I have some news for you—Foxtail has left you for *Douglas Fir*. She told me that she was *sycamore* of you and needed a new *manzanita*." Good old Amigo, how did he maintain such cheerful creativity while hiking? And what was he doing moving in on my woman?

Amigo's note mobilized a thought that had been percolating in my heart and mind for some time. While eating breakfast at the Black Bear Diner, I resolved to set aside a few minutes to visit a jeweler. I'd been carrying an engagement ring with me since Campo, and I wanted to be prepared in case the perfect opportunity presented itself. Maybe at Forester Pass, or on top of Whitney? It hadn't seemed right, though, not perfect; we were always in a rush, or too tired, or too dirty, or Angela had a large piece of freeze-dried chicken stuck between her front teeth. Even if the perfect opportunity for a proposal had arrived, we would have been celebrating it with a ten dollar stainless steel circlet from Miller's Outpost. I wasn't sure how well that would go over.

At the local jeweler, I was educated on the four C's of diamond picking. All of you marriage-age males out there are probably familiar with this simple guide to choosing the perfect diamond. It goes like this: *C* for "cost," *C* for "costly," *C* for "cut the crap, it doesn't cost that much," and *C* for "you can't be serious, it doesn't really cost that much, does it?" Or something like that. I never really got past the cost part. I am not really a good impulse shopper, so I didn't purchase a ring that day. For the time being, I would have to keep carrying the excess piece of Miller's Outpost baggage. The thought of a marriage proposal would continue to be a nebulous one, at least for now.

My next stop was a bookstore, where I found a copy of the guidebook and jotted down as much Section P information as possible. I bought a map and hatched a shortcut that I hoped would get me to Etna in time to meet Angela.

My brilliant scheme was to follow Forest Service Road 40N30 along the South Fork of the Sacramento River from Lake Siskiyou eleven miles up to the PCT. This route would save me fifteen miles of trail, not to mention the hassle of a hitchhike to Castle Crags.

In retrospect, I am not sure what I was thinking; perhaps all that diamond shopping had gone to my head. I walked over Highway 5 past a fish hatchery and an Evangelical Free church to Lake Siskiyou. Then I hiked along dusty North Shore Drive under droopy-branched Douglas firs and looked for Forest Service road 40N30. I looked and looked and looked some more. I ended up circling the Lake Siskiyou area and nearly all of its dirt roads and trails, for two entire days. I hiked many miles—I am not sure how many, but many—and pretty much all of them in circles. At the point when I realized that Road 40N30 didn't actually exist but instead was a figment of a mapmaker's imagination, I decided that I'd just walk, it didn't matter so much where. I hiked seven miles up to Castle Lake and then half-heartedly attempted to clamber over a ridge where the map showed the PCT. I suppose the trail was up there somewhere, but I didn't find it; instead I discovered a nice meadow where I sat down with my diary.

I stretched out, back propped up by Big Red, and gazed at a field of long grasses, purple and yellow daisies, Indian paintbrush, buttercups, and scattered pines. The meadow was spotted with Queen Anne's lace—fine white flowers that make a slightly domed clump. Plump black bumblebees danced around the clumps, their landings causing the flowers to bend over dramatically, nearly to the ground.

To the northeast I had a fantastic view of 14,162-foot Mount Shasta, the second-highest mountain in the Cascades. On the PCT, Mount Shasta is viewed for 300 miles of trail, a testament both to the mountain's magnitude as well as to the crazy zigzagging the trail does in northern California.

"Lonely as God and white as a winter moon," poet Joaquin Miller wrote of Mount Shasta, and I guarantee that this quotation isn't lonely; it's included in everything I've ever read about the volcano. And now it's in my own writing as well. The streets of Mount Shasta City are lined with flags that declare, "Shasta, where Heaven and Earth meet," which just scratches the surface of the mystical feel that surrounds this mountain. Some think Shasta is sacred; others believe that lost civilizations live in the old lava tunnels that crisscross her innards. Native Americans of the region rarely dared to venture into those dark, winding caves because they believed Sasquatch, the legendary ape-man, made his home in them. From my idyllic meadow I looked at the lonely and gigantic mountain and vowed to someday climb to its peak—maybe I'd even see Bigfoot along the way.

X ▪ ▪ ▪ X

My exploration as Solo-man drew to a close with a dip in Lake Siskiyou, a night in a grove of incense cedar and Ponderosa pine, and finally a several-mile road walk back to where I started—Mount Shasta City.

My plan was to surprise Angela at the Greyhound station in Yreka, and then, happily reunited, we'd travel to Etna by rural bus. I couldn't wait to see her. Six days without her playful chirps, nuzzles, and pats had been extremely difficult. I needed to reconnect the umbilical cord; I hadn't functioned well without it. I was happy to retire Solo-man and his routeless blundering. This is not to say that my solo-hike hadn't been memorable— I'd hiked many miles, meandered the hills above and around a beautiful lake, and written prolifically in my journal. It was just that, much like my vision quest ten years prior, this solo experience had been all about girls. Well, actually, *the* girl, and getting her back.

[13]

Cuddles

 THE TRIP FROM REDDING TO YREKA was picturesque and pleasant—something I never imagined possible on a Greyhound bus. Traveling on Interstate 5 we passed red-banked Shasta Lake and sneaked under the formidable granitic spires of Castle Crags before arriving in Yreka, a town whose greatest claim to fame may be that it was once the capital of America's fifty-first state—but more about that later.

I'd never been to Yreka before, but as soon as I stepped onto its oil-stained pavement, I felt like I belonged. Yreka had a PCT-feel—it was the kind of place where people still wore cowboy hats and Wranglers and where you just might see a mule-train in the Wal-Mart parking lot.

Before I even had a chance to look for my bus I caught a glimpse of a familiar silhouette. Turning, I was greeted by a hearty wave, toothy grin, and prominent ears. He was still three blocks away, but I yelled "Duffy!" and sprinted. There on the sidewalk we collided in a hug so fierce that for one ecstatic, exciting moment we forgot to breathe.

"What are you doing here?" I asked, "I thought we were meeting in Etna! How'd you get here?" I was shocked, relieved, and overjoyed. Covering 180 miles in a week had been a lofty goal and I'd figured I might have to wait for Duffy in Etna.

"It wasn't the same," Duffy said when I asked him about his adventures as Solo-man. The freedom and spontaneity had been fun at first, but day to day, he said, he enjoyed hiking with me much better. I can't tell you how pleased I was to hear that.

194

Ideal hiking partnerships are mutually beneficial in that each member of the party contributes to the experience of the other and benefits in kind. Partners split decision-making and burdens; lend each other encouragement; and share their thoughts, feelings, fears, and hopes. "A good partnership," writes Jardine in *Beyond Backpacking*, "leads to a deeper knowledge of oneself, and of one's companions, as well as a better understanding of the journey as a whole, its hardships and triumphs, its daily delights." For couples this can be a make-or-break proposition because on-trail they face extremes they'd probably never encounter at home. This makes teamwork crucial not only for physical survival but for the survival of the relationship and the expedition.

Looking back on our rocky desert start, I was surprised that we'd made it this far. Baptism by fire can work, but it can also backfire. And, as I later realized, there may be better ways to learn how to backpack.

In a section of *Beyond Backpacking*, Jardine explains how a more experienced hiker should introduce backpacking to a neophyte. "Teach beginners how to enjoy hiking and camping by ensuring that the experiences will be pleasant." Does hiking twenty waterless and heat-exhausted miles through the desert count?

"The person with [genuine outdoor skills] will foresee and avoid any unpleasant incidents," Jardine continues, "he or she will keep from exhausting the partner with a heavy load and a fast pace." And finally, some words about how to react to a novice, "lend gentle encouragement while extending illimitable patience. Ignore the inevitable mistakes, and give recognition to the many accomplishments."

Because Duffy and I jumped on the PCT without either of us having much backpacking experience, we missed the opportunity to "avoid unpleasant circumstances" or "keep from exhausting [ourselves] with a heavy load and fast pace." And certainly, because we'd been so focused on learning the basics, we hadn't had enough time or energy to provide each other with encouragement. Despite our ignorance of such matters, however, we'd managed to muddle through and in the process discovered that, as Jardine says, "Each failure teaches more of what you need to know in order to succeed."

We were still miles and miles from success, however—1,055 miles to be exact. Yet I was proud of our accomplishment thus far—of all the thousands of steps we'd taken and of the lessons we'd learned. Duffy continued to push me to go longer and stronger while doing so with more loving kindness and patience. As for me, I tried not to take the frequent moments of silence or physical distance personally. Instead of continually rushing to catch up, I trundled along as fast or as slow as my feet wanted to go.

X ▪ ▪ ▪ ▪ X

We got back on the trail at Etna Summit on August 8, the ninety-third day of our pilgrimage north. Here in the Marble Mountain Wilderness, the PCT cuts along narrow river valleys and climbs forested ridges. Against these deep green forests, the limestone peak of Marble Mountain stands out brilliantly, like a diamond set amongst emeralds. In fact, all of the 214,500-acre Marble Mountain Wilderness seemed like treasure.

In the company of deer and wildflowers so tall they tickled my elbows, we followed the PCT across steep rock-strewn and colorful slopes into wooded valleys. Sugar pines abounded, with their spires reaching 200 feet toward the sky, the thick canopy blocking out nearly all light. Large, airy, oval-shaped cones littered the path, and we kicked them like footballs as we went. We had fifty-six miles to cover before our next brief stop in civilization, at Seiad Valley.

Our first night back on the trail we camped near a murky green lake. Hard thunderclaps woke us before dawn and we scrambled out to put on our rain fly and cover our packs with garbage bags. Lazily, we lay under our sleeping bag until nine in the morning, waiting for an end to the pitter-patter and eating several meals in the process. Finally, we realized that since Canada wasn't going to come to us, we had to eventually get moving, rain or no rain. Conveniently, soon after we packed up our gear the skies cleared.

My body was still readjusting to the thru-hiking schedule, so we made camp early that night, under a gnarled and stately pine. In the distance a black cloud giving off streaks of gray cut into a pink, sunset-infused sky. As the evening progressed the sky became entirely black. I sat on a root that undulated in and out of the earth like a sea serpent and tended our pasta. Usually, we didn't eat and sleep in the same location. Fearing hungry bears, we typically utilized Jardine's "stealth camping" technique—cooking our dinner miles before choosing a (less established) campsite. Theoretically, this practice helped prevent bear invasions by limiting the number of tasty scents that emanated from our camp and keeping us away from campsites that bears habitually raid. But that night, because of my exhaustion and the imminent rain, we not only camped at a well-worn site but also cooked right outside our tent. At the time, we didn't think much of the indiscretion. So far we hadn't had much trouble with bears. Actually, our confidence was such that we had gotten in the habit of sleeping with our food bag nestled in the tent. I think it's part of the thru-hiker mentality to ignore conventional wisdom when it comes to bears; after all, thru-hikers tend to ignore conventional wisdom regarding a lot of things

Since the desert I'd slept soundly in our tent, falling asleep quickly and not waking up until Duffy's watch alarm went off. But during the darkest hours of that night, I awoke—not with a start, but slowly and disoriented, wondering whether I had to pee, or was cold—why on earth was I awake? And then I heard it.

Not three feet from my head, with only a thin layer of nylon to protect me: heavy steps and snuffling. The steps were slow, the sniffing erratic, and while I couldn't see our visitor, I knew immediately it was a bear. I could tell by Duffy's breathing that he was awake, too, but neither of us spoke or moved. My foot rested on the green nylon bag that held our food—a veritable feast of peanut butter, raisins, Snickers bars, and instant pudding mix. The intruder could have it all with one swipe of his paw. But slowly, the footsteps quieted and we were left with just the rustling of leaves in the wind.

"Oh, my God," I squealed, after I hadn't heard anything bearlike for a couple of minutes. "What if he'd ripped into our tent?"

"At least we have a tent," Duffy said.

He was right. Even though the nylon didn't provide any real protection from bear claws, I felt safer inside.

"Yeah, I couldn't handle staring a bad-breathed bear in the face. I'd pass out."

"Then you'd be bear food." Duffy tried to lighten the mood.

"I can't believe that Casey and Toby still sleep out after what happened to them."

While our late-night visitor either wasn't hungry enough or didn't like the aroma of our MREs enough to relieve us of our heavy food bag, Casey and Toby hadn't been so lucky. While in the Sierra, day hikers gave Crazy Legs and Catch-23 a foot-long salami, which they devoured in one sitting. "The only problem with receiving the salami," Catch-23 later wrote, "was that with it we received the salami wrapper . . . and we were in bear country." Like many thru-hikers, Crazy Legs and Catch-23 slept with their food. On the evening of their salami snack, just as Catch-23 zipped himself up in his sleeping bag, he heard a strange ripping sound. Poking his head out he came face to face—in fact within inches—of a drooling bear. The bear was in the process of tearing into the food bag he'd just extracted from Catch-23's pack by neatly slitting it open with a single claw. In an effort to scare away their uninvited dinner guest, the Seattle boys started singing, banging on their cooking pot, throwing rocks, and clapping. After a few minutes the bear moved away and Toby rescued what was left of their food supply. But still the bear lingered in the bushes, as if waiting for them to go back to sleep. That didn't seem like a "keepin' it real" sort of scenario, so the boys packed up and left.

X ▪ ▪ ▪ X

We didn't sleep much the rest of the night, and when morning came we bolted quickly out of camp. The trail down to Seiad Valley led us through a tunnel of blackberry brambles and tall pines. It was early afternoon and we were cruising. Rounding a switchback, our ears were suddenly assaulted with the sound of something crashing through the trees, scratching on bark and breaking branches. At first I thought it was two squirrels fighting. But as we got within ten feet of the commotion I saw something large and brown shuffling up a sugar pine's trunk. When the furry creature reached a height of about fifteen feet, it stopped and peered down at us. "A cub!" I squeaked, delighted that my first face-to-face bear contact was with a cuddly baby. His perked-up ears stood out against the bright blue sky. Duffy whipped out the camera and started snapping photos. I cooed at the cub and called him "Cuddles." He was on our right, and suddenly to our left we heard a much louder ruckus.

"It's momma," whispered Duffy. "We gotta go." As if we could hide our presence now. He scooped up a handful of rocks, started singing "Heigh-ho, heigh-ho, it's off to work we go" at the top of his lungs, and began hurrying down the trail—all in the same instant. I grabbed some rocks, too, joined in the song, and scurried behind. Black bears are rarely violent, but if there's anything that can set those fangs a-gnashing, it's getting between momma and cub.

In his chillingly titled book *Bear Attacks: Their Causes and Avoidance,* author Stephen Herrero, Ph.D., provides a comprehensive review of two decades' worth of maulings. Herrero reports that between 1960 and 1980, black bears caused five hundred human injuries and twenty-three deaths. But despite those twenty-three deaths, Herrero asserts that sudden encounters with black bears don't usually end in injury. More commonly, when a person surprises a black bear, the bear will charge and swat the ground with a front paw or make loud huffing noises but ultimately disappear. That said, it's not unheard of for a mother black bear to maul a human in an effort to protect her young. Herrero cites a 1973 incident in Yellowstone Park in which a momma bear pulled a fleeing man from a tree by his foot and "proceeded to maul and bite him." The man required seventy-one stitches.

Flying in the face of conventional backpacker wisdom, Herrero gives another (more gruesome) example that demonstrates that black bears can be just as ferocious as their grizzly, Kodiak, and polar counterparts. In 1950, sixty-five-year-old Athabascan Indian Alexie Pitka was hunting black bear in Alaska. After firing a shot, he waited to make sure that the bear was motionless before approaching. When he walked to within several yards of the downed bear, the creature suddenly rolled to its feet and leaped on him. Pitka survived the attack but the "entire right side of his face from the eye across to the nose and down to the chin was torn away. The right eye was ripped out of the socket. . . . His nose was torn off, with cartilage sticking out of raw flesh. The right cheek and part of the left were gone. . . . Three teeth were left in the jaw; the rest were dangling loose." This mauling, writes Herrero, "is a stark reminder of the power that black bears can unleash." In fact, black bears can bite through trees thicker than your arm and kill a full-grown steer with one chomp to the neck. The most dangerous blackie, says Herrero, "appears to be one that attacks a person who has been hiking, walking, berry picking, fishing or playing during the day in a rural or remote area."

That sounded awfully familiar. We were glad to escape the momma bear encounter without testing the strength of her bite.

X ▪ ▪ ▪ ▪ X

It was my third day back on the PCT, and my trail legs were coming back to me. That, combined with the adrenaline released by two bear encounters in less than twelve hours, helped to speed me along. The terrain was beautiful and the weather hot—just another day on the PCT, or so it seemed. But something was different—we were walking our last California miles. A new state, Oregon, lay on the horizon. But really, we were already in a new state; we just didn't know it yet. We were in the fifty-first state, the State of Jefferson.

Located in the mountainous border regions of what is "commonly known as California and Oregon," the State of Jefferson dates back to a secession movement in the 1940s. Mostly, the first Jefferson secession movement was about roads—or lack thereof. Migration brought settlers to the region in the 1840s and 1850s, and mining and agriculture convinced them to stay. But the people of Jefferson were, and are, miles away from centers of commerce, and this led to feelings of isolation and neglect. In the 1940s, Jeffersonians complained that poor roadways hindered their logging, mining, and agriculture industries and that they were being "double-crossed" by the leaders of California and Oregon. Today, the "double-cross," or "XX," is a common Jefferson symbol found on tee shirts, hats, suspenders, bumper stickers, signs, and graffiti-ridden walls.

The name "Jefferson" was chosen for the state in 1941 via a popular vote conducted by the *Siskiyou Daily News*. The inspiration was, of course, Thomas Jefferson, who championed the rights of states to govern themselves.

After choosing a name, the residents of Jefferson took immediate action by blocking Highway 99 outside of Yreka and levying "taxes" on those who tried to enter. At the roadblocks they handed out a *Proclamation of Independence*, which began:

> You are now entering Jefferson, the 49th State of the Union. [This was before Hawaii and Alaska became states.] *Jefferson is now in patriotic rebellion against the States of California and Oregon. This State has seceded from California and Oregon this Thursday, November 27th, 1941. . . .*

In Yreka, on December 4, 1941, Judge John L. Childs was inaugurated governor of Jefferson. Signs all over town signs read, "Our roads are not passable, hardly jackassable; if our roads you would travel, bring your own gravel." Three days later, the tragedy at Pearl Harbor changed everyone's perspective and the movement was temporarily forgotten while most of the region's men went off to war.

Today, State of Jefferson supporters live on and continue to criticize government officials in the state capitals of Sacramento and Salem for imposing environmental and land-use regulations on a region they don't know or understand. "People from the Bay Area and southern California," a Yreka resident told a reporter for the *Contra Costa Times*, "have no idea of what actually transpires in rural America." Indeed, to the uninitiated, entering the border region of Interstate 5 near Oregon can be like an episode of the *Twilight Zone*. Suddenly signs, graffiti, and twelve-foot black letters painted on the roof of a highway-side barn proclaim "The State of Jefferson"—a whole "state" most of us have never even heard of.

This is not to say that the State of Jefferson is merely a pipe dream amongst gun-toting rural anarchists. On the contrary. During sixty years of secession attempts, Jefferson proponents have come remarkably close to achieving their goal. In the early 1990s, California Assemblyman Stan Statham of Redding publicly advocated the division of California into two or three separate states and pushed the process far enough that an advisory plebiscite over the state's division appeared on the statewide California ballot. The logistics of getting statehood, however, remain a large hurdle. New states can't be carved out of existing ones without the approval of the state legislature and Congress. Beyond that, there are no laws on the books to govern such a procedure. Duffy joked that it was too bad that the measure hadn't gone through; if it had, we'd be finishing up our second or third state rather than just our first.

The PCT crosses the California–Oregon border in the middle of nowhere—approximately halfway between Seiad Valley on Highway 96 and Ashland, Oregon, on Interstate 5. Climbing out of Seiad Valley we followed interminable switchbacks through Douglas fir, incense cedar, Oregon oak, and poison oak as well as western white pines. We climbed approximately 3,000 feet and reached a saddle where the only place to put our tent was right in the middle of the trail. Figuring it was too late for anyone to be climbing behind us and that we'd be up and moving before any morning hikers could complete the climb, we pitched our tent literally on the PCT. Remembering that when Tweedle, the crazy goatee'd hiker from Agua Dulce, had once slept on the trail, he'd been stepped on by a stampeding buck and ended up in the hospital, I hesitated for a second. But as usual, I was too tired to argue.

The next day, crossing into Oregon felt like a significant occasion. But really, things looked the same on both sides of the border. Cows in either state were munching on meadow grass, noticing neither our presence nor our quiet celebrations. Standing at the wooden sign that marked the border, I waved good-bye to California while Duffy snapped a photograph.

Trail Mix

 AS WE APPROACHED THE OREGON BORDER, I saw an unpleasant face peering from the bushes ten feet away. His disheveled appearance and wild stare startled me. He wasn't a hiker—he wore ripped jeans and a hooded gray sweatshirt. I had no idea why he was cowering in the undergrowth, but I assumed his past to be checkered and intentions less than pure. Twenty yards up-trail I stopped and turned, gesturing for Angela to move quickly. She gave me a quizzical look and chugged her way up the hill. At the border I explained.

"Sorry to rush you, but I didn't like the look of that dude."

"What dude?" she asked.

"You didn't see that vagrant leering from the bushes? I though he might jump you."

"Nope, didn't see him. . . . Yikes, that's scary."

"Yeah, we should probably keep moving."

Amazingly, nearly 1,700 miles into our hike, this was the first suspicious person we'd seen. Sure, there'd been evidence of illegal immigrants and stories of vagabonds, but we'd never felt truly threatened on the trail. And while Chris and Stacey had seen a homeless man wandering the PCT north of Warner Springs without food or gear and severely sunburned, he was just asking for handouts and seemed more unfortunate than anything else. Angela *had* been accosted, but that was on the mean streets of Redding, far from the PCT.

The PCT travels through mostly sparsely populated territory so I hadn't worried all that much about strange men with evil intentions. The Appalachian Trail, however, is another story. Along much of its route, the AT is easily accessible and provides convenient shelters, which are especially convenient for people seeking asylum from the law. Over the last thirty years there have been numerous assaults, including nine murders, on or close to the AT. The most recent homicide (a double murder in the Shenandoah Valley) occurred in 1996—the same year that Bill Bryson hiked the trail. Eight years before that, Rebecca Wight and Claudia Brenner were stalked and attacked in the Michaux State Forest of south-central Pennsylvania by known fugitive Stephen Roy Carr. Wight was killed by a rifle shot at the scene; Brenner was wounded but escaped and reported the crime to authorities. In September of 1990, again in Pennsylvania, thru-hikers Molly LaRue and Geoffrey Hood were murdered at a shelter by fugitive P. David Crews (now on death row).

In contrast, the PCT hasn't seen a single murder in its nearly forty-year history, and I hadn't come across much evidence of any other type of violent crime on the trail.

Before our hike, a good friend asked whether I planned on packing heat while on the trail. I was skeptical. "A gun?" I said. "That's a heavy-ass piece of equipment." Furthermore, I explained, you'd need to bring a rifle to expect protection from crazed bears, and you'd be crazy to think you could shoot enough small game to feed yourself. And as for crazy people—I was more likely to encounter them outside my South Street apartment than on the PCT.

Several months before setting off from Campo I was mugged at knifepoint just thirty yards from my front door. This was profoundly frightening, but it hadn't provoked me to play Center City Dirty Harry. If I wasn't going to carry a gun in Philly, why would I on the PCT? Besides, it's illegal to carry a firearm in or through a national park. At the time, this argument made sense, but now, for the first time since the Mexican border, I wished I had some protection. We'd long since sent home our Counter Assault "grizzly tough" pepper spray and now all we had to defend ourselves with were beaten-up trekking poles and cross-trainer-clad feet. So we put them to use and after several quick photos strode quickly into Oregon, hoping to leave the wild-eyed stranger behind. We were following the extremely practical advice of Michael Bane who, in his book *Trail Safe: Averting Threatening Human Behavior in the Outdoors*, writes, "Distance is good, more distance is better. . . . You get a chance to run, you take it."

For several hours we walked briskly without a break, not looking back, using our fleet feet to deter altercation. Finally, I began to relax and appreciate that at last, at long last, we'd reached a new state. We'd walked the entire length of California. A truck driver on Interstate 5 could clear the state in sixteen hours or so; it had taken us three months.

X ▪ ▪ ▪ X

In general, the PCT is gentler in Oregon than in California, without brutal climbs or long, knee-rattling descents. For most of the state, the tread stays at comfortable altitudes of 5,000 to 6,000 feet. The PCT's highest elevation in Oregon is a benign 7,000 feet. Re-supply opportunities are primarily at remote backcountry lodges that beckon the thru-hiker to stop and relax for several days. In fact, there's only one major town, Ashland, near the Oregon trail, and we soon found ourselves on its outskirts. Ashland, home to an annual Shakespeare festival and a collection of quirky artists and hippies, is a mandatory stop for many hikers. It's a place where many plan their entire Oregon re-supply, packing and sending boxes on to Crater Lake, Shelter Cove, Olallie Lake, and Timberline Lodge. But our boxes were already packed and in the mail from Philadelphia, and as much as Ashland tempted us, there was no pressing need to visit. So we spent our first night in Oregon camped in the backyard of Callahan's, a homey restaurant and lodge a mile from the trail along Highway 99.

The next morning we followed the trail through rather mundane scenery and clear-cuts, catching several final glimpses of Mount Shasta to the south. The first fifty or so miles of Oregon's PCT are through BLM land and well below the Cascade Crest. In part because BLM land is managed with a "multiple-use" principle that permits a variety of recreational and economic activities (including timber harvest and cattle grazing), much of the old-growth forest in this region had been leveled, making it less than ideal for hiking. I couldn't wait to get to higher and more scenic ground and looked forward to reaching the crest near Mount McLoughlin, the next sky-reaching volcano.

That evening, at Green Springs Inn near Hyatt Lake (mile 1,745), we enjoyed delicious beer bread and chicken salad while chatting with the inn's owner, Diarmuid. The hot topic was President Clinton's designation of fifty-two thousand acres of wilderness surrounding Pilot Rock as a national monument. Pilot Rock, a gray stump of an old volcano, is just a short side hike from the PCT. Nationally, environmentalists applauded Clinton's use of executive power (through the Antiquities Act of 1906) to protect Pilot Rock and its environs, but many in the Hyatt Lake area were upset. Some locals apparently didn't agree with the rationale for banning off-road, all-terrain, super-suspension, rock- and dirt-busting vehicles from pristine roadless areas. It was probably some of these same residents who demonstrated their appreciation of the PCT by surrounding it with electric fences and signs that threatened trespassing hikers.

Diarmuid was an exception to the prevailing sentiment, though; he seemed to enjoy talking about the trail and its hikers.

"Catch-23 and Crazy Legs were here a couple days ago," he announced, and then whispered, "so were Sunrise and Mirage."

Sunrise and Mirage were an Israeli couple we'd initially met in Kennedy Meadows and then bumped into a few times in the Sierra. Now, according to Diarmuid, they were on the verge of breaking up. This didn't surprise me; I hadn't thought they were a particularly good match. Sunrise was no-nonsense; she'd served her mandatory Israeli military service driving tanks and had been driving Mirage hard all summer. Mirage, tall, lanky and brittle-looking, on the other hand, tried to take a leisurely approach to thru-hiking; he never appeared to be in a great hurry to get anywhere. This irritated Sunrise, and she'd often resort to verbal abuse to keep them moving, but Mirage's waifish ass was proving to be more difficult to move than an Israeli tank. Now, said Diarmuid, there was a new, unnamed love interest in Sunrise's eye and Mirage might soon be heading home. Their ill-conceived umbilical cord had dried, frayed, and snapped. Meadow Ed's skepticism was justified; the thru-hiking business was tough on couplehood.

The evidence was continuing to mount and I was reminded of Dan White's story of love on the rocks, recounted in the *San Jose Mercury News*. In 1996 Dan and his girlfriend Rebecca set off to thru-hike the PCT. His expectations were high. "I thought of great dinners, fresh air and endless lust in the woods. I imagined Christopher Atkins and Brooke Shields eating guavas and shacking up with abandon in *The Blue Lagoon*." Well, it didn't work out quite so nicely for Dan and Rebecca; differences in hiking style, motivation, and appreciation of dirt all contributed to the downfall of their hike and their relationship. At the end of it all, Dan offered this advice to lovers on the trail: "Lighten the mood in any way you can. Rebecca and I did this with terms of endearment. I called her 'Rat Face' and she called me 'Fish Body.'"

If playful nicknames were the key to success, Angela and I were on the right track. Sometime back I'd started calling her "Piggy Mouth"—in reference to her delicate but rapid style of food shoveling. In the Sierra this had been a highly contentious issue—the nightly ritual of speed slurping had turned dinners into races, and what started as a minor annoyance eventually became a bitter article of debate. Since then, I'd consistently made comments (perhaps some of them snide) about Angela's table manners and she grew increasingly resentful of the nitpicking. As it turns out, women don't appreciate having their eating habits questioned. Perhaps if I'd read *Men Are from Mars, Women Are from Venus*, I would have already known as much.

In his relationship guide, author John Gray, Ph.D., intimately explores the root causes of conflict between men and women. Of particular interest to clueless guys like me is Gray's chapter on "101 ways to score points with a woman." After our summer on the Crest, I scanned the list with interest and while I wasn't surprised to see suggestions such as "If she is tired offer to make her some tea" (number eighty-three), and "Leave the bathroom seat down" (number 101) on the list, I was shocked that "Sarcastically call her 'Chiggy the Piggy'" was left off. And for that matter, so were "Demand larger portions of food," "Accuse her of starving you," and "Compliment her on her burgeoning armpit stubble." No *wonder* we'd ended up in an ugly food fight.

Despite the abundant practical advice I found on Gray's list, some of the suggestions just weren't applicable to relationships on the trail. For example, on the PCT it would be impossible for me to "Sharpen her knives in the kitchen" (number sixty-three) and extremely difficult, not to mention extraordinarily chilly, to "Wash before having sex" (number thirty-three).

Perhaps the reason why our calorie conflict ballooned into a larger argument about differences is better captured by a passage from the *Tao Te Ching*, said to be the world's oldest and most widely read book of wisdom. "All that is negative and injurious to your relationship is born of fear. Fear births jealousy, fuels anger, and prompts harsh words. The most difficult times contain the greatest fear. If you would live in love, do not be afraid." My fear of wasting away and our mutual fear of failure drove us to fight and provoked harsh words. Eventually, and without supplemental reading, we'd reached a compromise. I was content to stuff a few extra supplies into our food bag as long as Angela made some acknowledgment of my greater caloric needs and a token modification to her high-speed consumptive technique. It was a simple (if not perfect) solution to the problem, and an example of how simple life on the trail can be. Now if only we could stop making simple things so complicated.

In reality, on any given day there were only so many choices for us to make—how far to travel, how fast to travel, where to camp, and which of three types of dehydrated meals to eat. It's just that the disagreements we *did* have were magnified by the physical and emotional stress of thru-hiking. Hence, after two months on the trail, Angela and I had bickered over many small incompatibilities, most of which stemmed from discrepancies in hiking style and physical endurance. But so far we'd been able to handle them all and in my opinion were doing quite well. Much better, I think, than many expected.

Angela's parents had been outwardly critical in the beginning, but there were also plenty of others who were doubtful, just more subtly so. My parents, despite being extremely emotionally and financially supportive, were among these. In fact, it wasn't until just recently that they'd announced their intention to meet us on the trail—at Odell Lake Resort in Central Oregon. This was highly unusual, considering my mother's tendency to plan all vacations nine to thirty months in advance. Looking back, I'd recalled that as the start of our hike had drawn near, my parents' skepticism had become more tangible. I could vividly remember one evening in early May when they'd treated me to a humorous recollection of my family's outdoor heritage.

I suppose this topic came up as a warning; Ma and Pa weren't sure how far we would make it and wanted to go on record about the sordid history of the Ballard men and outdoor courtship. The reminiscences began with my Grandpa Bert, whom I remembered as a practical and frugal man. Grandpa was the sort of guy who considered a camping trip to be the perfect vacation and couldn't comprehend the sense of spending a night in an expensive hotel room. Unfortunately for Grandpa, Grandma Charlotte didn't share these sentiments—she was fond of classy hotels, fine restaurants, and indoor plumbing. Grandpa tried his best to convert her, first by arranging a car-camping honeymoon in Yellowstone National Park.

Even in such a memorable location, things got off on the wrong foot. Curled up in the backseat of Grandpa's Model A, the newlyweds were enjoying a romantic evening—that is, until the car started rocking violently from side to side. Gramps and Grammy may have been young and lustful at the time, but this was far more than either had bargained for. It turns out that Grandpa had had the clever idea of storing the food bag beneath the car and a bear had discovered that with a little wriggling he could claim the prize. In Grandma's opinion, poor Grandpa had failed to follow Gray's helpful tip number eighty-nine, "Create special time to be alone together." An unfortunate precedent had been set, and from then on it became difficult for my grandfather to persuade his wife to go camping. Every so often, though, Grandma would humor him with a weekend outing. Such outings never went particularly well, and Grandma would consistently assert her preference for the indoors and her distaste for doing "number two" in the woods.

Grandpa, being a resourceful, inventive gent, put his mind to devising a way to make his wife's outdoor experience more enjoyable. His solution was a multi-purpose campstool—a wooden seat with a circular hole in the middle. Placed over a cat hole, he was confident that this would remedy one of his wife's major objections to camping. It was a fine idea that resulted in a fine mess. When Grandma went to use her throne over the ditch, she collapsed the stool and was unceremoniously ditched. From then on, plumbing became a vacation prerequisite.

As if Grandpa Bert's ordeal wasn't enough, I was next regaled with my own father's story. His difficulties, like Grandpa's, began shortly after matrimony. My parents were planning a budget-conscious honeymoon and decided that a night of camping would be a good way to stretch their funds. My father generously offered the use of his tent. Dad had many fond memories of this "pup" tent and related boyhood adventures. The tent had been his shelter on many a chilly Midwestern fall night in the woods, near the cornfields. He'd bring along his little terrier, Tiny, and after an evening of exploration, they'd both crawl into the tent and snuggle into his sleeping bag. Buoyed by these childhood memories, Pops proudly pulled out his pup tent at a Cleveland area campground on his wedding night. After nearly ten years in the closet, this pup tent was going to help him make the transition from boy to man. There was only one small problem: Small indeed, was the pup tent. My mother was and still is an outdoorsy sort of gal, but nevertheless, it took only one look at the diminutive tent for her to doubt that her husband and a dog (even one named Tiny) could ever have fit in it. The newlyweds proceeded directly to a nearby motel.

I cut my parents short before being exposed to further historical amusement. It was clear that I was destined for misadventure, but Grandpa and Dad had made it through, so I supposed that I would, too.

X ▪ ▪ ▪ X

We were sitting outside the Lake of the Woods resort, eating lunch. At an adjacent table a middle-aged man wearing a tank top that exposed sunburned shoulders was talking to another man in khakis while gesturing at a two-hundred-foot red fir.

"You see that, Bill, you see that tree? If they had a tree like that in Illinois, they'd build a state park around it."

"No kidding," said Bill.

"Yessiree, that's a giant redwood."

"I'll be. I've heard of 'em. They've got a big ol' one in Yellowstone. Name's General Sherwin."

I nearly coughed up my sandwich. I glanced around to see if anyone else was following this conversation.

"Do you mean General Sherman?" said the first man.

"Yes, yes, that's right, General Sherman. Lives in Yellowstone."

"Right-o." They both seemed pleased. I didn't have the energy to tell them that there aren't any redwoods in Yellowstone National Park.

As much as I enjoyed the comfort of fast miles and frequent restaurant meals in southern Oregon, I missed wilderness isolation and found myself frequently longing for the serenity and solitude of the Sierra. Tourist banter was harmless and often entertaining, but the sounds of wind through trees, snowmelt over rocks, and feet through wet meadow grass were much more satisfying.

A day later we entered the peaceful woods of the Sky Lakes Wilderness. We set up camp not far from the banks of Island Lake and stared up and over red fir and mountain hemlock at the gentle 9,500-foot peak of Mount McLoughlin. Mist rose over the lake in the early morning, coalescing several feet off of its surface. The grove of trees on the lakes' small central island appeared to be floating in the fog. Only the looming visage of Mount McLoughlin reminded me that we were well below the stratosphere. I'd been warned about the swarms of mosquitoes often encountered in the Sky Lakes basin, but I saw only a few stragglers. The big skeeter hatch was evidently over, and we enjoyed this and more fir-sheltered lakes to follow without DEET immersion.

The next day, we made our way along the western edge of the Oregon Desert toward Crater Lake National Park. Buried underneath our feet, beneath layers of pumice, was a network of streams and rivers. Seven thousand years ago, Mount Mazama, at the time 12,000 feet high, erupted, spreading volcanic matter over 350,000 square miles of the Pacific Northwest. In the process, much of the surrounding landscape was drastically altered, and instead of striding through creek-fed meadows we traipsed over cinder and ash under sparse lodgepole and pioneer pine cover.

Next up was Crater Lake, the most incredible of the transformations brought on by Mount Mazama's eruption. The PCT, for equine-related reasons, gives the lake a wide berth. Neither Angela nor I had seen it before, so we followed the footsteps of many fellow hikers onto Rim Drive and to Rim Village at the lake's southern end. It was around eight in the morning when we arrived, and the tourist mecca of the Rim Village was coming to life. We approached a series of picnic benches outside the gift store and noticed two sleeping bag-covered lumps tucked into the bushes. A jut of blond hair protruded from the top of one of the sleeping bags. Several empty beer bottles sat on one of the tables. It was Casey and Toby.

"Breakfast time, boys!" I shouted

"Go away and come back in a few hours," groaned Crazy Legs from his bag.

No such luck. We roused the boys and goaded them to share their (guaranteed to be wacky) story. Unlike us, they'd celebrated the passage into Oregon in style, camping out right next to the border with a group of other hikers, sharing a potluck dinner and a round of beers—all packed in from Seiad Valley. Toby chuckled as he recounted what they had done with the empty Bud Light cans—"We threw them back onto the California side and Casey yelled, 'Keep Oregon clean!'" After the border bash (and yes, they did carry out the trash), they stopped in Ashland for a day and a half, taking in some of the local entertainment. They'd planned on some outdoor Shakespeare but found the tickets were too expensive, so instead opted for a few beers and an artsy movie.

We spent several hours with Casey and Toby at Rim Village, grabbing soggy burgers from the cafeteria and sharing stories and gossip. We learned that Amigo had left the trail shortly after entering Oregon; he was back in Chico pursuing his Master's in Education. He'd vowed to return to hike Oregon and Washington the next summer. We'd miss Amigo; he'd been a consistent source of entertainment and inspiration—providing a constant supply of silly jokes, trailside cries of *"Arrribbaa,"* trekking-pole drawings in the dust, and clever notes and cartoons in the trail registers. Drip was also home starting his junior year of high school, but Fallingwater, after a bout with an unspecified gastrointestinal ailment, was back on the trail and apparently not too far behind. Fish had returned to Tampa to attend to a promising business offer. Ryan and Daris remained on the trail although no one was sure where they were or if they were hiking together. We estimated that Chris and Stacey were a week or so back; they'd emailed us recently from Mount Shasta City. Chris was proud of their new trail names, Rise and Shine, a reference to their early morning hiking habit.

After some time, an encroaching sea of motor homes, khakis, flip-flops, and unflattering hats overwhelmed our conversation; the summer tourist season was at its height. And the tourists flocked with good reason; Crater Lake is an incredible sight.

$$\mathbf{X} \bullet \ \ ^{\blacksquare} \ \ \bullet \ \mathbf{X}$$

After Mount Mazama blew her top, she collapsed on herself, leaving a twenty-square-mile hole over 2,100 feet deep. Slowly, rain and snow filled the crater, eventually to a depth of 1,932 feet. Over hundreds of years, Crater Lake's depth has remained essentially unchanged, with the rate of precipitation matching that of evaporation.

At the western end of the lake is a remnant cinder cone—Wizard Island—that towers 763 feet above the lake's blue waters. And blue the waters are, deep and pure—so pure that when you see the lake you can't believe the color is possible without digital enhancement. The color of the lake is a result of both its depth and clarity. Indeed, the clarity of Crater Lake is unmatched; in 1997 it set the world record for underwater visibility, at 142 feet.

As we followed a trail and road around the lake I was mesmerized. It was nothing more than a large puddle of water, but it emanated mysticism. I could see why indigenous Native American cultures worshiped the lake as a holy site—even today some still believe that to lay eyes upon the lake means instant death. If that was true, I had died and gone to heaven, because all I wanted was to gaze out across the blue water. I yearned to find a sheltered cove of grass where I could enjoy the sunset and subsequent sunrise over the lake, stare into the blueness and enjoy a warm mug of hot chocolate. But, as had happened so many times before, we were tugged by the call of miles with not many days left to cover them. It felt incredible to have walked over eighteen hundred miles and still face over eight hundred more. Crater Lake would just have to be added to the list of places to visit again.

[15]

Of Slugs, Rats, and Women

 VEERING AWAY FROM THE SHARP CLIFFS above the mer-curial blue waters of Crater Lake made my heart ache. It was like saying good-bye to a friend, one you weren't sure you'd see again for a long time. For eight miles we'd watched the changing position of the sun alter the mood of the subtly rip-pling waters. It was entrancing. By evening, the once brilliant view into the crater had darkened to shadows, the water a deep and mysterious indigo. Strolling down the Rim Road, we walked in perfect sync with the world around us and with each other.

The harmony lasted until the lake was out of sight. Then I grew tired and wanted to camp. Duffy wanted to cram in a few more miles before darkness. The resulting terse disagreement was a prime example of the mutual bull-headedness that often led us to a cacophony of misunderstandings and in-jured feelings. At such times I wondered whether we were even speaking the same language.

In her book *You Just Don't Understand: Women and Men in Conversation*, Deborah Tannen, Ph.D., writes, "Talk between men and women is cross-cultural com-munication." Men, she explains, speak a language of status and independence, while women speak a language of connection and intimacy. For example, when I was run down (like I'd been prior to our blowout at Vasquez Rocks, and was the night we left Crater Lake), I wanted to talk about the things that were making my day difficult, things like heat, hunger, and malaise. Such talk was my way of sharing my intimate thoughts and fears with Duffy. It didn't mean

I was blaming him or wanting to give up, but rather it was how I asked for empathy, tenderness, and support. Duffy, however, may have seen my complaints as criticism, as a threat to his status, and as evidence that he was failing me. "A man," according to *The Complete Idiot's Guide to Understanding Men and Women,* "loves to be around a woman whom he feels he can make happy." Any evidence that he was ineffective in this regard seemed to make Duffy defensive, regardless of the fact that I loved him and the PCT madly.

In reality, Duffy had many of the same fears and inner conflicts that I did. The difference was that he rarely showed or shared them. He wanted to be on the trail, so he attempted to maintain a consistent cheeriness. Meanwhile, I showed him each and every one of my emotional peaks and valleys. Yes, I wanted to hike the PCT, but I also had to admit that some aspects of the hiking life were hard. As a matter of fact, some things about long-distance hiking sucked—like the weird, egg-sized sacks that were forming under the skin on my hips. I'd lost all the fat around my waist. This meant that nearly the full weight of my pack rested, via the hip belt, directly on my now-prominent hipbones. Perhaps to compensate for lack of cushioning fatty tissue, my body developed what seemed to be fluid-filled bags right where my pack hit my bones. These pads made me look like Twiggy with swollen love handles. Would they ever go away? Or was I doomed to go through life with mysterious, subterranean formations right where the strings of my bikini bottom should be? Then there was the sunburn. Despite vigilant application of SPF 30, my nose had been blistering since Campo. Was malignant melanoma to be my PCT legacy? Was the fact that I wasn't menstruating dooming my future reproductive health? These were valid worries and complaints. They didn't detract from the value of our journey, but they were worth venting about if only because venting provided some relief.

It's no secret that when women get together they often "bitch" about what's bothering them. They don't do this to hurt the people they're bitching about or even to find solutions to their problems, they do it as a form of catharsis. The act of purging negative feelings and receiving reassurance from friends makes us feel better. Without many women thru-hikers around for me to talk to, I turned to Duffy for everything—which wasn't really fair. I'm not sure any man can succeed in assuming the role of a woman's female friends.

Science has revealed that supportive social networks have a positive effect on health, lowering the chances of high blood pressure, cholesterol, and blood sugar, and also slowing cognitive decline related to aging. Recent research in rats goes one step further. In a study conducted among rats at the University of Chicago, female companionship was shown to benefit longevity. Put male rats together, the researchers found, and they'll battle for dominance—often to the death. But put female rats together and they'll actually live longer—in fact, forty percent longer than their isolated sisters.

Unfortunately for my feminine side, there wasn't much of a sisterhood on the trail, probably because there were so few of us sisters—so few that I could count the ones I'd met on my fingers and toes. Foremost among them were those who made it most or all of the way. Daris, our Canadian friend; Madame Butterfly, hiking with her deaf husband Improv; Stacey, of Chris and Stacey fame; Sunrise, the Israeli tank operator; Desert Rose, retired and traveling with her husband; Debbie, another retiree; Lady Godiva, who was riding the PCT on her horse Livingston; and Ginny, traveling with her Jim. And then there is the longer list of those who went home early: Lora, who bailed out with the flu in the Sierra, never to be seen by us again; Chris, a teacher from Bolivia who suffered injuries in the desert and was left, literally, to tend to them in the dust (we believe her partner, Natasha, went on to complete the trail); Nokona, who abandoned her hike due to altitude sickness; Marcy, who gave up hiking and hung out in towns along the way instead; Laraine, who got off the trail in Northern California because of severe lactose intolerance; and Rosey, whose companion (her sister, The Artist) had departed during the first few days and who herself quit before Oregon.

Intellectually, I'd known that the PCT's long-distance hiking community was male dominated. But it wasn't until late in our hike that I realized what this really meant. Talking with men, and only men, the vast majority of the time sometimes made me feel like I was the last woman on Earth. The attention could be an ego boost, but at the same time I missed my friends and looked forward to having more gender diversity in my life when I got home. Being out-numbered, it seemed, added one more level of stress.

For me, this was a negative situation. But not all women thru-hikers felt this way. Daris, for instance, found the ratio of men to women to be extremely encouraging. "I try to convince my friends to go do [the trail]," Daris wrote to me, "and tell them that it's like twenty to one . . . good chance of meeting a fine one." Besides, says Daris, thru-hiking seemed to bring out an abundance of old-fashioned gentlemanly spirit. This was true. Duffy carried more weight than me (it was the only way I could go at his pace), held my hand during dangerous stream and snowfield crossings, and much more.

As my manly protector, Duffy felt a big responsibility to keep me safe, healthy, and happy. To ease his burden I needed to be optimistic and strong. I mean, really, Duffy didn't *always* need to know that the blister on my toe felt like a hot coal stuffed in my sock. Now, if only he'd learn to listen and say "I understand" empathetically just a little bit more often. . . .

X ▪ ▪ ▪ ▪ X

Leaving the Crater Lake region behind, the trail rolled gently past lakes and meandered through forests, all the while continuing to follow a string of snow-bound volcano peaks. The days flew by, varying little except for the occasional chance meetings with other trail folk.

On one hot and dry afternoon (I continued to be amazed at how dry Oregon was), we turned a corner to find a sixtyish man ambling toward us with a shovel and pruning shears. Trailing behind him was an old dog. The man (named Lance), we learned, had adopted the twenty-mile section of the PCT that we were in the process of hiking and was out checking up on things, taking care of whatever maintenance needs he could.

"I left a cooler about five miles ahead," said Lance. "There's cold 7-Up, Gatorade, root beer, water, and whatever else my wife bought in there. Help yourself and don't forget to sign my register." Coolers and similar trail magic are common occurrences on the Appalachian Trail, where one might find them filled with sandwiches and ice cream as well as drinks, but they're rare on the PCT. In fact, this was our first hiker cooler and we rushed the five miles to get to it. Gratefully gulping down root beer, I read the entries in Lance's spiral-bound notebook and noticed that just three hours before Casey had written, "It's so nice to have something besides water to chase the whiskey with." We walked on, and I pondered whether Casey was really drinking whiskey on a hot day like this. I imagined that would make the steel-woollike lichen that dripped from the trees look even more like syrup over pancakes.

Over the next few days, we covered miles easily—so easily that we had time and energy to play around. I draped the ubiquitous, lime-green lichen over Duffy until he looked like the Sea Hag villain from Popeye. We lingered by misty lakeshores, listened to woodpeckers busy in the trees above, and counted baby grouse that scampered across our path—two dozen in one day. The going was easy in Oregon and it became even easier when, about halfway through the state, Duffy's parents met us at Odell Lake.

For the next five days, the Ballards shuttled us to the trail every morning and to a hotel each night, sometimes even meeting us for a picnic lunch in between. Because they transported our gear as well, we were able to hike while carrying only daypacks. And given that the Oregon terrain was rolling at its worst, we found that we could cover more than twenty-five miles in eight hours. Sometimes we'd jog. As you can imagine, thru-hiking purists frown upon such "slack-packing," but with our window of opportunity rapidly crashing closed we decided we'd rather walk some of the Oregon miles lighter and faster than not walk them at all.

Our slack-packing ended at Timberline Lodge on Mount Hood. The climb to 6,000 feet and the lodge took us over a sandy, gray debris fan, the remains of mud flows caused when Hood last erupted two thousand years ago.

Timberline Lodge was completed by the Works Progress Administration (WPA) during the Great Depression and provided hundreds of artisans with work. Its design is rustic, utilizing natural materials with Native American and Western motifs. Carved wooden animal heads decorate the outside while others sit atop banisters. Every nook and cranny of Timberline holds a craftsman's treasure—a stone fireplace, intricately carved railings, hand-wrought iron door knockers, brightly colored textiles on the windows and beds, paintings and mosaics of forest creatures. Iron gates mark the entrance to the Cascade Room, a four-star restaurant where organic blackberry syrup is served over blackberry pancakes, and for desert you can order alpine silk mousse. We celebrated Duffy's mother's birthday there, toasting her sixty years and our 110 days on the trail. It was good to get a taste of home and to receive a strong dose of moral support.

Seeing Duffy's parents made me think of my own. But really, they'd been on my mind all along. As I've mentioned, walking for a living gives you a lot of time to think. Take that time, mix it with a little deprivation and physical strain, add a splash of the type of peace one can only find in the wilderness, and you get a special perspective on life. It didn't happen overnight, but it seemed that each mile brought me closer to something (besides the Canadian border). Where distress had lived, I was finding understanding instead.

I spent a lot of time thinking about why I was the way I was. My parents had dedicated their lives to raising me to be strong, intellectually inquisitive, and loving. These were the things that enabled me to walk the length of two states and would keep me going for one more—strength of body and mind, insatiable curiosity to see what was over the next ridge, and the capacity for intimacy. Unwittingly, my parents had made this trip possible, and for that I owed them much. This realization didn't make everything right, but it was a start.

X ▪ ▪ ▪ ▪ X

On August 25, we continued north along the Pacific Crest and Timberline Trails, which run in conjunction for a few miles. Above us loomed the peak of Mount Hood. At 11,235 feet, Mount Hood is the tallest mountain in Oregon and one of the world's most frequently climbed snow-capped peaks. Each year more than ten thousand people attempt to summit Hood. While requiring some technical mountaineering skills and equipment (including an ice axe, avalanche beacon, and crampons), Mount Hood is regarded as a fairly simple climb. The South Side Route is actually nicknamed the Dog Route because, given the right conditions, your average Rover can make it to the top and back and still have energy for a game of Frisbee. But not all days provide the right conditions, and simple does not always mean safe. In 2002, three climbers coming down the Dog Route ended up dead.

The tragedy added to Hood's sordid history, which includes a snowboarder who slipped off an icy ridge and plunged 2,500 feet to his death (also in 2002) and seven high school students and two teachers who froze to death in 1986.

Mount Hood's deadly disposition was well disguised on the bright sunny day when we left Timberline Lodge, and skirted its slopes to the west. Cotton-ball clouds floated around the volcano's cone while wisps of fog settled in the uppermost gullies, giving the mountain a soft, hazy aspect.

Traversing Hood's flanks, we walked through fine sand and fields of yellow and purple flowers. Glacier-fed streams raging down steep canyons were milky white with "rock milk." Just as we crossed one of the streams, a dog came rushing out of the bushes barking viciously. Two curious goats and a man's yells followed him—"Bessie, Jasper, git back here." In a clearing just beyond the stream a fortyish man with a round, bald head and glasses sat amongst blankets, a tarp, multiple cooking pots, and sundry bags of other gear. He was a goat-packer, we learned, which meant that his goats (pint-size black and white Bessie and the large, brown Jasper) carried his gear. "Bessie gives good milk, too," he told us, while she pulled a straw hat from a bag and began eating it. "Goats can walk about fifteen to twenty miles a day and they graze like deer, so you don't need to carry much food for them."

"Besides straw hats," I thought as I watched Bessie nibble the hat's rim daintily.

Leaving the goats, we descended into a deep, lush forest blanketed with ferns and came upon Ramona Falls. Here a sheet of water rushed over a dark volcanic cliff and broke on a bed of rocks, emitting rainbows in myriad directions. The forest around the falls was so dank and gloomy that any light in the grove seemed to be emanating from the falls themselves.

On the advice of both our guidebook and a local trail maintenance crew, we veered off the PCT at Indian Mountain and headed down steep and muddy Indian Springs Trail to Eagle Creek. We hadn't gone far down the Eagle Creek Trail when Duffy, who'd taken off his pack and sat down on a rock, held out to me a manure-green, mini-wiener-size slug. I shied away but he kept shoving his mittened hand closer, holding the slimy thing in my face.

"Kiss it. . . . Come on, Chiggy, kiss the banana slug."

As I stared at the banana slug (which was busy secreting slime), I came to a few conclusions. One, no way was I kissing that mutant sludge ball. Two, since Duffy had already smooched his new oozy buddy, I didn't plan on kissing him anytime soon, either. And three, someone (possibly the Forest Service) was pumping steroids into the northern Oregon wilderness.

Everything about the area surrounding Eagle Creek (approximately thirty-five miles from Timberline Lodge and 15.6 miles from the Washington border) seemed immensely exaggerated, from the mammoth slugs to the lush undergrowth with leaves the size of dinner plates. I felt like Alice in Wonderland—no, make that Alice in Wonder-jungle.

Light, airy moss hung from the trees like beards. The rocks were covered with carpets of a thick, spongy moss. Countless varieties of fern tickled our legs. Drizzle and dampness augmented the rain-forest effect. But while the verdant wood, literally sweating with dense vegetation, was spectacular, the real star of the show was Eagle Creek itself.

Roaring below us, Eagle Creek was like a watery Rube Goldberg contraption, whipping around corners, cascading into pools that overflowed into falls (and vice versa), pouring over basalt flats, and cutting through cracks. Even the trail along the creek was a wonder. Blasted into the cliffs of volcanic rock and frighteningly narrow, the precarious footpath heightened our sensitivity to the power of the water below. At some especially harrowing stretches trail workers had installed iron hand cables for safety, and I took full advantage of them.

Like a fine piece of classical music, Eagle Creek's delights started subtly, with rock-bound washes, a fifty-foot cascade, and clear deep pools. Soon, though, the composition built to a crescendo with a two-stage hundred-foot fall sliced into a gorge and hiding around a corner. And the finale, Tunnel Falls (a popular day-hiker attraction) brought us scarily close to the heart of a 150-foot waterfall with the trail actually leading to its showery edge about halfway up, and then ducking, via a narrow, wet tunnel, behind the thundering cascade. And then came the encore, an eighty-foot fall and then the Punch Bowl, a huge pool with a sapphire hue fed by a boisterous, forty-foot plunge.

The bowl would have tempted Duffy with a swim if he could have found a way down to it.

Eagle Creek is a hydrophile's delight. And if we'd stuck to the PCT we would have missed it. While we were down by the creek, the PCT was high and dry above us, plodding through the same pine-forested terrain we'd seen a lot of in Oregon, proving once again that the PCT is not always the most scenic route to Canada.

Because horses and other pack animals are permitted on the PCT, it's often forced away from major sites such as Eagle Creek and Crater Lake. And rightly so. Heavy hooves can damage trails; hikers and horses are often skittish around one another, making injuries a distinct possibility; and stock (when improperly attended) have a tendency to muddy water sources and defile campsites. This is not to say that the PCT should become horse-free; on the contrary, that would be quite unfair considering that equestrian groups played a critical role in building the trail in the first place and continue to be instrumental in its maintenance.

From Eagle Creek Trail we took a 2.4-mile bike path into the town of Cascade Locks, where I picked up a package from my friend Lisa that contained a new pair of sneakers. With my new shoes hanging off my pack, we headed to the Bridge of the Gods over the Columbia River Gorge. Made of metal and painted blue, the Bridge of the Gods didn't quite live up to its name; the only godlike thing about the bridge was the fact that when cars whizzed by me on it (there was no sidewalk), I screamed, "Oh, my God!" The risk of becoming road-pizza made taking photographs difficult.

The 1,243-mile Columbia River begins in Canal Flats, British Columbia, and empties into the Pacific Ocean at the Washington coast. Along the way, water temperatures range from thirty-eight to seventy-three degrees. From our vantage point on the bridge, the water appeared clear and inviting, but I knew that it was heavily polluted with neurotoxins and other nasties. According to the Environmental Protection Agency, there are zinc levels sixty times greater than the safe limit for aquatic life in the Columbia River, along with thirty-five different types of pesticides, sixteen at levels higher than is deemed safe for human consumption, and some, like DDT, that are banned. Fourteen dams have created thirteen lakes along the river that are polluted with arsenic, chainsaw-bar oil, slag from metal smelters, sewage, and even nuclear waste. Downriver, in Portland, it's not safe to swim in the Columbia, eat its fish, or drink its water. The once mighty Columbia, the famous watershed, is in a sorry state, but the boaters below appeared to be blissfully ignorant.

Arriving safely on the other side of the bridge, I looked across the river back into Oregon and couldn't really wrap my head around the fact that this was it. We were in Washington—the homestretch. I was melancholy yet proud that we'd made it so far. I was excited to see what Washington would bring, but frightened, too. What would happen when this was all over? We'd go home, to Philadelphia. But what then?

[16]

Wet!

I COULDN'T BELIEVE ANGELA WOULDN'T DO IT. I was shocked. Didn't she trust me? Why was she so inhibited? I mean, what was the big deal about a little protein-rich slime on the lips? It would be easy to clean off. To demonstrate the harmless nature of the proposed act, I squatted down and did it myself—gave that slimy chunk of mustard-green slug a big kiss.

As a middle-schooler, I'd taken a weeklong trip to the Pescadero Conservation Alliance in the Santa Cruz Mountains. There, on trails running through redwood forests, naturalist guides encouraged us to join the "Banana Slug Club" by giving one of the slippery buggers a kiss. They told us that because slugs do the dirty work of decomposing the forest floor, kissing one was an excellent way to get "in touch" with nature. As an added bonus, it made singing the "Banana Slug Song" around the campfire even more fun—"The way you wiggle your antennae, you know you give me such bliss. Come on, come on, come on banana slug, oh won't you give me a kiss? BA-NA-NA-NA-NA-NA, BA (clap) NA (clap) NA (clap) SLUG!"

My entire seventh grade class smooched slugs that week, including all of the pathologically color-coordinated twelve-year-old girls. But Angela, my hardened mountain lady—she refused to even touch a slug. Nothing I said, did, or attempted to sing could convince her otherwise. "Blaaah . . . yuck!" she responded, and kept walking down the Eagle Creek Trail. Eventually, my persistence started an argument. Neither of us could understand why the other was being so darn stubborn, and so naturally we locked horns.

I accused Angela of not trusting me, and she demanded that I be more sensitive.

John Gray, Ph.D., that noted logician of love, would recognize this as a classic case of men and women failing to communicate. "Most couples start out arguing about one thing," says Gray, "and within five minutes, [they] are arguing about the way they are arguing." How true. I didn't really care whether Angela kissed a slug or not, but I was angry that she wouldn't even consider it. She resolutely dismissed the notion, and this caused me to feel as if she was resolutely dismissing me. I needed her to appreciate that *I was right*, that kissing a slug *was* a pretty cool thing to do.... "Some people think that she's gross, but I don't hear that jive. If it weren't for my baby now, the forest might not survive. BA-NA-NA-NA-NA-NA-NA...."

Even though I was singing at the top of my lungs, thinking this was an effective way of expressing myself, I should have realized that I'd fallen into another communication trap. "When a man feels challenged," Gray writes, "his attention becomes focused on being right and he forgets to be loving as well.... A man unknowingly hurts his partner by speaking in an uncaring manner and then goes on to explain why she should not be upset."

Well, once again, it was too bad that I hadn't read *Men Are from Mars, Women Are from Venus* before the hike. If I had, I might have understood why we were having such a stupid argument. Ironically, according to Gray, intimacy aggravates conflict. The more intimate we are, the more difficult it is to listen to one another's opinions without reacting to emotions instead. Automatic defenses come up to protect us from feeling that our partner's disrespect or disapproval is deserved. And so, "Even if we agree with their point of view, we may stubbornly persist in arguing with them." Absolutely right! It really was a shame that this John Gray fella hadn't been hiking with us; he could have helped put everything in proper perspective. But I suppose he was too busy with his own sickly perfect relationship—you know, all open and honest and that kind of crap, making his wife tea when she was tired and dutifully sharpening her knives. The only "gray" with us this day, as it turned out, was the cloud over our moods. We continued to bicker and pout our way to the Washington border.

X ▪ ▪ ▪ ▪ X

Eventually the wonders of the Eagle Creek Trail distracted us, and by the time we'd passed over the Columbia River via the Bridge of the Gods our fight was nearly forgotten. I say nearly, because if I'd seen a banana slug on the bridge, inching its way over the metal grates, we'd have been right back where we started. . . ."The way you slide through the forest, you know you look so fine. Come on, come on, come on banana slug, let me follow your slime!" The bridge, however, appeared to be slug-free and so did the town of Stevenson on the northern bank of the Columbia, so we spent a bicker-free night at one of our favorite hospitality establishments, the Econo Lodge.

The following morning was gorgeous—clear and sunny with a crisp taste of fall. We sat in a breakfast booth at Dee's Kich-Inn, gazing at the windsurfers and para-sailers that dotted the Columbia River, discussing what lay ahead. Many hikers both rave and fret about the 508 miles of Washington's PCT, especially the last 250 through the Northern Cascades, past Mount Baker and Glacier Peak. As we progressed north, the terrain would become more difficult, with increasingly steep, abrupt climbs followed by rapid descents. But the scenery and ambience would be worth it: Brilliant fall colors, snappy September air, and magnificent mountain vistas awaited us. Provided, of course, that the weather continued to cooperate. So far, our summer had been blessed with meteorological good fortune. For almost four months, while covering 2,100 miles, we'd experienced fewer than eight hours of precipitation—so little, in fact, that we'd nearly forgotten to worry about it. That would soon change.

Several hiking days into Washington the blue skies began to fill with clouds. We passed through the Indian Heaven Wilderness and into the Sawtooth huckleberry fields, where Yakima Indians were harvesting the fall crop. Joining in, we picked handfuls of the tart berries, staining our fingers pleasantly purple in the process. The trail led us through acres of multihued bushes and we tried to grab and swallow berries without breaking stride. On several occasions, Angela performed a black bear impression, squatting to eat the berries directly off the branches. Huckleberries are said to turn bear scat purple—Angela assured me that it had no such effect on Chigger scat.

Finally leaving the Yakima behind, we swept around the west side of Mount Adams, the third-highest North Cascade volcano. Despite being over 12,000 feet high, Mount Adams appeared plump and squat, its girth expanding laterally as if hefty gods had sat on its peak. Past the flanks of Mount Adams, we hiked through an early morning frost over Cispus Pass and into the Goat Rocks Wilderness. From across a wide valley we spotted a herd of white mountain goats, barely distinguishable from patches of snow on the rocky ridge.

Soon we stood at the remnants of the Dana Yvelteron Shelter on the south side of Old Snowy Mountain. Nearly forty years ago, Dana Yvelteron and a group of high school friends were hiking near this section of the PCT when inclement weather descended on them. With Dana unable to hike out because of hypothermia, her friends left to find help. When they returned, she was dead. The rock shelter, completed in 1965 in Dana's honor, was now missing a roof and large chunks of its walls. It, too, had become a victim of the wild and unpredictable weather of the Goat Rocks Wilderness.

Departing from the stone rubble of the Yvelteron Shelter (which, in the two years since our hike, has been completely removed by the Forest Service), the PCT climbs up to and traverses scree and talus above the Packwood Glacier. The 7,930-foot peak of Old Snowy towers above. And as if the scree, talus, and glacier weren't scary enough, the trail then proceeds along a knifelike ridge—for two miles. This ridge is a thirteen million-year-old leftover of a volcano that once stood as tall as Mount Hood. All this adds up to a dangerous stretch of trail, especially in bad weather.

I'd watched the skies somewhat nervously over the last twenty-four hours. Wispy cirrus clouds had evolved into pregnant cumulus ones. And then, just as we began the traverse underneath Old Snowy, the wind picked up and snow began to lightly dust our shoulders. The footing was slippery and the drop-off was steep. My nervousness quickly escalated to fear as we stepped deliberately across several hundred exposed yards of trail. Snow transformed into sleet and wind gusted violently from the northwest. Bowing my head, I pushed forward, frequently stabbing out my trekking poles to maintain balance. Halfway across, I looked back; Angela was moving slowly, chin tucked into her chest. I turned forward and the wind blasted my mouth so forcefully that it carried the saliva right out of it. So here it was—loud, cold, and wet and windy as hell—our introduction to Washington's unpredictable weather.

A harrowing hour later, at Elk Pass, the trail dropped into whitebark and juniper forest, leaving the ridge and its fierce wind behind. A thick drizzle enveloped us as we marched the last sixteen miles to our re-supply at White Pass. To help pass the time, I turned to my now trusty friend, the AM/FM radio. From the NBA finals to major league baseball to NPR's *Talk of the Nation* and *All Things Considered,* the radio helped ease the monotony of many tough miles. For the last couple weeks, though, I'd had a hard time finding anything but the most frivolous of talk shows. After listening to the inane radio personalities that saturated the airwaves of Oregon and Washington, I'd decided that being a radio talk-show host was a pretty sweet gig. From what I could tell, all it required was spending five minutes or so each night thinking up a topic or two that might rile up folks.

For talk-show host Bill Gallagher, the topic du jour was Blockbuster's five-day rental policy. Bill had recently been charged $24.13 in late fees for *The Hurricane,* a movie he was sure he'd *never* rented. Bill clearly felt that he was victim of a horrible injustice and he'd taken his revenge by formulating a theory: Blockbuster's five-day rental policy is diabolically designed so that renters will forget the return date and hence return movies late. This, of course, means more late-fee revenues for Blockbuster's coffers. I reluctantly listened to Bill and his callers debate this theory for nearly an hour before I found Dwight Jones on 860 AM. That day, Dwight was wondering if "age matters in love," and whether "Dennis Miller dropped the f-bomb on his Monday Night Football broadcast, and if so, do you care?" Finally, a couple issues of national importance! Profanity associated with a football game—oh, the horror. I mean, imagine all of those naïve fortyish-year-old men, innocently swilling their six-packs and being unexpectedly bombarded with offensive language.

As I was preparing to loudly drop my own f-bomb on Dwight Jones, my radio trance was interrupted by a stampede. Branches cracked and the earth trembled. A herd of furry white rumps was bounding down the open slope— a rumbling, bumbling team of elk. Elk are one of the largest members of the deer family. Bulls can weigh up to a thousand pounds, and compared to the whitetail and mule deer, elk can make a major ruckus during a downhill crusade. I'd read in Clyde Ormond's *Outdoor Lore* that elk migrating out of high country in the fall season signifies an impending snowstorm. I sure hoped Clyde was wrong.

It was gloomy and nearly dark by the time we reached White Pass. Slipping and sliding, we went straight down grassy wet ski slopes to Highway 12 and then across the road to the ski lodge. It was still overcast and drizzling the next morning as we sat at the One-Stop Mini Mart, hoping for clearer skies. With us were a group of other thru-hikers, mostly new faces. We spoke about the weather.

"They say that Rainier gets more than seven hundred inches of snow a year," said Ken Powers, a thin, middle-aged man with a white beard that made him look a little like Santa Claus after a crash diet.

"That's fine . . . just as long as it waits until October," said his wife Marcia. She was even thinner than Ken and wiry as a wood elf.

"Fat chance," Ken replied. Looking at him as he said this, I couldn't help but smile at the irony of the comment. There was no fat on his frame or his wife's, or ours for that matter; there hadn't been for a long time. That was probably part of the reason we all felt perpetually chilled.

"You know, the weather was great in ninety-eight. Not a single drop of rain the entire time. September's a good month; it'll clear." This prognostication was from Weather Carrot, a tall hiker with a bushy red beard. Weather Carrot had been a long-distance hiker for ten years. He did trail work in the off-season to earn enough money to hike in the summer. This kept him on an extremely tight budget, but he didn't mind. With obvious pride he declared that he'd taken less than ten showers all summer. Judging from the odor emanating from his vicinity, he wasn't exaggerating.

"I don't recall too much about the weather back in seventy-seven; after so much time, it's all a blur," Chad chimed in. Chad was returning to re-hike the trail twenty-three years after his first adventure and doing so with the same backpack—the only external frame I'd seen on a distance hiker the entire summer.

"Well, the guidebook keeps advertising these vistas of Rainier, but yesterday all it got was *rain-ier.*" As I said this, I wondered how many people had used this joke before. Casey would have been disappointed; he once declared the pun to be the lowest beast on the humor food chain.

"You know what they say . . . locals tell the weather by looking at Rainier. If you can't see it, it's raining, but . . . if you *can* see it, it's about to rain." Ken's joke was slightly better.

"I can't see it," Angela glumly stated. She wasn't happy about sitting here in limbo, ready to walk, but waiting. Evidently, she could sympathize with Mark Twain's quip that "Everybody talks about the weather, but nobody does anything about it."

Morning turned into afternoon, and the other hikers ventured out into the wetness. Although it was still drizzling, occasional shafts of sunlight illuminated the One-Stop parking lot. It wasn't likely to get much clearer than this, so we walked down Highway 12 and then up a muddy trail trenched with hoof marks.

Just as we entered the William O. Douglas Wilderness, the drizzle escalated into a shower, and soon a full-fledged rainstorm was pelting us. The trail underneath our feet rapidly deteriorated—slippery mud gave way to puddles as the earth became saturated. Balanced on the puddles' surfaces were thin sheens of dirt and pine needles, giving the illusion of dry trail. These illusions resulted in repeated splashes, submerged sneakers, and yelps of discomfort. After about forty-five minutes, the puddles morphed into a frothy torrent of muddied water racing down the trail. At first, I tried to hopscotch around the flow, but soon the entire trail became an ankle-high current and I was forced to just struggle upstream, wincing as chilly rainwater enveloped my toes. After several hours of this misery we were cursing not only our waterlogged feet and bitterly cold hands but also our earlier decision to leave the One-Stop. Nearly all of Angela's fingers had turned blanch-white, the worst Raynaud's flare I'd seen. Every ten minutes or so, I'd pause and she'd wedge her hands under my shorts and onto my bare but toasty butt cheeks. In the past, this cheek-grabbing maneuver had always relaxed her blood vessels, allowing her fingers to regain their normal color. But not today—my magical buttocks were useless against Washington's wet fury.

We hiked on and evening further darkened the skies. Making camp in this deluge was not an option; movement was the only way to stay somewhat warm. Sooner or later, though, we'd have to stop. I could only hope that by then the rain would have abated. "Perfect setup for hypothermia," I muttered to myself.

I'd been warned of the dangers of hypothermia (abnormally low core body temperature), particularly in conditions like these. Many people associate hypothermia solely with blizzards, icicles, and arctic weather, but the combination of cool and wet can be just as deadly. This is especially true when clothing gets damp, thus intensifying the cooling power of evaporation. Evaporation, one of the four primary mechanisms by which the human body dissipates warmth, refers to heat loss from wet surfaces (in this case, skin). Evaporation makes sweating an effective means of cooling down, but given the wrong conditions, it can also turn wet cotton garments into death suits. The colonel, our old hiking instructor, had adamantly warned us about this. "Cotton kills," he'd said again and again.

Hypothermia strikes quietly and insidiously. It doesn't jump out of the woods and claw like a cougar or strike from underneath a rock like a rattlesnake; rather, it slowly weakens the mind and body. Someone suffering from mild hypothermia (a core temperature loss of two to nine degrees) will shiver uncontrollably and may suffer from unsteadiness or impaired judgment. If the wet clothing isn't removed and a source of warmth found, the condition may progress to moderate hypothermia (a loss of nine to seventeen degrees Fahrenheit). A moderately hypothermic person becomes increasingly confused and eventually stops shivering. In fact, the person might feel flushed and start undressing in order to, of all things, *cool* off. It's as if that song by Nelly dances restlessly in the mind, "It's getting hot in here (so hot), so take off all your clothes, I am getting so hot, I wanna take my clothes off. . . ."

If this seems counterintuitive, well—it is. Some of you may have read about Scott Fischer, one of the Mount Everest guides portrayed in Jon Krakauer's book *Into Thin Air.* Fischer had already summited Everest and was following his group down the mountain when a fierce storm swept in and left him stranded on an icy ledge at 27,200 feet. Later that night, fellow guide Anatoli Boukreev climbed up from the expedition's camp to rescue him. Krakauer quotes Boukreev, "I find Scott at seven o'clock, maybe it is seven-thirty or eight. . . . By then it is dark. Storm is very strong. His oxygen mask is around face, but bottle is empty. He is not wearing mittens; hands completely bare. Down suit is unzipped, pulled off his shoulder, one arm is outside clothing. There is nothing I can do. Scott is dead."

The disheveled state in which Boukreev found Scott Fischer is a morbid illustration of the phenomenon of "paradoxical undressing." At 27,200 feet, and assaulted with ice, Fischer (paradoxically) had unzipped his down suit and ditched his mittens. Why? Because hypothermia had caused his brain's temperature regulation system to shut down. Instead of restricting blood flow to peripheral tissues to preserve blood flow to vital organs such as the brain, his thermoregulatory center had relaxed them. Blood rushed to his arms, legs, and skin, just as it would on a hot day. Fischer suddenly felt uncomfortably warm, like an Eskimo in Haiti. And his brain was too oxygen-deprived to question the logic of shedding his clothing in the middle of a snowstorm.

Soon, Fischer entered the realm of severe hypothermia (defined as a core body temperature of less than 80.6 degrees Fahrenheit) and by this point was about as lively as a Popsicle in a meat locker. Fluid filled his lungs, his blood pressure fell, his heart thumped irregularly—and he felt none of it because he had lost all perception of pain. His death was painless, and in this respect I suppose it's not a terrible way to go. I can certainly think of worse. Nevertheless, a paradoxically undressed death was not high on my summer agenda.

It was seven o'clock. The rain had eased a bit but we were both thoroughly drenched. I assumed that the garbage bags draped over our packs were keeping our gear relatively dry, still, I didn't see us warming up without a fire. But how could we start a fire? There wasn't any dry timber to be had in this soggy forest. We could light our stove, but propane was a precious commodity. Who knew how many rainy days lay before us on this nearly hundred-mile walk to Snoqualmie Pass? We couldn't decide what to do. So we kept walking, hoping the rain would eventually stop.

As we approached Buesch Lake, my nose caught a whiff of good fortune. Wet, thick smoke, the smell of damp wood overwhelmed by bonfire. Saved! A sweet inferno! How our perspective had shifted since Whitewater Canyon in Southern California. Back then we would have recoiled from a campfire like Superman from kryptonite.

Seated on a log next to a fire pit at the edge of the misty lake was a very large man in full camouflage fatigues, rifle in hand. I was taken aback, but we had little choice—we had to approach him or risk shivering the night away. The imposing figure greeted us with a smile. His name was Travis, and he was a native of Olympia. He was waiting for a friend to join him for a week of elk hunting. One elk would be enough to feed them both for the entire winter, he said. A full-grown black bear would provide just as much meat, but neither Travis nor his buddy liked the taste or texture of bear meat. Too tough to chew, Travis said. We stood silently by the fire for some time. Angela's fingers regained a pinkish hue, and the rain softened back to a light drizzle. Travis offered to share his camp spot with us, and we gladly accepted. I was extremely relieved—if we hadn't found Travis it would have been an unpleasant and perhaps hypothermic evening.

X ▪ ▀ ▀ ▪ X

"I can't believe you use those things." Travis was cleaning his rifle the next morning, watching us as we prepared to leave.

"Which things?" I wasn't sure what he was talking about.

"The Walkmans." I was in the process of strapping my radio to my backpack's chest strap.

"Why's that?"

"Cougars. They're everywhere and they're aggressive."

"Have you seen any?" asked Angela

"Oh yeah, last summer a big'un nearly jumped me. I turned just in time, because I sensed something. He was only ten feet away.... Scared the crap out of me."

"Have there been...."

"Attacks? Oh, yeah. This kitty would've had me if I hadn't been paying attention. I'd be careful with those Walkmans."

I made a mental note to use only one earphone.

"Did you shoot him?" Angela's face got longer and her eyes got wider.

"Oh, no, that's illegal. I just stood my ground and tried to look big." Looking big came natural to Travis.

I was sure that I'd hear more about this from Angela. But to me, wet weather remained a bigger threat than a cougar attack. We thanked Travis and strode back to the trail through a dense fog. We still had ninety-three miles to cover before Snoqualmie Pass—ninety-three soggy miles.

Over the next two days we covered forty-seven of those miles, to Government Meadow and the Mike Urich Shelter—a large wood shelter named after a 1940s trail worker. It was only five in the evening when we arrived, but given the recurring pattern of fog-drizzle-fog-shower-drizzle-fog-shower, we decided to stop and give our gear a chance to dry out. Hopefully, a shelter would also cure Angela's sudden bout of late-night illness. The previous night, at Sheep Lake, she'd rushed outside the tent twice in the middle of the rainy night to throw up.

Almost as soon as we'd laid our packs inside and set up the stove on the porch, the rain started again. We scuttled our dinner inside and were shoveling down mac 'n' cheese when Weather Carrot arrived, gasping for breath, having run from a now-driving storm. Soon Chad appeared, his entire body and pack covered by a gigantic parka. After dinner we all laid out our mattresses and sleeping bags on the wood floor. The rain pelted the roof and tinkled down the chimney of the wood-burning stove. Mice scurried in the corners. Weather Carrot was giddy to have company for the night, like a young boy at a sleepover. He launched into a long stream of trail stories, full of strange trail names. I tried to pay attention, as I thought it would make great material for our book. But my focus was worthless; my thoughts turned to Angela, to our life on the trail, to our lives off the trail, and to ... banana slugs.

How long would it take a banana slug to hike the PCT? Could one do it in a lifetime? Or would it have to be a several-generation relay, passing the slime baton off to the next slug in line? Banana slugs were slow; it most surely would take several banana-slug lifetimes. At top speed they probably could cover—what, a hundred feet an hour? Less than half a mile a day. What was their life expectancy? I didn't know. I decided that it would probably take hundreds of slug lifetimes to hike the PCT. "She's got just one foot, she ain't got no toes, she hangs out in the forest, and helps it decompose. BA-NA-NA-NA-NA-NA, BA (clap) NA (clap) NA (clap) SLUG!"

Really, I couldn't believe that Angela and I'd argued so bitterly over a slug kiss. A strong dose of unruly Washington weather had cooled us off. Petty arguments were forgotten now that Angela's fingers were turning to ghosts, hypothermia haunted us, and cougars waited around every corner.

The challenge of the Northern Cascades lay in front of us, and I wasn't sure what would stop first, the rain or our hike. We had a little over three hundred miles to go before the Canadian border. I didn't realize it yet, but those miles would be filled not only with rain, snow, and pain, but also with an unexpected reunion.

[17]

Panic and Precipitation

 I COULDN'T MOVE. WORSE, I COULDN'T BREATHE. *Gasp. Heave. Gasp.* No good. My throat was closing up. "This must be what it feels like to be buried alive," I thought. I tried to scream but nothing came out. I hyperventilated. I gagged. The feeling of being trapped was overwhelming. I was zipped tight in my mummy bag, swaddled in rain gear, two layers of fleece, long underwear, and two pairs of socks. "If I don't get out," I thought, "I'm going to die."

When I'd climbed into my sleeping bag (a new mummy-style bag we'd bought in Oregon in anticipation of Washington's cold weather), I'd been shivering, unable to get warm even after putting on every article of clothing in my pack. Now I was boiling. Rain pelted our tent, which was zipped up, too—like a coffin. The nylon hung heavy and close to my head. I had to get out. *Now.*

Thrashing and unzipping, I wiggled out of my sleeping bag, tore off layers of clothes, and stepped on Duffy's hand as I crashed out of the tent into the rain and mud. My bare toes sunk into the earth as I bent over to vomit, dry heave, and vomit again. In my desperation to escape I'd taken off nearly everything I was wearing. I stood shaking in the darkness. A man camped across Sheep Lake yelled to see if I was okay. I crouched to expel diarrhea and vomit simultaneously and meekly replied, "Sorry to wake you."

Duffy was dumbstruck. "Chiggy? Chiggy? What's wrong? Are you okay? Come back in the tent, you're going to freeze."

Still hyperventilating, I paced outside the tent door. I didn't want to go back inside, but my bare limbs were covered in goose bumps and rain. It couldn't have been more than thirty-five degrees out. Tears ran down my cheeks. What was wrong with me? Finally, dizzy and thirsty, I crawled into the tent and my sleeping bag, but no matter how cold I was, I couldn't put my clothes back on and I couldn't close my bag. I was too scared of that *feeling.*

Tremors plagued me the rest of the night. Lying beside me, Duffy wondered whether we should hike two miles south, back to Chinook Pass, and hitch a ride to the nearest hospital. The farther north we went, the more remote we'd be, and if I were seriously ill, getting help would be difficult.

The next morning, I was tired and dehydrated but capable of moving on. I knew that if we went to the emergency room, we might not come back—with 325 miles to cover in thirteen days, the sand (and dirt) in our hourglass was running low.

It drizzled on and off the entire day, and we covered the twenty miles to the Mike Urich Shelter as fast as we could. As we climbed onto the shelter's large raised porch and dumped our packs inside, the heavens started dumping water. Subsequent thunderclaps were as loud and piercing as rifle shots. Soon, Weather Carrot came running out of the forest, followed within minutes by Chad. As the four of us ducked into the mildew-scented cabin, we rejoiced at our good fortune. The grumpy weather gods could piss the night away; we'd be safe and dry, for the next ten hours at least.

Warming my hands around a mug of our favorite hot drink (hot chocolate mix, an envelope of Sanka, and dehydrated milk), I watched my cabin-mates, including Duffy, drift off to sleep. The Urich Shelter was relatively large, with a high ceiling; still, I was a little frightened of curling up in my mummy bag. I was sure it was going to come back—the sense of smothering—I just wasn't sure when. Eventually, with my body half out of my bag, I fell asleep. When I awoke in the morning the sun was out, and I'd had a peaceful night.

The following evening, however, I wasn't quite so lucky. Leaving the Mike Urich Shelter, we began the two-day hike to our next re-supply at Snoqualmie Pass. That night, in our tent, it happened again. Sweating, panting, shaking, panicking! I woke with a start. "I've got to get out of here," I screamed. There wasn't enough air. There wasn't enough room. *"Let me out!"* Out in the cold rain, throwing up freeze-dried chicken with rice and then dry heaving when there was nothing left—this was becoming a late-night ritual. Over the course of the forty-odd muddy Washington miles since my last conniption, Duffy and I had tried to figure out what mysterious illness had stricken me. During the day, while we hiked, I felt fine—a little sleep deprived, but otherwise as healthy as anyone who'd just walked 2,350 miles could expect to be. But at night—well, we weren't sure what to expect.

"I don't mean to sound unsympathetic," Duffy said as we stepped off the trail to allow a mule team to pass, "but I think it's all in your head."

"No way," I said. "Whatever's going on, it's real."

"I'm not saying it's not real. I just think it's more complicated than the stomach flu. I think you're probably having panic attacks."

A panic attack is roughly defined as the abrupt onset of intense fear which peaks in approximately ten minutes and includes at least four of sixteen possible symptoms, the worst of which are sweating, trembling, choking, nausea, fear of going crazy, fear of dying, the urge to flee, and intense dread that something terrible is going to happen.

Although we don't hear about panic attacks very often (besides on HBO's *The Sopranos,* in which they plague mob boss Tony Soprano), the "spells" are fairly common. In fact, one out of every fourteen people will experience a panic attack in his or her lifetime. In Tony's case, the attacks are precipitated by an inciting event, such as eating antipasto that reminds him of a gruesome finger-chopping incident. In many other cases, the attacks seem to just come out of nowhere.

Although a panic attack in itself is not dangerous, it is terrifying, and people who've had attacks often live in fear of them. Such dread can lead to phobias, depression, substance abuse, medical complications, and even suicide.

No one really knows what causes panic attacks. Some research suggests they occur when a "suffocation alarm mechanism" in the brain erroneously fires, falsely reporting that death is imminent. Why this happens is unclear, but according to the American Psychological Association, there does seem to be a connection with major, potentially stressful life transitions such as graduating from college, getting married, or having a child. Looking back, I wonder whether our imminent return to the "real world" after a summer of adventure triggered my attacks, or perhaps it was fear that, given the weather conditions, we might not reach Canada at all. Certainly Travis' warnings about mountain lions (also known as cougars or pumas) didn't help to put my mind at ease about anything.

Snippets of a dream I'd had just before my first panic attack were coming back to me. In it, I am hiking alone in dark woods, the type of woods where evil might lurk. I feel small and vulnerable, like a lost child. Suddenly, I can see myself from a great distance; I can also see a cougar, eight feet long from nose to black-tipped tail, creeping behind me, occasionally stopping in a crouched position, all the while intently staring at the back of my neck. His tail is twitching and his ears are erect. I realize that he's been stalking me, stalking me for miles. His legs start pumping gently up and down as he gets ready to leap. I scream to warn myself—and then wake up, screaming.

X ▪ ▀ ▪ X

Over the past few years, mountain lion attacks in North America have increased dramatically. Between 1991 and 1999, there were thirty-six recorded mountain lion attacks in North America. Seven of these were fatal. Two major theories are used to explain why such incidents are on the rise. First, as suburbs continue to sprawl, mountain lion habitat is disappearing. This means that more and more humans and lions find themselves in the same place at the same time. Second, conservation laws that prohibit the killing of any mountain lion except in self-defense are blamed for allowing the population to grow and to become increasingly aggressive.

According to the Mountain Lion Foundation of Texas, mountain lions are more likely to prey on people who are less than four feet tall. Children between the ages of five and eight have been the targets of greater than sixty percent of mountain lion attacks on humans. Additionally, the majority of lion–human confrontations occur when a person is alone. Given that Duffy and I often hiked a hundred or more yards apart, this fact did little to alleviate my fears. Neither did the knowledge that while I was over four feet tall, I was still rather petite (weighing in, at the time, at a meek 105 pounds).

One of the things that scared me the most about mountain lions was that they have a nasty habit of silently tracking people, sometimes following hikers for days. During this time, if the opportunity arises for the kill, a mountain lion will do so from behind, with a bite to the neck that severs the spinal cord.

While statistics may show that an American is ten times more likely to be killed by a domestic dog than a cougar, more and more PCT thru-hikers are seeing mountain lions. In fact, in an informal survey of articles written about the trail, I found that the majority of hikers interviewed mentioned at least one mountain lion encounter, often occurring at twilight, one of the cougar's favorite hunting times.

I didn't think that my fear of lions was causing my panic attacks, but I did think it contributed to stretching my nerves tight—so tight that, sometimes, at night, they snapped.

X ▪ ▪ ▪ ▪ ▪ X

The forty miles between the Mike Urich Shelter and Snoqualmie Pass are said to be the ugliest on the entire PCT, a checkerboard of clear-cuts, punctuated by muddy roads deeply rutted and churned by logging trucks whose wheels have jagged, earth-shredding teeth. We tried walking on these roads for a while, thinking they'd get us through the tortured landscape a little faster, but due to the shoe-sucking mud and crevasselike tire tracks, our progress was slow and we returned to the overgrown trail instead. Weather Carrot's constant banter occupied us for a while, and as long as the wind was blowing the right way, his company was a pleasant diversion. Still, we tired of fighting our way through dense huckleberry bushes that dumped water down our legs and into our shoes. My toes started each day white and achy then turned blue and became so cold that I couldn't feel them at all. We needed to get to Snoqualmie Pass, the lowest and busiest pass in Washington's Cascades, quickly. There we would find a motel.

My panic attacks and Raynaud's were wearing us both down, and we hoped that a night in town might warm me up and jump-start me out of whatever funk it was that I'd fallen into, or at least that sunnier skies might be on the horizon. At Snoqualmie Pass, we checked into the Summit Inn. After taking a scalding-hot shower, I called my parents from the pay phone in the lobby.

"I got a note from Meadow Ed," my mother said almost immediately upon answering the phone.

"Meadow Ed?" I said. "What the—? How the heck did he find you?"

"He returned a card I sent to Independence for you with a note that you'd left the day before and looked well. Who is this Meadow Ed?"

"He's a trail angel, Mom, he looks after us hikers."

I was astounded; trail magic was powerful enough to stretch around the world!

"We bought a map," my mother continued, "and have been following you on it. Where are you now?"

"Snoqualmie Pass in Washington."

"Oh yes, I see it. You're almost finished!"

"Yup, we're almost there. I'll be seeing you again soon," I said, and I knew I would.

There was a quick pause, and just before she hung up the phone my mother said, "And give our love to Duffy."

"I will, Mom. We'll call you from Canada." Turning away from the phone I steadied myself. For more than a year my parents had rarely talked about Duffy. Relief at having him acknowledged in a loving way—having us acknowledged—washed over me, and I happily headed to the inn's restaurant to meet Duffy. I found him talking with several other thru-hikers—Weather Carrot, the Abominably Slow Man, and Feather Dave, whose pack was as light as a feather.

When we left Snoqualmie Pass the next morning it wasn't raining—not one drop. The warmth of the sun on my face felt like the tender touch of a long lost friend. Climbing out of the pass and toward the high ridges of the Alpine Lake Wilderness we gained 3,000 feet in eleven miles. But despite the physical strain, I couldn't stop smiling. The sun was out, we'd spent a panic-free night in a soft bed, my relationship with my parents was on an upswing, and, finally, we were entering the North Cascades—America's Alps.

Unbroken by rivers and traversed by only a handful of roads, the North Cascades are characterized by craggy peaks, ice-plucked cliffs, serrated ridges, plunging valleys with rain forests at their bottoms, and 750 glaciers. Clinton C. Clarke described the landscape of the North Cascades as "the most primitive and roughest in the contiguous United States."

Atop an exposed ridge, we looked down into the Alpine Lakes Wilderness and ahead to Canada. At 5,000 feet, the trees were thin and the cliffs severe. I was sweating and relishing it. Duffy grinned and timed his steps with the beat of the music on his Walkman. We had seventy-five miles to cover before our next re-supply, in Skykomish; with weather like this we'd easily be there in three days and two nights—or so we thought.

Our first night in the North Cascades we camped under a dense cover of trees on moist, soft duff. We'd hiked twenty-two miles since noon and were feeling quite giddy. In fact, we were so drunk with sunshine and views that when clouds started to block out the moon, we barely even noticed.

In the early morning, though, I did notice gumdrop-size raindrops pelting our cooking pot (which I'd left on a tree stump), making metallic pings.

Over the next three days we walked approximately fifty-three miles, but to be honest, I don't remember that much about them. I mean, other than the views we got on our first day out, I never got the big picture of the area. Actually, my only picture of the area was taken through the small oval opening of my rain hood, and it looked like rain, sleet, and snow. I'd like to be able to write a vivid description of the North Cascades—really, I would—but all I can offer are visions of slushy puddles, drips off my hood, and a solid wall of gray cloud on the horizon.

I think the hardest thing about hiking in the rain is that you can't stop. Taking a break is not only pointlessly unenjoyable, but it's also dangerous. As soon as we stopped moving, our damp bodies caught a chill. Duffy's lips turned blue and I shivered. For three consecutive rainy days between Snoqualmie Pass and Skykomish, we hiked for six to eight hours straight, without sitting down, without lunch, and without feeling dry or warm. In our sneakers, our Smartwool socks were soggy sponges—the tired, dirty kind that linger by the laundry room sink for a while before finally getting thrown away. Our fleece mittens were equally soaked.

I was accustomed to getting Raynaud's in my fingers and toes; their blood-less pallor was a familiar sight. But on those rainy days, my entire palms went pale and I couldn't feel the cork handles of my trekking poles. In my sodden shoes, the Raynaud's was creeping across my feet, too. At night, while my panic attacks had thankfully subsided (I must have gotten used to the close conditions or, having now defined them as panic attacks, was somehow able to head them off), my feet continued to feel like dead fish.

In the morning, we didn't hear birds, just howling wind, rain through the trees, and rain against our tent. As we hiked, we listened to the Gore-Tex of our hoods swishing next to our ears, the squish of saturated earth under our feet, the clanging of our trekking poles as we clumsily rushed along, and each other's gasps of frustration and cold. At higher altitudes, sleet and hail pum-meled us and our feet crunched over ice. I wore my rain pants, but Duffy wore shorts (saving his rain pants as an extra dry layer to wear at night), and his legs turned ruddy and raw.

During two of our rainy nights between Snoqualmie and Skykomish we camped with Ken and Marcia and a gnomelike section hiker, Mike. I think it gave us all comfort to have company in such extreme conditions.

On our 125th night, as we made camp by Deception Lakes, I noticed steam rising off Mike's tent like a sauna. "He's using his stove in his tent," I whis-pered to Duffy, shocked and intrigued. We'd been taking turns standing out-side in the rain over our stove when we cooked dinner, or chose not to cook at all. I knew that using a stove in a tent was unsafe, as tents and sleeping bags are highly flammable. But I envied the warmth Mike must have been feeling. Warm, dry air in our tent would be blissful, and perhaps some of our clothes might even dry out. Soon all three tents, clustered in a muddy site next to the lakes, were emanating steam.

The next day, we headed down to Stevens Pass (at 4,062 feet in elevation), from which we'd access the small railroad town of Skykomish, fourteen miles to the west on Highway 2.

As we walked along the flooded trail, we saw bowling ball-sized mushrooms in fluorescent orange hues clinging to the dank bark of huge trees whose boughs were hanging heavy with raindrops. Stumbling down the trail, I tripped over exposed roots and hidden stones. My feet whizzed out from underneath me too many times to count, landing me on my butt in puddles and mud bogs. Each time I cried out like it was the first. Finally, after getting lost, we scrambled over a highway barrier onto the road's shoulder. Cars whizzed by, spraying water. We stuck out our thumbs for a ride, but it seemed hopeless. Who in their right minds would pick up two drenched, muddy hikers and their equally sodden packs?

Headlights blazing, windshield wipers whipping, car after car sped by without so much as a sidelong glance. Suddenly, though, the traffic ceased, and in the distance we made out the shape of a van. Its headlights were off and it was going only about twenty miles an hour. Behind it, cars were lined up, crawling. "That's our ride," Duffy joked. I knew he was right and was excited and scared all at once. If anyone was going to pick us up, it was going to be the wacko driving that broken-down van. We'd learned a lot about hitchhiking since May.

But the van drove by us, causing me to let out a cry.

"What? Is he crazy?" Duffy exclaimed several seconds later. I followed his eyes. The van had stopped about a hundred yards beyond us and was backing up, on the highway. "He's either going to give us a ride or kill himself," Duffy said. "Come on!" He started running to the van. Horns honked and brakes screeched.

"Hey, you guys need a ride?" asked a pale, sunken-eyed man of perhaps thirty-five.

"Yeah, Skykomish?" Duffy replied hurriedly.

"Get in, throw them packs on the backseat."

I looked at the backseat; it was clearly the guy's bed. An old tan and orange sleeping bag and a grungy flat pillow lay on it.

"Lemme just move your stuff," I said, not wanting to get his home muddy.

"Nah, just get in." I felt bad, but Duffy was already in the front seat and the van was beginning to roll, so I jumped on his bed and slammed the door shut.

Without so much as a glance in the mirror, our driver pulled out into the highway and started cruising—at a mean twenty-five miles an hour. The rain was coming down harder, and without headlights or windshield wipers the road ahead appeared as just a blur. Only the oncoming headlights warned us of curves.

"Man, I don't feel right," our driver groaned. "I've been up in the hot springs for a couple days. Man, I don't feel right."

Duffy looked at him. "Hot springs?"

"A couple days?" It was my turn to groan.

"Yeah, Kennedy Hot Springs, you should check 'em out, man, you'd dig 'em. But I think I stayed in too long. I started hallucinating and shit." As he spoke, he looked right at Duffy, who, in turn, stared at the road ahead, as if willing the Himalayan-sweater-clad hippy to look where he was going. Later, I learned that the Kennedy Hot Springs (where clothing is optional) are filled with "ill-rumored" water. In fact, according to the *Seattle Post-Intelligencer*, hikers should avoid them in the summer "when the bacteria count can be high."

"I, uh, like your van," I said, trying to change the subject.

"Got it for a hundred bucks and been living in it for a few months. Brakes and lights ain't so hot, but for a '68 Ford it runs pretty good."

"How about the windshield wipers?" Duffy asked, "They work?"

"Man, I need a jolt or something. I'm out of it."

The next few minutes felt like eons. Finally we pulled into the gas station in Skykomish, a town so small that it doesn't have a grocery store, drugstore, barber, or doctor. We both jumped out of the van like it was on fire while our hallucinating chauffeur went inside to get a cup of coffee. Duffy had urged him to get Gatorade rather than a diuretic like coffee, but there was no reasoning with this guy; he was, as he said, out of it.

When we checked into the Sky River Inn, the motherly woman at the front desk said she'd wash our clothes for us if we brought them over. So, as usual, Duffy sat naked on the bed while I threw on my sundress and delivered our muddy, wet bundle. We hung our tent, rain fly, and sleeping bags all over the room and made macaroni and cheese on the stove. Ken and Marcia were in the room adjoining ours, and the section-hiker, Mike, came in to use our shower before catching a Greyhound bus home. Later, we opened the door between our room and Ken and Marcia's and, sitting on our respective beds, we chatted through the doorway, reliving the deluge and watching bad movies on TV.

The next day, the sun came out and we laid our gear out on the grass behind our rooms, which were near the Skykomish River. On any other occasion, we would have been ecstatic to spend the day reading and writing by a river, but with our trail days being numbered, we were grumpy that the sun had only decided to come out while we were in town.

Back in our room, we quietly sorted through our second-to-last re-supply package. Now, with our journey coming to an end, everything smacked bittersweet. We'd been on the PCT for 127 days but it felt like a lifetime. I could barely remember what life was like before the PCT. Due to the rain, we were behind schedule and would have to skip another section of trail—ninety-seven miles, in fact. Neither of us was happy about it, and the decision hung over us like another dark stormy cloud.

"What if we hiked thirty-five miles per day, no rest days?" I suggested.

"Chiggy, be realistic. If we had perfect weather—maybe. But probably not; the terrain's going to get rough, and with foul weather, we'll never make it."

I knew he was right, and while Duffy was running errands I was on the phone with Greyhound, figuring out the schedule between Skykomish and Lake Chelan, where we could take a ferry to Stehckin and pick up the PCT at mile 2,570.

"When we reach Canada, let's turn around and hike back," I joked.

"Oh, yeah, you wanna go back to the desert?" Duffy asked.

"I would. I'd go back and do it all again." Our showdown at Vasquez Rocks, the sunburns and blisters, my knee injury, Duffy's incredibly shrinking waistline, even my panic attacks—they all seemed like distant memories.

[18]

Monument 78

FROM A DISTANCE, IT WAS HARD TO TELL WHAT IT WAS. Though it resembled a hiker, it moved slowly and close to the ground, waddling rather than striding. We were north of Hart's Pass at mile 2,620, trekking across the rock-strewn sidewall of Slate Peak under clear skies. Mount Baker's 10,778-foot glaciated peak dominated the western horizon. The creature advancing from the north appeared to be bluish in color, all blue except for one small patch of white. As I came within a hundred yards, the beast sat down. It was then that I realized it was a man, a man resting on a boulder and awaiting my arrival.

"Meadow Ed!"

"Duffy-me-boy."

"Whoa. . . . What are you doing out here?" I was as surprised to see Ed out there as I would have been to see Rush Limbaugh.

"I'm hiking south, checking up on y'all." Ed was dedicated, that was for certain. "How's the umbilical cord?" he asked with a wink.

"Strong as ever. She's right behind me, can't seem to lose her. Trail's been tough, though. Especially the last few weeks, with all the damn rain. Doubt my shoes will ever dry out."

"'Tisn't easy for anyone, me-boy, but you'll make it. Monument 78 is just a day or so away." It seemed like Ed might actually be proud of us. I decided that I shouldn't disappoint him by mentioning that we'd skipped a big chunk of Section K. But there was one item that *did* need to be addressed.

"Ed, I gotta' tell you—remember you said the trail would make us cry? Well, I haven't, not yet. I've been close, but...."

"Yeah, well, I made up for you. I've cried. Lots." Angela placed her big fuzzy mitten on my shoulder. "Ed, I can't believe you're here! How are you?"

"Good. I'm just checking up on y'all. Angela, you're looking strong. Those tears toughened ya up, eh?"

"Yep," Angela smiled. It had taken over two thousand miles, but she finally had gained Ed's respect.

"How's it look from here to Manning Park?" I asked.

"Trail's in pretty good shape. Weather's been good, real good.... Section L is usually mild anyway... Mount Baker catches the storms. You'll stay plenty high, with nice views. Anyone behind you guys?" Ed was an information-seeking machine.

"Ken and Marcia, Weather Carrot, Feather Dave.... They're probably a few days back. And we saw Daris going south. Have you heard anything about Casey and Toby or Chris and Stacey?"

"You mean Crazy Legs and Catch-23? They're still on. Chris and Stacey got off at Cascade Locks. Sounded like they'd gotten tired of it all."

"Can't blame them. Like you said, Ed, this trail can break you down," I replied.

"Sure can." Meadow Ed scratched his beard thoughtfully.

I was excited we had happened upon Ed. As much as I'd poked fun at him and used his doubt as a motivational force, I was fond of the guy. It was fitting to see him now, just a couple days from the Canadian border. Every thing was coming full circle. The end of our adventure was near.

As we parted ways, a touch of melancholy fell over me. I wondered if I'd ever see Ed again. He wasn't the type of guy we were likely to bump into on the streets of Philadelphia. I didn't even know if he had a permanent home or a telephone number. He was a relic of the Pacific Crest Trail, a treasure of sorts—a portly treasure, badly in need of a good tooth cleaning. My mind swept back over all of the generous characters we'd met along the trail: Bob in San Diego, Donna Saufley, Butch Wiggs, and so many others that bestowed trail magic upon us. I'd never experienced such a culture of good will and trust before, and doubt I ever will again. "Someday," I thought, "I'll return to the PCT as a trail angel, and maybe, a few gifted six-packs at a time, I can help the magic live on."

X ▪ ▪ ▪ ▪ X

Our reunion with Ed wouldn't have been possible if we hadn't skipped most of Section K. We hadn't wanted to, but given our time frame it seemed like our only option. According to what we'd read, Section K was fantastically scenic but also extremely rigorous. "With a combination of rugged terrain, many climbs, isolation, and potentially stormy weather," writes Karen Berger in *The Pacific Crest Trail: A Hiker's Companion*, "[Section K] is often considered one of the most difficult on the entire PCT. It's also one of the most varied and beautiful. The landscape ranges from glacier-scoured bowls to old-growth forests; elevations range from 1,550 to 7,126 and the weather can challenge hikers with four seasons' worth of conditions, sometimes in a single day."

Given our impending Canadian deadline, we decided that we couldn't risk getting stuck in the middle of Section K, post-holing our way through snow-drifts. My parents were scheduled to meet us either September 16 or 17 in Manning Park, and after that we'd have to find our way to San Diego for a September 19 flight to Philly. I was due to be in class on September 20, and Angela needed to be back at work a couple days later. As it was, we'd already lost the opportunity to be pure "thru-hikers," at least by any reasonably strict definition. Hiking or not hiking Section K wouldn't change that fact. Thus, it seemed reasonable to give ourselves a chance to end our hike at Monument 78 rather than risk having it end in the Glacier Peak Wilderness—chased backward by snow.

Our detour took us from Skykomish to Lake Chelan via bus and then across the lake to Stehekin via ferry. In the process, we completed our summer tour of the three deepest lakes in the United States. Lake Chelan, a glacier-carved gorge, is number three on the list, after Crater Lake and Lake Tahoe. At the northern tip of the 1,149-foot-deep lake sits the small settlement of Stehekin, a town accessible only by watercraft or footpath. We reunited with the PCT at the Agnes Creek trailhead (mile 2,569) after a bumpy ride up a dirt road on a Park Service bus.

The PCT took us along Bridge Creek, across Highway 20 at Rainy Pass, and up to Cutthroat Pass. Meanwhile, unbeknownst to us, several inches of snow were being dumped in the Glacier Peak Wilderness of Section K. We hiked under dry but overcast skies on a high crest, traversing mountainous graywackle ("muddy sandstone") scree and rounding glacier-carved bowls. Periodically we'd drop through a patch of bright forest tapestry—larch, maple, and spruce leaves in seasonal colors. The night before seeing Meadow Ed we'd camped at Brush Creek and finished off our very last Mountain House dinner. It was the summer-long favorite—chili mac—nutritious, delicious, and still gassy as hell.

The next day, after a strenuous climb to a shoulder of Tatie Peak and a descent to Hart's Pass, we had our unexpected reunion with Ed. And that night, camped at a heavily wooded saddle near Holman Pass, nostalgia struck fiercely.

I lay awake, listening to an unknown animal scratch its claws on a tree outside the tent. I didn't dare wake Angela—those claws sounded suspiciously cougar-esque. The clawing soon ceased, but still, I couldn't sleep. We were twenty-two miles from the Canadian border at Monument 78 and twenty-nine miles from a comfortable bed at the Manning Park Lodge. In many ways, I was anxious to be finished; I was sick of the dampness and ready to immerse myself in the luxury of home-cooked meals, trips to the movie theater, and Sunday afternoons watching football. But at the same time, the reality that something special was ending was setting in.

I'd walked for an entire summer, testing my feet, legs, and mind along a challenging roller coaster. I'd hiked through the devil's heat, despite Indra's rain, and with Giardia's affliction. I'd seen sparkling desert in early dawn and brilliant alpine lakes as pure as the snowmelt from which they formed, and gazed from Whitney's peak at miles of free wilderness, an unparalleled expanse of granite, ice, and green. I'd tossed pinecones the size of melons, stepped over beetles the size of small rodents, dodged raspy rattlers and run from ursine mothers. I'd hiked nearly a marathon and a half—in one day. Nearly one hundred marathons—in one summer. And I'd done it all with the woman I loved. We did it together. We'd share this forever; nothing could take away this experience. We'd fought, we'd bickered, she'd cried, and blisters were formed and incised and formed again. But it was more than worth it—it was the adventure of a lifetime, with the love of a lifetime.

X ■ ▪ ▪ ■ X

The weather was clear and the skies were blue as we reached Lakeview Ridge. We turned slowly in a circle, admiring the views. To the north, the Cascades continued far into Canada—the crest, unlike the trail, didn't end at the Canadian border. Craggly Three Fools Peak rose from the south and more mountains loomed to the west. Reds, golds, and oranges painted the valley to our east.

Our last six miles were a blur. We snaked down a series of switchbacks, and then I saw it: Monument 78, a four-foot replica of the Washington Monument. I broke into a run and a whoop, twirling my trekking poles like a drum major's baton.

"Canada! Canada!" I yelled.

"Canada! Canada! Canada!" cheered Angela, close behind. I reached the monument, dumped my pack, and met her for a big bear hug. We jumped up and down together, continuing our chant.

The Canadian border couldn't have presented a more stark contrast to the trail's southern terminus. There was no fence, no barbed wire, and no desert chaparral. Instead, there was just a fifteen-foot-wide swath cut through rolling evergreen forest. Other than the thin strip of deforestation and a sign welcoming us to British Columbia, there was no evidence that we'd reached an international border. No guards, no roaring crowds, no beers to crack open, not even a bench to sit on—just us and Monument 78. But for the last four and a half months, during the toughest and most memorable moments, "us" had always turned out to be enough.

We arrived at the monument around four in the afternoon and didn't leave until after five. During our hour at the border, we finished up our last roll of film and then pulled off the top of the monument, discovering a trail register in its belly. We read through it and composed our final entry.

The JourneyFilm Crew—well, at least part of the crew—had finished. "August 21: JourneyFilm Crew rolling through. Mexico to Canada 2000. It was worth it," wrote J. B. Kimmo added, "My toes frickin hurt and my shoes are full of frickin holes." There weren't many other familiar names in the register; our recent trail jumping had left many of our friends behind. As I scanned the register, an August 19 entry caught my eye: "The PCT reminds me that it is important to stop just being a human being, and become a human doing."

Our entry was a hastily composed poem (I use this term generously) based on a song from the *South Park* cartoon:

September 16
The March of Pines (Blame Canada!)
Feet ache, shirt reeks.
Legs ache, socks defiled.
Blame Canada! Blame Canada!

Bugs in my face
Bugs in our food.
Bugs in my bowel.
Uh-Oh, quick pass me the trowel.
Blame Canada! Blame Canada!

Snickers for breakfast.
Snickers for lunch.
Dinner out of our pot.
Watch our teeth rot.
Blame Canada! Blame Canada!

Over 2,300 miles,
And 132 days too.
Through mountain, desert and rain.
So much potential for discomfort and pain.
Blame Canada! Blame Canada!

Danger here, danger there.
Ever since Kennedy Meadows Store
I've believed I could end up dead
If I didn't remember what "Meadow Ed said."
Blame Canada! Blame Canada!

The Mojave was steaming,
Washington was drenching,
The Sierra was rugged,
And Crater Lake is deep,
Now we are done
And don't know whether to laugh or weep.
Blame Canada! Blame Canada!

X ▪ ▪ ▪ ▪ X

As we composed our masterpiece, Feather Dave arrived at a jog. Although he'd just completed forty trail miles in ten hours, he somehow looked fresh. Soon after, Lady Godiva and her 1,200-pound quarter horse, Livingston, appeared. We'd unknowingly passed them earlier in the day. Their trip wasn't over; they planned on returning to the Sierra to complete several hundred unfinished miles.

We'd have dallied by the monument longer, but unfortunately we still had seven anticlimactic miles before reaching Manning Park Lodge. Reluctantly, we replaced the register and hoisted our packs. As a final gesture, I stuffed my mildew-soaked Nerf football into the monument—a gift that I hoped Casey and Toby would eventually appreciate.

Several hours and many shades of darkness later, we were at a road, and lost. It was a final insult, a reminder that the trail gods weren't always benevolent. The trail had been rerouted, and instead of emerging on Highway 3 less than a mile from the Manning Park Lodge as expected, it emerged at a poorly lit two-lane road. After half an hour of wandering, we finally received directions from a passing motorist and embarked on what we figured would be our last road walk.

But, oh no—there was one final surprise waiting for us at Manning Park Lodge. My parents hadn't arrived; they were at a hotel several hours away. They hadn't expected us to finish until the next morning and we'd had no way of contacting them. Even worse, there were no rooms available at the lodge; it was Saturday night and they were booked solid. One last night in our nylon blue home awaited us at a nearby Canadian campground. We set up camp in the pitch black on hard, gravelly ground.

At seven the next morning a campground ranger roused us. He needed twelve Canadian dollars.

"But we're thru-hikers," Angela said, spoiled by months of special treatment.

"Trail ends here, ma'am," he said, holding out his hand for payment. The Canadians didn't seem so keen on the trail angel concept.

X ▪ ▪ ▪ X

But no matter how inglorious our ending, nothing could dim the unforgettable memories. Weeks later, back in Philadelphia, I flipped through William Gray's book, the one we'd found at my parent's cabin in Big Sur. It had been, and still was, an inspiration.

I reread the epilogue and felt a strong kinship with Gray. "My thoughts went over our long journey, and I felt again the joy of walking through the land, observing, contemplating, marveling. I remembered the hour-to-hour changes in terrain, the day-to-day changes in weather, the week-to-week changes in season—and even more gradual changes in myself. Along the way I had learned to set aside some habits of my city life and to heed the advice of Ralph Waldo Emerson: 'Adopt the pace of nature. Her secret is patience."

I, too, had found patience on the trail, and perspective. These acquisitions helped me adapt to the stresses of returning to my city life. But there was one task that I shouldn't, couldn't be patient about any longer.

Epilogue

COYOTES *YIP, YIP YA'ROO*'D as a full desert moon began its ascent across the quickly darkening sky. The trail meandered among the fuchsia blooms of prickly pear cactus, blood-red Indian paintbrushes, and fragrant sagebrush. Jittery pushup lizards and emerald hummingbirds kept us company as we set up camp on a sandy exposed ridge in the Colorado Desert.

Five hundred and fifty miles later, from glacier-polished, snow-blanketed High Sierra slopes, we gazed down at a turquoise, ice-crusted tarn, breathing air so crisp it made our lungs ache.

In the Trinity Alps, a burly bruin cub peered at us from his treetop perch. Four hundred and sixty miles north, in Oregon, sheets of crystal water plunged over a black volcanic cliff that dripped with moss. In Washington, bright orange mushrooms flourished in a dense muddy rain forest. On the slopes of the North Cascades, larch trees donned autumn hues of gold.

We'd been living, breathing, and walking the PCT for four and a half months. You'd think that would have given us enough time to prepare. But nothing can really prepare you for coming to the end of (in the words of a fellow thru-hiker) your "life's best journey (so far)." When we arrived, our hearts burst with happiness, but also broke.

Monument 78 sits in a small clearing in the forest between Washington and British Columbia, about seventy-eight miles east of Monument 1, which is the westernmost point of the U.S.–Canada border. It had taken us approximately 6,300,000 steps, 528 doses of ibuprofen, 180 Snickers bars, thirty-six popped blisters, seven pairs of shoes, four pairs of shorts, two stoves, and one titanium pot to get there. But really what it took was love (albeit a somewhat blistered kind) and determination.

At the end of it all Toby, also known as Catch-23, wrote, "We walked from an arbitrary line in the sand to an arbitrary cut in the trees. It is not a particularly meaningful accomplishment when you boil it down. It is somewhat of a ridiculous thing to do. But it was meaningful to us, for some reason, and that is why we did it."

Like many before us, we felt joy and exhilaration but also sadness upon finishing. We had renewed faith in the generosity of strangers and in humanity at large, but we also dreaded going back to crowded urban streets. We felt like we'd discovered a simpler view of life and yet longed for creature comforts. We couldn't wait to get home; we were sad to go home.

We'd had adrenaline rushes, we'd conquered things—our fears, our differences, and a mountain or two in between—but mostly we'd strived, long and hard. We'd strived to become better hikers, better lovers, and most importantly better people. And even if we only succeeded in these things just a little bit, it was worth every ache and pain. As Walt Whitman once wrote, "Now I see the secret of making the best persons, it is to grow in the open air and to eat and sleep with the Earth."

If you've made it this far in this book, you already know that our trail life wasn't all sunsets, starry nights, and self-development. Sweat, stench, gritty skin, and exhaustion killed many otherwise profound moments. Simply put, the day-to-day trekking wasn't always bliss, but the romance of our thru-hike turned out to be more concrete than any Hallmark sentiment. The romance was in what we accomplished together. Climbing Mount Whitney, the tallest mountain in the contiguous U.S.; helping one another through thirty-mile days; holding hands across ice, snow, as well as treacherous fords, and knowing limb—if not life—depended on our grip; even carrying a little extra weight when the other person was hurting. These and other situations created a bond and partnership that candlelight dinners and strolls on the beach couldn't match. We're not against such luxuries, of course; in fact, we couldn't wait to enjoy them again. But as Ginny Owen (who had met her husband, Jim, while thru-hiking the AT) once told us, "On the trail, you don't have masks and you don't have distractions and you don't have games. You're just being yourself. That leads to a level of intimacy that is way beyond what you might develop during the same time period at home. You spend six months with somebody on the trail and you'll know that person better than you'll know most people in twenty years." And if you still like each other when you hit the border—well, you're in pretty good shape.

In Judaism, after reading and studying the Torah, members of a congregation often recite, *"Chazak, chazak, venitchazek,"* which can be translated as, "May we be strengthened from this experience and move from strength to strength." Because the Torah has been read publicly, the listeners are said to gain strength not just from the words but also from the community that reads the words together. So it was with our long walk. Each of us gained much from walking from Mexico to Canada, but by doing it together we gained even more—most importantly, we gained each other.

X ▪ ▪ ▪ X

They were clouds with something to prove—gray, brooding, and headed our way. Although our backs were to the storm front, we could see it reflected in the way the maple leaves were flopping upside down, exposing their silver underbellies in the wind. Still holding hands, we laughed and looked into the heavens as fat drops began to fall—first scattered like petals in the wind and then steady and straight. It was perfect—the perfect end to one adventure and beginning to another.

We've got a picture from that day permanently etched in our hearts and minds. In it, we are clasping hands with our two sets of parents in a circle of unity. Thunder punctuates the moment with loud joyful claps. Rain courses down Angela's smiling face, mixing with tears of joy. As husband and wife we run down the aisle, throwing birdseed out of our titanium PCT pot and laughing. All of our loved ones are there ready to join us in a new future—together. Later, the clouds part to reveal a warm, summer sunset.

X ▪ ▪ ▪ X

Thirty million Americans and three million Canadians live within a hundred miles of the PCT, yet only about three hundred people set out to hike from Mexico to Canada each year. In 2000 (according to Meadow Ed's records), approximately 103 people reached their goal—105 if you include us. Afterward, we all went home to different cities, states, and even countries. But even now we remain connected by our shared experience. When the PCT was officially completed in 1993, then Secretary of the Interior Bruce Babbitt said, "It seems to me that what this day and this occasion is all about is the way trails connect not just land and ecosystems, but people."

Over the course of our summer on the PCT, we grew extremely attached to the trail angels and to many thru-hiking compatriots. We've lost touch with some, but we think of them all often and still greatly admire their strength and accomplishments.

Ken and Marcia Powers began their PCT thru-hike on May 1 and finished on September 21, after 144 days. "The scenery is what kept us going," Ken once said. Since returning home from the PCT the couple, in their fifties, has completed the 3,100-mile Continental Divide Trail (CDT). They plan to thru-hike the Appalachian Trail during the summer of 2003.

Amigo hiked the length of the California PCT during the summer of 2000. In 2001 he returned to hike the PCT through Oregon, and in 2002 he finished his thru-hike by completing the Washington portion of the trail. He now teaches outdoor education in Northern California and during the summer months he and his parents run a trail angel operation on the Hat (Hot) Creek Rim, caching water for thirsty hikers.

We saw Daris for the last time just north of Stehekin, Washington. After losing both Fish and Ryan, she had gone home to Canada to take care of some logistics before continuing her hike. She finished on October 3 after switching directions (to beat the impending bad weather) and heading southbound from the border. She's now studying forestry in British Columbia and hopes to eventually complete the CDT—with her dog.

Fish finished the California PCT, but then returned to Florida for business reasons. Ryan reached Canada without him on October 4.

Crazy Legs and Catch-23 stumbled upon the Canadian border on September 30 after 147 days, having achieved their goal of hiking one percent (twenty-seven miles) of the trail while intoxicated. The next day they returned home to Seattle to recover from the hangover. Catch-23 claims he never experienced any re-entry shock. "I just adjusted the couch in front of the TV and then adjusted my ass to the couch, and hey, I was readjusted." Later he would adjust himself to teaching English in Japan for six months. We don't know what Casey is doing, but are pretty sure it's something crazy.

Fallingwater (Ron) completed the trail on September 14, sans Drip (Brandon), who had to return home in time for the first day of high school. And while Drip is now too fully immersed in being a teenager to do much hiking, his father continues the fine family tradition, hiking portions of the CDT and designing lightweight packs, tarps, and tents.

Chris and Stacey got off the trail in Cascade Locks after finishing 2,150 miles. They have since broken up.

Five months after completing the PCT, J. B. asked his girlfriend to marry him. The couple now lives in Los Angeles. They're hoping to hike the AT together in the near future. Kimmo eventually returned to Finland. He remains committed to endurance feats and is training to swim from Finland to Sweden, across the Gulf of Bothnia. Work on the JourneyFilm Crew documentary continues.

Trail angels Bob, Meadow Ed, Donna and Jeff, and Don and Helen are still going strong. Pat and Paul's Hiker's Oasis was forced to move after Kamp Anza RV Park became a "resort." The Oasis now operates about a mile from its original location. Paul is installing outdoor showers for hikers and Pat's roses, after being transplanted, continue to bloom. Vermilion Valley Resort maintains its hiker-friendly status but sadly without one of the hikers' dear friends: Butch Wiggs committed suicide in January 2001. He is sorely missed.

Duffy graduated from medical school in May of 2001 and has since moved on to complete his training in Emergency Medicine. Angela continues to write, for herself and for others. After getting married in May 2001, we headed cross-country (by car, not by foot) to make our home in Northern

California, just an hour and a half drive from where the PCT meets the shores of Echo Lake. Over weekends and extended weekends we're slowly filling in the missing pieces of our PCT thru-hike. On such excursions we are now attached, as Meadow Ed would say, "by an umbilical cord" to a third hiking companion—a gender-confused Labrador retriever named Gary. She loves chili mac, too.

Recommended Reading

Ballard, Chris. *Hoops Nation: A Guide to America's Best Pickup Basketball.* New York: Henry Holt and Company, 1998

Bane, Michael. *Trail Safe: Averting Threatening Human Behavior in the Outdoors.* Berkeley: Wilderness Press, 2000

Berger, Karen. *Advanced Backpacking: A Trailside Guide.* New York: W.W. Norton & Company, 1998

———. *Hiking the Triple Crown: How to Hike America's Longest Trails.* Seattle: The Mountaineers, 2001

Berger, Karen, and Daniel R. Smith. *Along the Pacific Crest Trail.* Englewood, Colo.: Westcliffe Publishers, 1998

———. *The Pacific Crest Trail: A Hiker's Companion.* Woodstock, Vt.: The Countryman Press, 2000

Bryson, Bill. *A Walk in the Woods: Rediscovering America on the Appalachian Trail.* New York: Broadway Books, 1998

Croot, Leslie. *Pacific Crest Trail Town Guide.* Sacramento: Pacific Crest Trail Association, 2002

Go, Ben. *Pacific Crest Trail Data Book.* Sacramento: Pacific Crest Trail Association, 2001

Gray, William R. *The Pacific Crest Trail.* Washington: The National Geographic Society, 1975

Hall, Adrienne. *Woman's Guide: Backpacking.* Camden, Maine: Ragged Mountain Press, 1998

Herrero, Stephen. *Bear Attacks: Their Causes and Avoidance.* New York: The Lyons Press, 1985

Jardine, Ray. *Beyond Backpacking: Ray Jardine's Guide to Lightweight Hiking.* Arizona City, Ariz.: AdventureLore Press, 1992

————. *The Pacific Crest Trail Hiker's Handbook.* LaPine, Ore.: AdventureLore Press, 1992

Jenkins, Peter. *A Walk Across America.* New York: Fawcett Crest, 1979

Meyer, Kathleen. *How to Shit in the Woods: An Environmentally Sound Approach to a Lost Art.* Berkeley: Ten Speed Press, 1989

Muir, John. *My First Summer in the Sierra.* San Francisco: Sierra Club Books, 1998

Pelton, Robert Young. *Come Back Alive: The Ultimate Guide to Surviving Disasters, Kidnappings, Animal Attacks, and Other Nasty Perils of Modern Travel.* New York: Doubleday, 1999

Rawicz, Slavomir. *The Long Walk: The True Story of a Trek to Freedom.* New York: Nick Lyons Books, 1956

Ryback, Eric. *The High Adventure of Eric Ryback: Canada to Mexico on Foot.* San Francisco: Chronicle Books, 1971

Schaffer, Jeff, and Andy Selters. *The Pacific Crest Trail: Oregon and Washington.* Berkeley: Wilderness Press, 2000

Schaffer, Jeff, and Thomas Winnett, Ben Schifrin, and Ruby Johnson Jenkins. *The Pacific Crest Trail: Northern California.* Berkeley: Wilderness Press, 2003

————. *The Pacific Crest Trail: Southern California.* Berkeley: Wilderness Press, 2003

About the Authors

Angela Ballard has written articles about hiking, health, and business for *Men's Health* and other publications, as well as *GORP.com*. Prior to focusing on freelance writing in 2001, Angela worked at Medical Broadcasting Company in Philadelphia, where she wrote about health and medicine for the Internet. Today she writes extensively for the Pacific Crest Trail Association's *Communicator* magazine and related publications.

Raised in Westchester County, New York, Angela's favorite childhood toys were a stuffed lamb named Lamby, and a crying baby doll named Victoria. But even though her bedroom was filled with dolls and papered in pink flowers, Angela climbed trees with the best of them (i.e., her big brothers). This meant that, more often than not, she could be found (or conveniently not found) playing in the woods, where she built forts and snacked on wild onions. Still, the Pacific Crest Trail fare of jerky and raisins came as quite a shock. She adapted, though, and even now can sometimes be caught eating food she's dropped in the dirt.

Duffy Ballard grew up in the suburbs of San Francisco and attended Marin Academy high school. Later he moved to Philadelphia to attend Haverford College, meet Angela, major in Political Science, and play three years of extremely average Division III basketball. After college, Duffy remained in Philadelphia for medical school and, in 2001, graduated with an M.D. and a master's degree in bioethics from the University of Pennsylvania. Soon afterward he and Angela were married and moved cross-country to Sacramento, where he is completing his residency in Emergency Medicine at the U.C. Davis Medical Center.

Duffy has always enjoyed a good camping trip, especially if someone has had the forethought to bring along a twelve-pack of cold beer. Having his wife along is nice, too. It would be even nicer if she could carry more beer.

BARBARA SAVAGE
MILES FROM NOWHERE
MEMORIAL AWARD

★ WINNER ★
MEMORIAL
AWARD
BARBARA SAVAGE
Miles from Nowhere

I nitiated in 1990, this ongoing biennial award is presented for an unpublished work of non-fiction written as a personal narrative. The program commemorates the late Barbara Savage, author of the book, Miles from Nowhere, published by The Mountaineers Books in 1983.

Barbara was killed in a cycling accident shortly before the book's publication; the story of Barbara and Larry Savage's two-year, 23,000-mile, round-the-world bicycle adventure continues, however, to embrace a wide readership and to generate letters from readers who have come to know Barbara through her book. The author's husband, Larry Savage, created this award in cooperation with The Mountaineers Books by donating royalties to encourage adventure writing in the genre of Miles from Nowhere.

THE PRIZE AWARD
The prize consists of a $3,000 cash award, a $12,000 guaranteed advance against royalties, and publication by The Mountaineers Books.

ELIGIBILITY CRITERIA
The winning manuscript will be a compelling non-fiction account of a personal, muscle-powered outdoor adventure. It will vividly convey a sense of the risks, joys, hardships, disappointments, triumphs, moments of humor, and accidents of fate that are inevitably a part of such a journey. It will recognize the fact that we are all, like it or not, unwitting adventurers in a strange landscape.

SELECTION PROCESS

All entries meeting the basic criteria will be read by a panel of reviewers who will select the top candidates to go on to a panel of judges outside of The Mountaineers. The judges selected include people knowledgeable both in outdoor subjects and literary matters. The sponsors of the award reserve the right not to make the award for any given period if, in their opinion, no entry during that period is sufficiently outstanding.

For more information, contact: The Barbara Savage Miles from Nowhere Memorial Award, The Mountaineers Books, 1001 SW Klickitat Way, Suite 201, Seattle, WA 98134; (206) 223-6303; *www.mountaineersbooks.org/*

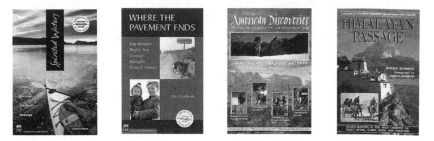

THE MOUNTAINEERS, founded in 1906, is a nonprofit outdoor activity and conservation club, whose mission is "to explore, study, preserve, and enjoy the natural beauty of the outdoors. . . ." Based in Seattle, Washington, the club is now the third-largest such organization in the United States, with 15,000 members and five branches throughout Washington State.

The Mountaineers sponsors both classes and year-round outdoor activities in the Pacific Northwest, which include hiking, mountain climbing, ski-touring, snowshoeing, bicycling, camping, kayaking and canoeing, nature study, sailing, and adventure travel. The club's conservation division supports environmental causes through educational activities, sponsoring legislation, and presenting informational programs. All club activities are led by skilled, experienced volunteers, who are dedicated to promoting safe and responsible enjoyment and preservation of the outdoors.

If you would like to participate in these organized outdoor activities or the club's programs, consider a membership in The Mountaineers. For information and an application, write or call The Mountaineers, Club Headquarters, 300 Third Avenue West, Seattle, WA 98119; (206) 284-6310.

The Mountaineers Books, an active, nonprofit publishing program of the club, produces guidebooks, instructional texts, historical works, natural history guides, and works on environmental conservation. All books produced by The Mountaineers Books fulfill the club's mission.

Send or call for our catalog of more than 500 outdoor titles:

The Mountaineers Books
1001 SW Klickitat Way, Suite 201
Seattle, WA 98134
(800) 553-4453

mbooks@mountaineersbooks.org

www.mountaineersbooks.org

OTHER TITLES YOU MIGHT ENJOY FROM
THE MOUNTAINEERS BOOKS

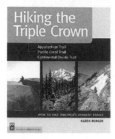

Hiking the Triple Crown, *Karen Berger*
For anyone planning hikes on the Appalachian, Pacific Crest, or Continental Divide trails, this is an indisputable, must-have resource

Best of the Pacific Crest Trail: Washington, *Dan Nelson*
A useful mix of day hikes, overnighters, or weeklong outings for hikers who want to enjoy the best of Washington's section of the PCT

Don't Forget the Duct Tape: Tips & Tricks for Repairing Outdoor Gear, *Kristin Hostetter*
Find all the tools you'll need to be an outdoor fixit guru in this pocket-sized guide

Everyday Wisdom: 1001 Expert Tips for Hikers, *Karen Berger*
Expert tips and tricks for hikers and backpackers selected from one of the most popular Backpacker magazine columns

More Everyday Wisdom:
Trail-Tested Advice from the Experts, *Karen Berger*
More tips for enhancing backcountry trips

Trekker's Handbook:
Strategies to Enhance Your Journey, *Buck Tilton*
Contains pre-trip, during the trip, and post-trip strategies for long-distance hiking

Available at fine bookstores and outdoor stores, by phone at
800-553-4453 or on the Web at www.mountaineersbooks.org

THE MOUNTAINEERS BOOKS